SMALL PEARLS
BIG WISDOM

PALMETTO
PUBLISHING
Charleston, SC
www.PalmettoPublishing.com

Copyright © 2024 by BethAnne Kapansky Wright, PsyD

All rights reserved

No portion of this book may be reproduced, stored in a retrieval system, or transmitted in any form by any means–electronic, mechanical, photocopy, recording, or other–except for brief quotations in printed reviews, without prior permission of the author.

Hardcover ISBN: 9798822967618
Paperback ISBN: 9798822960756
eBook ISBN: 9798822960763

Small Pearls Big Wisdom

365 reflections on the heart of being human

BETHANNE KAPANSKY WRIGHT, PSYD

Advanced Praise

As a clinical psychologist, I feel fortunate when I find a book I can recommend to my patients and my students. What makes *Small Pearls, Big Wisdom* even better is it's a book I also recommend to my friends and myself! Dr. BethAnne skillfully weaves together reflections and anecdotes in twelve sections that empower you to select the right passage for wherever you are on your journey. These pearls are shared with such fearless authenticity that they nourish your strength and inspire your growth. Her lessons on humanity and strategies for connection vibrate off each page, making this gem a welcome resource for your office, your nightstand, or wherever else you can designate a few minutes for your journey toward self-compassion and peace. Invest in yourself, embrace your imperfections, and invite Dr. BethAnne to support you with her Small Pearls.

—Diane Logan, PsyD Board Certified Psychologist

Dr. Kapansky Wright is a board-certified clinical psychologist and spiritual educator with an incredible gift. She has the intuitive ability and use of language to translate the wisdom of the heart and soul. Her latest book, *Small Pearls Big Wisdom*, is another example of her ability to facilitate insight and connection to a deep inner knowing while also healing the wounded parts of self in a profound way. I know I will use the passages in *Small Pearls Big Wisdom* for guidance and inspiration and will recommend it to friends, family, colleagues, and clients. It will take you on a journey of connecting to the deep wisdom and insight of your heart while also celebrating what it means to be human.

—Jennifer Jepson, PsyD, LCSW Counseling Psychologist and Licensed Clinical Social Worker

BethAnne's book *Small Pearls Big Wisdom*, is eye-opening and heart-expanding with a touch of whimsy and humor. One of my favorite things about it is how the author reveals so much of herself and her story. It's down-to-earth and relatable. Odds are that the reader will see themselves in this book. And one cannot help but feel that the musings contained in the pages of this book confirm some of the thoughts held deep within one's own soul. A joy to devour from cover to cover.

—Ivory LaNoue, Intuitive Medium and Author of
Let Your Angels Lead

Insightful, authentic, and inspiring. *Small Pearls Big Wisdom*, offers a collection of essays that guide readers through life's complexities with grace, strength, and compassion. Each of the twelve sections explores different aspects of the human experience, helping readers to navigate change, discover meaning and happiness, and be their authentic selves. Dr. BethAnne utilizes her amazing skills as an empowering psychologist to connect with the reader on a deep, resonant level. She genuinely sees the potential in people and encourages them to believe in themselves and chase their dreams. As an endurance athlete and high-performance coach who knows the value of a positive mindset, overcoming adversity, and finding resilience in life's challenges, I highly recommend her work. Her pearls of wisdom are a valuable resource and a wealth of inspiration that will touch many and be a guiding light in your life.

—Rebecca McKee, Performance Coach and Endurance Athlete

To Mom and Dad. Thank you for all your love
and support, always.

To Eric, Rosie, Frodo, and Shire— my heart, my home,
my joy— thank you for the love.

Table of Contents

Introduction 1

Pearls of Wisdom on Authenticity and Following Our Hearts 5

   1   What's at Stake 6
   2   The Rainbow Tea Party of Sincerity 7
   3   Heartcentric Living 9
   4   Terms of Engagement for Sacred Heart Rebels 10
   5   How the Heart Speaks 11
   6   Authenticity and Endless Reservoirs of Joy 13
   7   A Love Relationship Life 14
   8   First, Value Yourself 16
   9   The Map of You 17
  10   Experts 19
  11   Learning to Walk Our Truth 21
  12   Challenging Our Status Quo 23
  13   The Trifecta of Heart, Psyche and Soul 24
  14   So Noble and Significant 26
  15   A Daisy Chain of Light 27
  16   Living the Questions 28
  17   From Junk to Jewel 30

18	The Astounded Soul	32
19	Your Heart is Magic	34
20	The Juiciest Peach	36
21	Write, Tell, and Live Your Own Story	37
22	An Old Friend, This Truth	39
23	Truth's River	41
24	YOU Are Your Permission	43
25	Fields Unseen	45
26	We Belong to Love	46
27	The Gifts of Loneliness	48
28	The Necessity of Owning Our Experience	50
29	Your Magic is Your Own	51
30	How To Know Your Soul	53
31	Anyway	55

Pearls of Wisdom on Dreams, Hopes, and Possibilities ... 57

32	Seed of Possibility	58
33	The Matter of Dreams	59
34	Toolbox	60
35	Beyond the Gate	61
36	Take a Chance on You	62
37	The Signature of Hope	63
38	Deep Sea Diving	65
39	Thickets and Wild Roses	67

40	Bigger Dreams	69
41	On the Nature of Wings	70
42	Protect the Seed of Your Dreams	71
43	The Gift of Transformative Possibilities	72
44	Hope's Hum	74
45	The Making of a Dream Begins With You	75
46	The Expansion of Possibility	77
47	Red Doors	78
48	Rose Gardens in the Stars	80
49	With Hope	81
50	A Shero's Point of View	82
51	Dream Your World	84
52	That's Hope	85
53	The Restoration of Wonder	87
54	On Underdogs and Finding Inspiration in Quiet Ways	89
55	The Things Dreams Have to Teach Us	91
56	Lessons in Life From The Girl With The Curious Heart	93
57	Dreams Are a Living Thing	95
58	Leap	96
59	This World Needs Your Light	97
60	Mantra of My 2013 Self	99
61	Start, Just Start	100

Pearls of Wisdom on Growth, Transformation, and Becoming 103

62	On Caterpillars and the Essence of Growth 104
63	The Gift of You 106
64	Breaking Out 108
65	Reidentification 109
66	I'm Just Not Myself 111
67	New Moons 112
68	You Are the Reason 113
69	New Eyes 114
70	Bigger Beings of Light 115
71	Because You Can 117
72	Unpacking the Backpack 118
73	Who We Wish to Be in This World 120
74	Spiral of Becoming 121
75	This Process Called Life 122
76	Divergence and Displacement 123
77	In the Darkness 125
78	New Wings 127
79	Tending to Our Inner Gardens 129
80	Shapes 130
81	The Courage to Surprise Yourself 132
82	Metamorphosis 133
83	Upside Down and In-Between 134

84	Breaking Ourselves Awake	136
85	Deconstruction	137
86	No Longer Willing	139
87	The Butterfly Effect	140
88	The Bold Stroke of Reinvention	142
89	Creatures of the Deep	144
90	The Destination is the Path	146
91	Mud or Stars	147

Pearls of Wisdom on Self-Love, Self-Belief, and Self-Trust 149

92	Canvases of Grace	150
93	Shine Bright for Yourself	151
94	Don't Abandon Yourself	152
95	To Learn Self-Trust	154
96	To Live at the Pace of Love	155
97	Cultivating Self-Love: a few how to's	156
98	Sacred Circles	158
99	Building Our Inner Home	159
100	The Way of the Heart	160
101	Mosaic	162
102	Let Your Smile Be Your Guide	163
103	Your Beat of Purpose	164
104	Don't Drink the Poison	165

105	Got Comparison? Try This.	167
106	Self-Love Affirmation for Difficult Times	169
107	Canon in Trust	170
108	Manifesto of Belief: a letter to my younger self	172
109	Cartwheels and Spirals	174
110	Questions of Self and Feeling States	175
111	Truth-Living and Truth-Speaking	177
112	Core of Self-Honesty	178
113	Excess Baggage	179
114	Just Say "Yes"	181
115	In Wholes, Not Halves	182
116	Compass of Love	183
117	Self-Trust Requires Continual Surrender	184
118	Success Can Be Found in Sitting Still	186
119	It is All Sacred	187
120	Self-Care on a Saturday Night	189
121	Self-Love is an Ongoing Journey	190
122	My Dear One, I Believe in You	192

Pearls of Wisdom on Being, Receiving, and Patience in the Process 193

123	Come Together	194
124	On the Value of Being and Receptivity	195
125	In Flow	197

126	On Cycles and Process Living	199
127	Sacred Spaces	201
128	Equilibrium	202
129	Nature's Teachers	203
130	Great Expectations	204
131	To Bring Balance	206
132	The Gifts of a Free and Clear Heart	207
133	On the Mountainside	208
134	On Stillness	210
135	Sea Surfers and Beachcombers	211
136	Bruises and Pearls	213
137	Life Cycles of Grief and Love	214
138	A Blessing of Peace	216
139	Just Take Class	217
140	The Direction of Water	219
141	Under the Surface	220
142	My Serenity Prayer	222
143	Water Wisdom	223
144	Balance: an ongoing renegotiation	224
145	Keys	225
146	Into the Woods	227
147	Parachutes	229
148	Ecosystem	231
149	In Nature, We Remember Ourselves	233

150	The Beauty Way	235
151	To See and Receive the Answers	236
152	We Are Golden	238
153	Nomads in Time	240

Pearls of Wisdom on Relationships, Connection, and Love 243

154	How We Wish to Be Loved	244
155	The Work of Change, Growth, and Love	246
156	Compassionate Detachment	247
157	Score-Defying	248
158	You Knowing You	250
159	Move Yourself Forward Instead	252
160	The Great River of Life	254
161	Delicious Unmet Sides	256
162	The Path of Greater Presence	257
163	Gaze	258
164	Score One for Team Love	259
165	Free to Be You and Me	261
166	In the Trenches	262
167	Exit Plan Out of the Ghostlands	264
168	Respectful Dialogue as an Act of Love	266
169	Lessons on Relationships Learned as an Empath	268
170	The Whole Story	270

171 Questions for Evaluating Relationship Exchange . 272
172 Permission to Remap Boundaries 274
173 Loving Kindness Meditation for Clearing Space . 276
174 Without Limits 277
175 Rainbow of Shades 278
176 A Multidimensional Responsibility and Necessity 280
177 Beautiful Things 282
178 Choosing to Travel Light 283
179 Making Broken Things Whole 285
180 Happy, Uncluttered, and Free 287
181 Listening to Our Hearts in a Divided World 289
182 Evolution of Love 291
183 Paint the Sky with Stars 293
184 Strut on My Friend 295

Pearls of Wisdom on Compassion, Sensitivity, Courage, and Grace 297

185 What Courage Is and Isn't 298
186 What's Grace Got to Do with It? 300
187 Gifts of Strength 302
188 Grace Rebels 304
189 Snowflakes 305
190 Words for Open-Hearted Living 306
191 Freeing Ourselves of Fakery 307

192	Bigger and Brighter	308
193	Perspective for the Hard Days	310
194	Diamond Souls	311
195	Reservoirs of Love	312
196	Magicians	314
197	The Voice of Compassion	316
198	Weep	318
199	Guidance for Times Life Doesn't Seem to Get it Right	319
200	The Direction of Hope and Light	321
201	Fierce Gentleness	323
202	What Is Sacred Every Day	324
203	Grit and Glitter	326
204	The Great Web of Light	327
205	Expanding Into Courage	329
206	An Exhortation for the Tender-Hearted	331
207	Tangled	333
208	BIG	335
209	Stress Cycles and Great Seas of Light	337
210	May Grace Flow	339
211	Superheroes	340
212	Bloom	341
213	Those That Shine the Brightest	342
214	Galactic-Hearted Supernova	343

Pearls of Wisdom on Healing, Wholeness, and Finding the Light in Darkness 345

   215 The Importance of Feeling Our Feelings 346

   216 Unicorns and Mud 348

   217 Excavating Our Hidden Lights 349

   218 Embracing Brokenness as a Natural Process in Life 351

   219 The Core of Being Whole 352

   220 Shadowlands 354

   221 Building Bridges 356

   222 Broken Birds 357

   223 Embrace It All 359

   224 You Are Not Alone 360

   225 On Healing Wounds 362

   226 Listening to the Inner Voice 364

   227 Making Friends with Sadness 366

   228 The Potential of Night 368

   229 Boxes of Darkness 370

   230 Pain as Teacher 372

   231 Becoming a Friend to Ourselves 373

   232 Tricksters 374

   233 Tuning Into the Frequency of Love 375

   234 Someday, Someway, Somehow 376

   235 Broken and Whole 377

236	From Grit to Pearl	379
237	Sunshine in Winter	380
238	Darkness is Magic, Too	382
239	Transmuting Pain Into Love	384
240	To Find Our Way Home	386
241	Self-Forgiveness	388
242	A Healer Instead of a Hurter	390
243	Illumination	391
244	Purpose It to Love	393

Pearls of Wisdom on Grief and Finding the Light in Darkness 395

245	Heart	396
246	How to Grieve	397
247	Blank Spaces	398
248	Grief, The Great Equalizer	399
249	Small Ways to Help Care for Oneself in Grief	400
250	Sideways	401
251	Bounce	403
252	Watchtowers of Love	405
253	Get Over It	407
254	How to Swim	408
255	The Thick	409
256	Labyrinth	411

257	The Wasteland	413
258	Becoming	415
259	Break	416
260	Shine	418
261	Brambles AND Roses	419
262	Essence of Grief	420
263	Home	421
264	Wildflowers	422
265	Noodles	423
266	We Will Have Joy	425
267	Eclipse	427
268	Everywhere	428
269	If You Strike Me Down	429
270	All That Is Shabby and Bright	430
271	Honor Them	432
272	Grief's Doorway	434
273	What Loss Has to Teach Us	435
274	Non-Sequitur	437
275	Forever	439

Pearls of Wisdom on Letting Go and Embracing Change 441

| 276 | Change Cycles | 442 |
| 277 | Go, Be Your Change | 444 |

278	Who We'll Be	446
279	The Nature of You	448
280	The Importance of Tiny Anchors	450
281	Learning to Lean	451
282	Making Space for Uncertainty	453
283	Authenticity, Grit, and Light	455
284	Jump	457
285	Each Brave Step	458
286	Little Acts of Change	460
287	Chop Wood, Carry Water	461
288	Unsticking	463
289	Questions for Letting Go	464
290	Choosing Growth and Change	466
291	The Face of Change	468
292	A Clear Heart Ready to Receive	469
293	Breathing Our Way Through Anything	471
294	The Wild Unknown	473
295	Tides	475
296	Strings	477
297	Balloons	478
298	Moving Forward	479
299	The Love Inside	481
300	On Leave-takings, Becoming, and New Springs	483
301	The Sacred Totality	485

302	We Open at the Close	487
303	Dancing Leaves	489
304	Let the Shadows Fall Behind You	491
305	The Ongoing Unknowing	492

Pearls of Wisdom on Happiness, Creativity, and Meaning 493

306	On the Exploration of Happiness	494
307	Meaning, Whimsy, and Laughter	496
308	Here at the Intersection of Life and Grace	498
309	Every Day, a New Creation	500
310	Meeting Happiness Halfway	501
311	Finding Sunshine on a Drizzly Day	502
312	The Art That Is You	504
313	Progressions on the Path of Happiness Circa 2013	506
314	Resistance and Insistence	507
315	The Cultivation of Gratitude	509
316	The Places Joy Lives	511
317	The Palette of You	512
318	Celebrating Wee Victories	513
319	Happiness is the Act of Being Whole	514
320	You Are the Art	515
321	What is Unwritten	517

322 Aim for Peace 519
323 The Dance 521
324 Creative Adaptation 523
325 Snow Falling on Happy 525
326 You Are the Journey 527
327 Gratitude is a Gateway 529
328 Personal Artistry 531
329 Joy is Vital to Our Souls 533
330 Manifesto of Hope 535
331 Dream Your World, Create a Beautiful Reality .. 537
332 Write About the World We Wish to See 539
333 Lighthouses of Hope 541
334 Joy is Happening Right Now 542
335 A Life of Appreciation Is a Life Well Lived 544
336 On the Heart of Being Human 546

Pearls of Wisdom on Purpose, Presence, Impact, and Wild-Hearted Living 549
337 How to Live Wild-Hearted 550
338 A Life of Untamed Love 552
339 Little Deeds of Intention Compound.......... 554
340 The Vibrancy is Here 555
341 Change Your Heart, Change Your World 556
342 Let Your Purpose Be a Poem 558

343	Real	559
344	Let Your Heart Break	561
345	Starlight and Strange Beauty	562
346	From Cocoon to Sky	564
347	Soul Retrieval	566
348	Wild and Wise	567
349	The Beautiful Mess	568
350	Rewilding Our Souls	569
351	Wild and Free: a tiny essay on rewilding	571
352	Choose Love	572
353	Coffee Talk	574
354	Energetic Footprints	575
355	Sphere	577
356	Raising the Power of Love	579
357	How to Make a Difference	581
358	Earth Angels	583
359	On the Matter of Light	585
360	Purpose is Multifold	587
361	My Compass, My Questions	589
362	Love is a Holy Circle	591
363	Spokes on a Wheel	593
364	The Call of the Wild-Hearted	595
365	A New Cycle of Light	597

Epilogue 599
Acknowledgments 601
Addendum 602
Connect With Me 609

Introduction

Hello lovely readers,

This book has been a long time in the making, starting with the first time I had the idea to clickety-clack my fingers across a keyboard, piece together a little reflection on life, and press share.

I was at a pivotal time in my life. Coming out the other side of a profound crisis of psyche and soul and subsequent spiritual awakening left me feeling like I was starting all over again in many ways.

I knew something had radically shifted inside of me. I was standing at the crossroads of a new way of being, knowing I could never go back to how I understood myself before. I didn't fully have the language for it then. Still, I sensed I was rebuilding and re-piecing my life from a place of authenticity, vulnerability, and something intangible but very real that I could tap into when I took the time to listen to the voice within. *You're following the heart's way now, BethAnne*, I thought at the time.

I began to write to better understand myself, the world, and the relationship dynamics I experienced and observed. I realized my words felt medicinal during this time. Through blogging, poetry, journaling, and little wisdom reflections, I wrote to find my true self during this change and understand how to live with conviction, wholeness, and truth. Once I started writing and expressing my truth, it made space for more truths, and I kept writing.

This collection of words is a kaleidoscope of truths written over the last thirteen years of my life. Many are from those first brave years of fierce courage and vulnerable change. Some came later in my timeline, reflecting new lessons of growth, discernment, and learning to navigate life's twists and turns with more grace and creative courage. Still, others are newer and reflect the current soul cycle in which I find myself.

Regardless of when each piece was written, they compose an instructional manual on wild-hearted living and how to stay in our hearts. These truths have seen me through many seasons of change, love, grief, and transformation in my life, informed my psychological practice, and helped me return to the compass of the heart whenever I needed to center and recalibrate.

I believe in writing about the world I wish to see. I've noticed over time that when I use my words to process my pain, I almost always end each of my writings on a high note. As if on some level, I know I'm lost in the basement of fear and pain, and I'm struggling to see the light on the path, but I still know where North lays, and so I see to point my compass in that direction and carve out a path.

These words have been my way of carving out a path and understanding what lies at the heart of being human. While I might not always embody the words written on these pages, I aspire to. Each came through as a reflection of my truth to help me through the pages of my own life. As if my higher self, my wiser self, my most compassionate self, who knows that love connects us at the core, reached through and helped me find a fragment of truth in a moment that inspired me to live with more authenticity, compassionate courage, and grace.

I've found that wisdom, at its core, is usually simple. It offers us a facet of a greater truth that helps us find our center and stay connected to our moral compass. Wisdom helps us come back to a space of stillness and inner truth, and it has a way of cutting through the increasingly complex dynamics of our world and helping us find clarity.

Read this book in the way that works best for you. Go from cover to cover. Find a chapter that speaks to a current struggle and choose a passage that feels good for your heart. Read a reflection per day over the next year. Pick it up and allow it to fall open, trusting whatever words you're drawn to that day. Make this work for you; take whatever resonates.

True wisdom is fluid, malleable, and able to be shaped to meet the recipient where they are. If something doesn't quite work for you, then make it your own. Reflect on how your experiences might help you see things differently and use that as a jumping-off point into your journey and truth. Add your unique knowledge and wisdom to the verses. Use them as a journal or creative prompt and write, color, and create your world into being.

As always, and forever, just do you. Thank you for being here.
With Warmest Wishes,
Dr. BethAnne

Pearls of Wisdom on Authenticity and Following Our Hearts

1
WHAT'S AT STAKE

Sometimes, it takes a while to be our true selves and show the pieces for which we most fear we will be judged.

We find our courage in small and big ways, in tiny moments and bold gestures. Sometimes, we vacillate between bravery and fear before we find the confidence to claim something inside ourselves and transcend our fears.

We can't keep ourselves hidden just so somebody else doesn't feel uncomfortable— they are free to go their way if they differ, so release them with love and grace to keep exploring their life path and then get about the business of owning yours.

We are the only ones who can know who we are on the inside. We are the only ones who can learn to embody our truth and walk a path where our internal world is in alignment with our external world.

We will eventually find that each step and gesture becomes a relief, release, and revolution to be honest and live our truth. To step outside the weight of caring about what others may think. We embody the self-knowledge that our truth of self is not for others to understand.

It is for us to understand within our hearts and souls. When it's pressing upon our hearts, we must speak and share. The truth of our souls is what's at stake.

2
THE RAINBOW TEA PARTY OF SINCERITY

So, you want to dance with authenticity? Welcome to the party. You don't need anything special to be here; you don't have to clean yourself up, be a certain way, or know your truth; you just need to be willing to show up.

Stay open, flexible, fluid, and curious about who you are. Authenticity doesn't happen overnight; it is a process of trying to show up in the most genuine and sincere ways to live a life that aligns with our truth.

Authenticity isn't about being perfect or having ourselves perfectly figured out— we are an ongoing work in progress and an ongoing art of self-discovery, and authenticity asks us to show up and stay present for this discovery.

It invites us to learn the things that light our hearts up. To understand where we hurt and where we suffer. To take responsibility for healing ourselves and learning how to bring love and grace into the spaces inside.

It's not afraid to stomp around in combat boots and a tutu and be both fierce and fancy all at once.

Authenticity isn't terribly interested in fighting for breadcrumbs at the tables of image, prestige, or appearance; instead, it would rather find a side door to the rainbow tea party of imagination, sincerity, creativity, and light.

All you must do to engage with authenticity is show up for yourself and be willing to learn about yourself. Do the good work of you. Begin to listen to the voice of your heart, then follow the guidance within.

Welcome to the party, my friend. Grab a colorful stool. Let me pour you a mug of peppermint tea from the eclectic mismatched stack of fancy porcelain. Help yourselves to crumpets, cake, and jam. Put on your Mad Hatter's cap of discovery, wonder, and curiosity.

We are so glad you are here. Welcome, welcome, and come on in.

3
HEARTCENTRIC LIVING

Despite our best attempts, being in "control" of life and thinking we have it all figured out is merely a well-done illusion.

We will find when we let go of the reigns and stop trying to define ourselves by achievements, successes on paper, what others think, what others want us to do, or anything that keeps us bound to a one-dimensional dried-up structure that says life is supposed to look a certain way; AND instead start defining ourselves by how we are honoring our life— well, what a wonderful world that would be.

What if we evaluated ourselves by how we feel on the inside, how much we are speaking our truth, and whether we are living compassionately, soulfully, consciously, authentically, kindly, honestly, bravely, faithfully, vulnerably, and fearlessly— what kind of beauty might we create?

We will see that happiness, peace, and contentment must come from within. We must have the courage to look in, see the beauty within, and then live it.

We will see that our greatest contribution to each other is our authenticity and compassion.

We shift the paradigm to heartcentric living, where integrity is honored, self-scrutiny is encouraged, forgiveness is freely offered, and choosing the path of peace reigns supreme.

4
Terms of Engagement for Sacred Heart Rebels

Following the path, even when it's dark.

Following your intuition— even when you can't fully see.

Listening to your heart cycles and soul rhythms and unique take on life.

Choosing to find greater meaning in life's experiences.

Choosing to find personal meaning when greater meaning is hard to find.

Dancing in the direction your inner winds are blowing, regardless of season.

Trusting, trusting, trusting: yourself, your heart, your process, your unique relationship to life, and understanding of your path (even when, especially when, it doesn't make sense to anyone else).

You doing you, as authentically and truthfully as you can.

This is what it is to be a sacred heart rebel.

5
How the Heart Speaks

"The trick to life is to have the courage to walk down the path that's in your heart."
—Atticus

If we walk the path of the heart, then first, we must understand how to listen. Our hearts have a unique voice and language different from the mind. The heart doesn't speak in rational, sequential thought.

The heart speaks through feelings and resonance, intuition and inclination, nature, animals, color, art, numbers, symbols, and imagery. It speaks through emotions, inner knowing, and nudges that tell us when to act and move and when to rest and receive.

Our minds want to know the plan and how things will look and work out. The heart keeps curiosity as a companion and knows that all we need to do is stay open to our process. The heart knows that our deepest truths often don't make sense at first because it is only through living our truth that we begin to see and understand our bigger picture.

The heart's process isn't linear. It's non-linear, highly intuitive, creative, and intelligent. We can't think, quantify, and logic our way into understanding our hearts; we must feel, dream, and sense our way into them.

The heart's process is an experiential process and is best understood through personal encounters, self-exploration, and direct experience with your personal heart magic.

In other words— you are the keeper of an expert on your heart and your magic, and the more you dive and delve deeper into your heart, the more the energy of love continues to reveal itself.

Your heart magic becomes an ongoing journey that will continue to take you deeper into yourself, deeper into the heart of the universe, and deeper into a delicious life with soulful meaning and purpose.

6
Authenticity and Endless Reservoirs of Joy

An authentic life begins inside of you. It begins with taking the time to learn who you are. It begins with not lying to yourself about yourself. It begins with reflecting on your values, attitudes, and beliefs and not being afraid to scrutinize and challenge them.

It begins with permitting yourself to change. It begins by peering into your shadows and gently bringing those ugly, broken parts into the light so they can find healing.

It is investing and nurturing a relationship with the self through creativity, movement, self-expression, meditation, intention, and so many other ways that create space for the self to expand and become.

It is not being afraid of patience, hard work, and digging deep to find your gems of internal truth.

Above all else, it is learning a language of self-compassion and self-love to speak for yourself. Then, it is finding the courage to take all that you have discovered and start bringing it out into the world so the steps you take in the external world reflect the steps you take in your internal world.

Authenticity requires massive heart, guts, and courage. This is what makes it so hard and rare. It is also what makes it profoundly beautiful when we see it in others. And when we begin to find it in ourselves, we feel like we have found an endless reservoir of liquid joy.

7
A Love Relationship Life

I don't always like the phrase, "I love my life," not because there is anything wrong with such a wonderful, grateful sentiment but because it seems too absolute to me.

I always think about people who are struggling to find themselves in life or who might be having a bad day and think that life is hard. It's easy for any of us to lose perspective and have lows, especially when things aren't going our way.

Sometimes, life can be hard to love.

I don't know if I can always say that I love my life, but I can say I am in a loving relationship with my life, which continues to evolve daily. I see loving life not as a permanent residence but as a continual relationship we develop with our existence. Marked by ups and downs, punctured by aches and pains, sustained by resilience and beauty, and the choice to keep engaging with life, day after day.

It is letting our softness chisel away at our angles and plains, making us gentler, wiser, more compassionate, and more rounded. It's imperfect and messy, with lots of room for doubts and lots of room for growth. It is remaining open, adaptable, and gracious and learning to accept the whole of our experience, not just the parts we like.

That is the real journey of authentic love for our lives. Learning to embrace the whole of ourselves, not beating out and denying the parts we don't like to prove we are enough.

Whether you're happily sitting on cloud nine right now because life has been a bit extra magical as of late or at the other end of the spectrum, where you'd like to curl up in your blanket fort and stay there for the next month eating Rocky Road ice cream and crying over sad movies— keep your heart and stay your course.

You are authentic, valid, wild, and beautiful. Your willingness to continue engaging in life is an act of love for your existence. No matter where you are at.

8
First, Value Yourself

If you want others to take you seriously, you must take yourself seriously. If you want others to respect you, you must respect yourself. If you want others to value you and value the gifts of your heart you choose to share, you must first value yourself.

We can't delegate responsibility for determining our worth to others. Our worth is ours to claim, and if we devalue ourselves, how much do we truly expect others to value what we treat so carelessly? Each of us is worth great love and great value, and that work of worth starts within.

Don't know where to start with learning to value yourself?

Make a commitment today to sit quietly with yourself for two to five minutes. Start by saying, "Hello, I see you. I am listening. I am here. Help me see myself through the eyes of my heart today." Then, allow your heart to guide you from there.

9
THE MAP OF YOU

"There is an eternal landscape, a geography of the soul; we search for its outlines all our lives. Those are lucky enough to find it ease like water over a stone, onto its fluid contours, and are home."
—Josephine Hart

We create our inner map of self the more we get to know ourselves and begin to acknowledge and learn to accept all parts of ourselves: the good parts, the less desirable parts, the parts that feel ugly, the parts that feel little, the parts that hold secret dreams, the parts that feel scary and the parts that want more for our lives.

It is all a map of our inner world— a map we are continually graphing, cartographers of the soul, as we go on our journey of self-discovery and truth-seeking.

We treasure hunt for clues to our maps within our everyday lives. We find quotes and words that resonate and reveal a truth within ourselves. We watch movies, read books, hear others' stories, and see a piece of our own experience reflected that helps us better understand our scope.

We live and learn and grow in our experiences, and each time we take note and pay attention to ourselves, each time we find something that lights us up or creates a wave of feelings within us, each hope and dream and idle musing, these things all become guideposts on your map quest.

All the soulful territory we travel: a mountain of grief, a river or joy, a forest where you felt you'd lost your way and couldn't seem to find the path— this, too, is a part of your inner map. So are the tools you've learned along the way and the things that fill your heart, help you mend and heal, and bring you back to the center.

We live out this map as we seek authenticity and follow the heart's way. Because this is wild terrain, the landmarks and topography of our map keep slowly changing, for the map of the soul is fluid and expansive and interacts with us as we go. Shifting scope as we continue the ongoing process of self-discovery,

Just when we think we're starting to have ourselves figured out, we go into our inner lands and discover a small cairn of rocks. We notice a little hand-painted sign nearby that seemed to pop up overnight: "This way," it says, "to go deeper into the wild meadows of soul."

10

Experts

I can't stop being me just because somebody doesn't understand me, and you can't stop being you just because somebody doesn't understand you. We need to be ourselves in this life— it is the only path to authenticity.

Trying to stoop lower and reduce yourself to meet somebody where they are at will only make you small. Just as trying to reach down, do the work for them, and pull somebody up to meet you where you are will only make you realize how tiring it is to carry somebody.

We are who we are and where we are, each of us navigating our paths according to our dictates of heart and soul, and so it becomes important to recognize those who have a parallel journey we're meant to walk beside and those whose paths split from ours, each of us free to move in the direction that resonates.

I believe this is one of the hardest lessons to learn in life: to grow beyond a model where we seek others' validation and approval and to do the work of self so diligently that we turn inwards when our buttons get pressed. Instead of saying, "How can they act like that?" We learn to say, "What is this triggering inside of me, and how can I bring healing to this space?"

We begin to find the courage to simply be ourselves and to find the courage to let others do the same, recognizing this as a two-fold process of courage.

Because it takes courage to let go. It takes courage to recognize others will see you through a distorted lens and that you may see them through a distorted lens. That you can't do a thing about the cloudiness of their lens, but you can work to keep yours clean and let those times it clouds become a teacher.

We must do this work to free ourselves, embody ourselves, and learn to be our own experts. As time goes on, those who don't understand you may still sting, or hurt, or ache a bit, but the benefits gained from walking your own path will become so great you wouldn't want to go back.

And any words of dissuasion that others may say will begin to pale in lieu of the magnificence of *you* claiming your own brilliant light.

11
LEARNING TO WALK OUR TRUTH

The only way to truly live our truth is to learn to walk it on a day-to-day basis, so we can be aligned with it.

We can know something holds true in our hearts, but the only way to integrate our truth into the fullness of who we are is to experience situations that allow us to test and try out our truth so we can learn how to embody it, breathe into it, and put it into action.

For example, if your truth is, "I want to live more authentically," you'll be given opportunities to do so. This may happen when challenging situations and people show up in your life, offering you opportunities to speak your truth and express yourself in bigger, authentic ways.

We often feel challenges are there as punishment (why is the universe doing this to me?), when, in fact, on a soul level, we're just drawing in unique opportunities and experiences to facilitate the growth we are seeking so we can become the higher expression we want.

Our growth rarely comes how we think it will, so we must keep surrendering the how. We put our truth and intentions out into the universe, then allow whatever shows up on our doorstep to be a teacher, which helps us gain experience and perspective to live from a more conscious, awakened state.

This is how we learn to grow in love. Finding our truth is an internal experience, but the only way to live it is to take it out into the world and experience situations where we must choose to apply it. We must learn to walk it. I know we can. We've got this. We're meant to be our higher expression, and we're each growing in our own beautiful ways.

12
Challenging Our Status Quo

It is up to us to challenge our own status quo. To say no to mediocrity and insist on better for our own lives. To challenge ourselves to expand and grow into the potential we've been given. To get over our own sense of shame and rejection and how life wasn't fair.

To stop holding ourselves back with limiting beliefs. To give ourselves permission to change. To let love and life in, instead of keeping love and life out. To leap off the edge of the precipice.

To hold ourselves accountable for stepping outside of the shadows of the cave and seeing the sun with our own eyes. To try and then fail. To try and then succeed. To take responsibility for our actions and make amends for the hurts we've caused.

To take responsibility for the love we hold in our hearts, choosing to give it away and watch it grow exponentially instead of diminishing it through fearful, squandered hoarding. To do away with boxes and find the courage to live a life of imperfection. To find the courage to say no thank you to a humdrum life and insist on magic, mystery, and color.

If we want to create a beautiful world, that work begins inside us by embodying the qualities we wish to see, insisting on leaving no stone unturned in our quest to know ourselves, and becoming the beauty and growth we wish to be.

13
The Trifecta of Heart, Psyche and Soul

What if all you did was ask the question, "Who would I become if I allowed myself to be my highest expression?"

Then you took a single first step, and in so doing, you ignited the dominos of your heart who heard your words, knew your intent, and then set into motion every single thing you'd need to be your highest self.

What if life isn't doing it to you? What if it's the collective light of your heart, your psyche, and your soul? What if this trifecta of intuitive intelligence is helping you unfold all you need to self-actualize?

What if the chaos is really a storm to cleanse, clear, and reset all aspects of your being so you can create a new channel of self?

What if it is all the doing of the light inside of you? Not some outside force happening to you, but some inside force working with you. Who loves you infinitely and who heard your sincere commitment to become a fuller self, so they answered your commitment in the most unlikely ways, bringing you the ingredients you would need to birth your dreams.

Maybe nothing is as it seems, and we must look beyond the illusion. Be like the moon, which shines on all. See the truth waiting for us in the shadows. Realize the path to liberation can only be found through sieving away what no longer fits and allowing new skin to renew and redeem.

There is nothing more terrifyingly beautiful in this world than a heart that is whole and free, and the only way to achieve that is for circumstances to unbind all bounds so we can become vulnerable and tender in our needs.

Ready to release the old and rebirth ourselves free.

14
So Noble and Significant

You have nothing to prove to anyone, no status quo to meet, and no responsibility towards being what others think you should be.

However, you do have a responsibility to yourself, to be yourself.

You are the only one who can become an expert on your being. You are the only one who can take the reins of your change and steer yourself in a new direction or choose to find contentment exactly where you're at.

The choice is up to you. The knowledge is yours to find. Your inner voice of truth is something only you can tap into.

This is your sacred responsibility and accountability. This is the light you are called to understand and shine in the world.

The untarnished, unvarnished, authentic act of naming yourself, claiming yourself, and then finding the courage to be yourself.

And there is absolutely no one except you who can accomplish so noble and significant a task.

15
A Daisy Chain of Light

Radical self-belief is a lifelong work. It is one that is a continual work in progress. It takes courage to show up in this world and courage to show up for ourselves and follow the truths placed in our hearts.

We must learn to believe relentlessly in our vibrant vision of self and believe that the world needs that vision.

Little is gained when we don't show up in our lives.

Little is gained when we diminish our light because we think it will make somebody else accept us. Little is gained when we don't listen to our hearts.

Little is gained when we don't allow ourselves the space to expand and grow into more authentic creatures of truth and love.

Everything is gained when we allow ourselves to show up in the world in bigger, braver, and more real ways. Everything is gained when we fight for our right to believe in ourselves and refuse to give up on ourselves, no matter what our circumstances.

Everything is gained when we choose to honor the possibility of who we know we are and inspire others to do the same.

Our self-belief then becomes a light. Not only for us, but to other seeking hearts who are looking to color outside the lines and dream their world into being. We create a daisy chain of light. It helps us shine brighter and inspires others to live more sincerely, expansively, and freely.

16
Living the Questions

"Be patient toward all that is unsolved in your heart and try to love the questions themselves, like locked rooms and like books that are now written in a very foreign tongue.
Do not now seek the answers, which cannot be given you because you would not be able to live them.
And the point is, to live everything. Live the questions now. Perhaps you will then gradually, without noticing it, live along some distant day into the answer."
—Rainer Maria Rilke

The questions you have in your heart? Trust your heart. Trust its timing. Trust it to bring you the answers when the season is right.

Trust that it has a unique process all its own whose energy syncs with the world around you; pulling in what you need for growth and working its intelligence to bring good things to fruition in your life.

Stay with yourself and your journey. Stay your course and see what lies beyond the bounds of what you've previously known. Right now, you don't know what you don't know, but your heart knows and will help reveal it to you in time.

In the meantime, be in the moment, learn something new about yourself, collect a new facet of your unique shape, and remember— no matter where you wander, you cannot lose your way; you can trust your heart and know that all roads will eventually take you where you need to go.

Now, isn't that an affirming thought? You're not lost at all. You're simply following the heart's way and trusting in the intangible threads still guiding you home, and you are doing just fine, dear soul.

17

From Junk to Jewel

There is a lot more to authenticity than just skimming the surface by picking up a new hobby that you like, saying the first thing that comes to your mind, or even making changes in your relationship, job, or external circumstances.

These things can be a start to making positive changes, but we will fall short of true authenticity if we stop there.

True authenticity requires depth. It requires a person who is willing to do the work inside of themselves of diving down deep to the bottom of their own ocean.

Digging through the sediment. Unearthing the dirty, muddy diamonds found there that initially look more like lumps of junk than brilliant jewels. Then, bringing them back to the surface so they can clean them off and find a way to honor them.

It is a process of self-integration where your being becomes so ineluctably polished and rubbed by all your diving, mud scraping, excavating, examining, heart polishing, and soul shining that you carry the full of you wherever you go.

Others will begin to see your gleaming diamonds. More importantly, you will see them. You will carry and hold them and know them to be the beautiful, real, core part of yourself that nobody can take away.

This authenticity can't help but be reflected in all other aspects of your life. It becomes a natural extension of self, where you will find being real is less about what we do and more about who we are.

Real is an inside job. Perfect circumstances, the perfect partner, the perfect life, the perfect timing, the perfect achievement— they don't exist and certainly won't bring you inner peace.

Real starts exactly where you are at right now. It begins inside. Listen to it. Put on your hip waders and dig through your sediment. Dive down. Find your courage, begin seeing what lies in the deep, and go from there.

18

THE ASTOUNDED SOUL

Our ability to form genuine, real connections with others is a direct reflection of how real and genuine our connection is with ourselves. Transparency starts within.

It can be a messy process, unconstrained and unformed, not very pretty, not very nice feeling, real, raw, getting down to the brass tacks of your heart, soul, and voice. In fact, this process is the direct opposite of "having it all together."

Authenticity will place high demands on the pretty containers we have formed to package and present ourselves to others nicely. It will ask us to expand well beyond those containers and become bigger. It will challenge us to grow beyond caring about image and become more. It will push us to live life from the inside out and let our true self shine.

Expect the process to be highly uncomfortable. Decide not to care because comfort is overrated. Expect that many will not get it. Follow your heart anyway. Keep pushing even when it's hard. Know that joy and sorrow are opposite sides of the same coin; you will not have one without the others; they will be companions on this journey. Learn to create space for both.

Expect to be astounded by how life responds to this work of your heart. Expect to be astounded by what you find in your heart. Expect an astounded soul.

This world already has enough pretty containers. It is choking on them to breathe in something real. Pretty containers don't nourish impoverished hearts. Genuineness, connectedness, courageous transparency, vulnerability, relentless self-honesty, radical compassion, the courage to become— that is what opens our hearts to ourselves, this world, and this life.

This is where love resides: not in the pretty container, in the astounded soul.

19

Your Heart is Magic

I like to think of each of us as Cosmic Investigators, Soul Explorers, and Heart Adventurers who get to play Scooby-Doo with the cosmos as we search for the clues that resonate in our hearts and piece together our bigger picture of soul.

Our life then becomes a patchwork of silk scraps, love notes, and starry truths, which help us make sense of who we are and what our purpose is in this lifetime.

One thing I've learned is purpose is multilingual and open to many interpretations. It's not about one set path; it's about who we are, our daily choices, and how we choose to direct our energies.

After all, there are many ways to be a light. Or to be a motivator for peace. Or to be an unruly heart, who does things backward and out of the book, yet still states an elegant case for the cause of love.

Purposes are like the stars. There are billions of them, which means there are billions of ways to shine bright and light up the night.

Don't stop listening to the feelings whispering and calling to you. Follow them. Put on your spyglass and take a closer look at the things that make your heart sing. Collect those experiences and tapestry them together into the bigger picture of you, even if they don't make sense.

They don't need to make sense to your mind; they already make sense to your heart.

Allow yourself the grace to be a topographer of the universe. Take notes on the pages of your heart of everything you find and see. You're not foolish for seeking more: you are big, bold, beautiful, intuitive, and your heart is magic. Hang onto that and let that knowledge be your boon travel companion.

Trust yourself. Trust your heart. And you can always trust your magic.

20

THE JUICIEST PEACH

"You can be the ripest, juiciest peach in the world, and there's still going to be somebody who hates peaches."
—Dita Von Teese

I am continually reminded that in all things, just keep working on being yourself. Do things in a way that feels good, authentic, and aligned with your true self. You could turn yourself inside out trying to curry favor with others and still feel like you are constantly failing.

The good and freeing news is that we're not meant to be understood or liked by everyone, and that's completely okay. However, the right people, those who truly want to support us for our true selves, will.

Be yourself— no more, no less. Let whatever gifts life has given you shine bright, and keep working on your own heart and path. It's the one thing nobody else can do for you; only you can do your best.

Keep working on radical detachment each time you get stuck in another person's judgments of your path. Release them to life as many times as you need so you can keep bringing the focus back to yourself and creating a peachy life of joy, vitality, and curiosity just by being you.

21

Write, Tell, and Live Your Own Story

If you don't define yourself for yourself, others will quickly do it for you, telling you who and what you are about in this world.

The problem is that you are the only one who knows who and what you are about. You are the only one who can develop a meaningful vocabulary that resonates and a descriptive plotline that does justice to your scope and your truth.

You are a story in progress as you go. Do not be afraid to claim your words for yourselves and develop a narrative rich in truth, warmth, humor, and experience. Sometimes, the best thing we can do to embody our story is to get out of our way and rescript ourselves into a new way of being.

Release the expectations of how things should be and who we think we should be; pen a chapter in learning how to let go and find brave surrender.

Let go of our preconceived notions of self; pen a chapter on reinvention and finding the courage to embark on an odyssey of heart and soul.

Step out of the way of the ego, the old stories, and self-imposed limitations; pen a chapter on vision, expansion, and dreams.

Stop judging the process; pen a chapter on self-acceptance and radial compassion for the process.

We will only be as big as the stories we create for ourselves, and so if we wish to grow, we need bigger stories. When we choose to write them, we discover that life has been standing there expectantly— with nothing but a loving glint in its eyes and compassion in its voice— saying:

"Welcome! I've been here all along. I was simply waiting for you to get over yourself so you could see what comes beyond. Now that you've knocked down your old walls and preconceived notions of self, the real adventure story can begin."

22

AN OLD FRIEND, THIS TRUTH

There is this truth— it's not a new truth, just an old friend— that I keep coming back to again and again: we can be no more than or no less than ourselves.

It's so simple. Each of us feels called to be a certain someone in this world, and we are the only ones who can realize that path. At the same time, it is hard to realize that path, because there are so many levels of influence in our lives who tell us about who and what we should be.

I keep finding that while we can pull values and attributes into ourselves inspired by others, they must resonate with who we are, and we must make them our own: try and live somebody else's truth or value system or vision for your life, and you will gradually notice how out of alignment you feel. When things are out of alignment, they tend to crack, malfunction, or go off-course until we travel so far away from ourselves that we almost forget how to return home.

It is an old friend, this truth. One that I run into time and time again every time I feel like— because person A over there is doing things a certain way, perhaps I should be too. Or because person B believes something, maybe I should, too. Or because person C has accomplished this with their life, perhaps I should too.

Comparison is insidious and suction cups our energy. It is an easy trap to fall into for this world is ripe with influence, advice, and people willing to tell you how to live your life.

However, it is my face I must face in the mirror every day, and I am constantly reminded that regardless of what others are doing,

I am the only one who knows my requirements of soul, and I am the only one who can actualize the seeds of the person I'm created to be.

In those still quiet moments of self, I return to my truth and remember that on any given day, if we are doing life the best we know how, if we are trying to be ourselves the best we know how, if we are engaging with this whole "being human thing" the best WE know how:

It is enough. I am enough. You are enough. We are enough. Just as we are.

23

Truth's River

Throughout our timeline, we go through multiple iterations and incarnations, during which we might be trying to find, realize, or free something inside of ourselves that badly needs a voice.

We each learn to speak our truth in many ways. Hesitant bits and pieces where we still haven't figured out quite what we're trying to say. Incomplete phrases are connected by ellipses. Some truths take a while to divine, and their completion can only be answered by living and finding our words through our process of life.

Finding our truth will come with its ebbs and flows. Sometimes, truth unfolds slowly and peacefully through a gentle meander— a lazy river floating on an honest Sunday afternoon, where something resonates within us, and we feel a deep sense of rightness.

Sometimes, truth hits swiftly, like a giant raging swell, carrying us in its flows; we get wrapped up in the current during these times, and it might make us realize or say or feel called to act from a place of truth that feels like it is coming from a force greater than just us.

Truth is like that: sometimes gentle and peaceful and sometimes rapid and all-encompassing. Our task is to learn how to listen to ourselves and engage with our inner river and learn when to sit and observe, when to begin to dip our toes, when to dive clean in, and when to let the river carry us and move us to action.

Each time we collect a new aspect of truth— each small act of self-scraping, heart-baring, soul-exposing, and scrutiny— we help contribute to our greater truth, reveal another shade of self, and find a new key to unlock a door within.

It can take a while to piece together our truth. Sometimes fragments of truth add up to a greater truth, so it's important we stay patient with the process and give ourselves permission to let truth flow into our consciousness over time, deepening our awareness of its whole.

The more we invest in listening to ourselves, the more we grow in authenticity in accordance with our truth discovery. Our world becomes a little more authentic, our presence clearer, and our ability to live from a place of integrity and heart coherence continually shaped and aligned by our river of truth.

24

YOU ARE YOUR PERMISSION

Sometimes, it seems like we are waiting for life to give us permission to do something. We desire change, want to have a new experience, or secretly hold a dream in our hearts but keep waiting for everything to line up and show us the way.

Often, though, it doesn't work like that. There will be times when destiny marches into our lives and begins rearranging and disrupting the direction we were going, but often, the universe will pause with us for as long as we remain in a space of indecision.

During these times, you have to realize that you are the change. You are the one who is enough to give yourself permission. You are enough to change your life now. To say "yes" to the dream. To take the brave step. Nobody else is going to come along and do it for you, or hold your hand, or tell you exactly how to fly instead of fall.

This is your sacred work and beautiful responsibility to self. The gorgeous thing is that life will begin to line up to meet you once you give your consent. The universe will begin to unfold the path, so the details that lay unknown become clearer.

Your heart will begin to pull in everything it needs to create, do, and be the thing that is in you. The tangible will materialize from the intangible, once you say yes to manifesting the energy inside of you. You take one brave step in the direction of change and discover a solid step in a space that previously looked like thin air.

But it starts with you. It starts with your *yes*. It starts with being your own permission giver. It starts with you being all in, and when you do that movement happens.

You are the permission-giver and change-maker in your own life. Remember— you don't need to do anything grand to make a change, you just have to find one small way to move in a new direction and then allow things to begin to flow from there.

25
FIELDS UNSEEN

Learning how to be ourselves is a humbling process. One that takes place in quiet spaces and dark nights of the soul and demons wrestled to the ground again and again before we feel they are adequately conquered and permit ourselves to be free.

It isn't very elegant, it's not a change easily measured, and though sometimes we all need those moments where we leave an exclamation mark and shout, "I am HERE world," more often than not, becoming our authentic selves happens in the invisible choices we make.

The times when we find the courage to listen to something speaking inside and acknowledge our truth. The times when we go against the grain and carve out a new way with grit, mettle, and determination.

The times when we choose to fly in another direction simply because we want to feel how the wind changes when we leave the same behind and dare to go into fields unseen.

26

WE BELONG TO LOVE

Sometimes, walking our truth can be a lonely road. I've had many moments of feeling like a hungry ghost, palms pressed against the glass, yearning for a seat at the banquet table. The tea party of authenticity might be a juicy, wild ride, but it will require more of us.

It mostly requires us to continually tune out the chatter and buzz in this world, which tells us who to be, how to be, and how to do things a certain way. We will be asked to continually shed old ways of being and leave behind old skins.

We will be asked to keep living our authentic truth by taking things back to a space of ourselves. To engage in solitude to create space for our higher selves and truths to come in. To wade through the world's chatter— sifting the sands for our gems of wisdom.

It can get lonely in this solitude space, but please remember, above all else, that even in loneliness, we belong to ourselves, we belong to nature, we belong to our heart, and we belong to love.

You are not alone on the journey, and you can always keep tapping into your heart's wisdom, which is endlessly available to guide and direct us.

Please keep on doing you. Be intentional about creating space. Challenge external messages. Open your mind's eye and examine all things for truth. Place your hand on your heart often and ask yourself, "How do I feel about this?" and "What do I need to know for my highest truth?"

Invite your wiser self into the mix and ask for deeper wisdom. Live life from the inside out. Create rose gardens in your heart, plant seeds of authenticity in the entirety of your being, and water them with your faith, fortitude, and refusal to be anyone other than yourself.

Allow yourself space to grow. Place your hand on your heart in gratitude for all that you're becoming and all that you've become.

27

THE GIFTS OF LONELINESS

It's lonely not to belong. Not to fit a shape or tuck into a box or know where to find your tribe. Or to be part of a tribe that doesn't entirely fit you, so you always feel separate from the mix.

But maybe not belonging is an indicator of something else; maybe it means you are creating your own path, and you don't belong because nobody has walked this path before. Maybe not belonging means you aren't supposed to follow where others have tread but be the brave innovator who forges a new way and shines a light for others to follow.

Maybe loneliness can be a gift— a gift of void, creativity, and opportunity. After all, even Source was alone in its singular existence, and out of that space came multiplication, combustion, creation, and expression, so love could be more fully imprinted in billions and billions of forms.

Maybe loneliness can be a blank slate, clean canvas, or catalyst for creation that forces one to multiply, combust, and create something new in one's life to more fully express oneself— to express the love they have inside, which they are trying to uniquely imprint upon the world.

Maybe there is more to loneliness than meets the eye. Maybe loneliness is creation's gift, and if we learn to harness and channel it, we can learn what it means to be creators ourselves— innovators, magicians, trailblazers, visionaries, dreamers, and artists.

Walking on the fringes to shift shape so we can discover and navigate uncharted territory. Forever wandering outside the lines because lines were meant to be changed, and somebody has to be the changer. Always pushing at the endless bounds of the universe, trying to fathom infinity's grace so we can paint new pictures of love for the world to see.

28

The Necessity of Owning Our Experience

Reasons to keep doing the good work of owning your experience of self:

It is the experience that is going to be the most useful to you, for it is the nucleus at the core of your authentic journey.

It is the experience that will unlock your unique knowledge of your inner universe and understanding of your path.

It is an experience you can tap into to create an inner calendar of your seasons, so you stay aligned with your soul cycles and inner rhythms.

It is the experience that holds the keys to your intuitive knowing, your sacred gifts, and your holy purpose.

It is the experience that will shift you from being pulled in the direction of this world and help you turn inward and explore the inner terrain that is you.

It is the one experience with which you can develop unparalleled expertise because no other person can do you, experience you, or be you like you.

Most importantly, no other person can do this very sacred work— your very sacred work— of the psyche, heart, and soul and uncover the beauty, healing, and freedom waiting to be discovered in this space.

29
Your Magic is Your Own

Your magic is your own. Did you know you have magic in you: the ability to create, transform, alchemize, sense, and perceive?

Maybe you know how to walk into a room and change the energy through kindness. Maybe you sing for the joy of the music, and with each appreciation and love of the lyrics, become like the songbird, and you sing the world a brighter tune.

Maybe you dream in color and hold space for rainbows of diversity, the scales of justice, and the ability to envision a better world. Maybe you soar through the stars in your mind, speak with the numinous and know ancient things.

Maybe you sense the intelligent patterns being woven out as the moon and planets orb the wheel and weave together portals for change. Maybe you sit in holiness within your inner temple and anchor space for peace.

Maybe your empathy and sensitivity create the diamond light of fierce gentleness. Maybe you're working through grief and pain, and each step of brave courage creates a rite of passage through the shadowlands to bring more healing, wholeness, and truth to the world.

And maybe you're just working on being yourself— in the best way you know how— as much as you can, as often as you can, and in so doing, you're writing a story of authentic expression and willingness to be real.

It is enough. It is all enough. Our magic is enough. There is no better than or worse than; there is just all of us coming together, as a whole, to express the facet of the divinity that is inside of us.

So, just keep doing you and know— your magic is your own, and it is more than enough.

30
HOW TO KNOW YOUR SOUL

You have to keep showing up for yourself— again and again and again. Show up and do your own work of heart, mind, and spirit. Learn how to sit in silence and know yourself. Learn how to breathe through your uncertainty.

Realize all experiences of yourself are right and good and valid.

Learn what works for you until you become your own guru on you. Learn how to cultivate discernment and wisdom. Learn to differentiate between what the world says you should be and who you feel called to be.

Realize all experiences of yourself are right and good and valid.

Discover that if it doesn't resonate with you then it is not for you. Realize that you don't have to be anyone special. You don't have to do anything special. You don't have to search so hard for the answers— you just have to learn how to be yourself.

Realize all experiences of yourself are right and good and valid.

Do this and you cannot help but find the soul-directed path- your soul-directed path. Do this and you will quickly begin to learn what is right for you and what isn't. Do this and you will begin to see you always had the answers- written inside the depths of your heart— waiting for you to look within so you can remember what is true.

Realize all experiences of yourself are right and good and valid.

There isn't a single person out there who is going to show up, roll up their sleeves, do the work for you. Who can tell you how to live, or what your truth is, or the things that will light your heart most bright. It is just that easy and just that hard: to know your soul, you must cast off all that this world has told you about who you should be and then get down to the business of finding your truth.

Realizing all experiences of yourself are right and good and valid— the language of your soul only you can discover for you.

31

Anyway

There will always be somebody who says you're doing it wrong. Who thinks you love too much or love too little. Who thinks you're taking the wrong path, as if they know the right one for you and hold the grid to your map of self.

Maybe they'll think that you're too happy, abundant, successful, or talented, or maybe they'll think you're not enough of any of these things because your "enough" comes from something deeper and far more real, and they don't have the sight to see.

There will always be somebody who thinks you should be somebody else because it is more convenient for them or because it makes them feel better about their well-defended heart.

The trick is to hang on really tight to what matters, keeping your heart clear so you can hear its voice and, above all else, be yourself anyway.

Pearls of Wisdom on Dreams, Hopes, and Possibilities

32
Seed of Possibility

What would any of us dare to do if— even if scary and farfetched— we believed it was possible? Because all dreams that come to fruition start with a seed of possibility.

We either nourish or starve that seed with the ingredients we feed it. We have to cradle those seeds, blowing wishes, and hopes, and *yes you cans* into that dream.

We have to believe in our vision of self so very, very badly that we refuse to let anything get in the way. We have to refuse to take doubt and fear for an answer when faith and hope will better suffice. Refuse to believe that our dreams are anything but entirely possible.

Because all that composes our realities, at some point, was no more than the faintest wisp of a dream. A seed of possibility. Their creation falls to the only ones who can see them through to fruition— you and me.

33

THE MATTER OF DREAMS

I see the dreams we hold in our hearts as many things:

They are the treasures tucked in our hearts that we're meant to discover and bring out into this world. They are fragments and puzzle pieces of our heart and soul, which compose the greater whole of who we are and help direct our sense of purpose.

Dreams are a living energy inside us, continually beckoning, cajoling, aligning, and inspiring us to move in the direction of our deepest truth.

Dreams are the songs we've been given to sing in this world that somehow weave into the greater symphony of life; we join our notes and make a greater composition when we find others with who we can harmonize and rhythm.

Dreams are magic. They are seeds of creative possibility. They are the waters of joy for the soul. They are vital and life-giving and help us stretch the horizons of potential and possibilities.

Dreams are meant to be acknowledged with reverence and respect. They are not fantasies, foolishness, or any disparagement we sometimes get in a world that has forgotten how to speak the language of the heart.

When we acknowledge ourselves, acknowledge our hearts, acknowledge our dreams, and believe they are meant for us?

We reclaim essential pieces of ourselves, reawaken hidden knowledge, and remember wisdom and truths we forgot we already knew.

The dreams in our hearts are incredibly powerful. Follow them, trust them, believe in them, and be them.

34
Toolbox

Potential means little without dedication and action, and you hold worlds of potential inside of you—

You are the only one who has the capability to grow your heart, increase your mind, develop yourself, and harness the gifts you've been given to create a life authentic to you.

You are the only one who can actualize your goodness, strength, resilience, and perseverance.

You are the only one who can give yourself permission to dream— both tiny dreams of simple things and grand dreams of beautiful visions.

You are your own magical agency of change. You are a walking toolbox of possibilities; you only have to decide how to use those tools.

Isn't that an empowering thought? You are your own best resource.

Sometimes, all it takes is a deep breath, an upward gaze, and a reminder to set an intention to take your capable hands, clever mind, and open heart, then go make something magnificent out of your day.

35

Beyond the Gate

"Keep some room in your heart for the unimaginable."
—Mary Oliver

If you don't save space in your heart for the impossible, the unimaginable, the beautiful, unfathomable, and miraculous, how much room are you giving your life to grow?

Life meets us where we are. Expansive opportunities can be difficult to come by if we can't learn to think expansively or imagine a beautiful vision for our lives.

Prepare a place for hope to reside in your heart. Turn down the covers, tidy up its contents, and roll out the welcome mat for the ideas and imaginings that make your soul hum, thrum, and sing.

Give life a little room to run wild and rampant, tearing through the fences in your heart.

Some of the most beautiful, juicy, abundant gifts are waiting outside the safety of the gate. But we will not find them or be able to receive them— even if life's possibilities come knocking— if we don't first make space.

36

Take a Chance on You

How would your life be different if nobody was standing in your way, telling you something wasn't possible or practical or that you couldn't do it?

Would you chase a dream you've always had in life? Write a book, run a certain race, change jobs, return to school, save your pennies to take that trip you've always wanted?

Would you live the life you already have differently? Love more fearlessly, live more boldly, find more joy in the everyday moments, let go of the baggage you've been carrying around, and dare to give yourself permission to simply be happy?

Now, what would you do if you weren't the one standing in your way, telling yourself these things are not possible for you?

When we talk ourselves out of our dreams and why we think we cannot do something, we close ourselves to bigger possibilities and stay in a space of limited belief, ensuring a smaller and paler way of life.

We say: "I wish I could, but I really can't," "If only but—," "My obligations," "What would other people think?"

What it comes down to is that we must keep freeing ourselves from the expectations of others so we can keep finding the courage to be ourselves in a world where anything is possible.

Choosing a different path starts with taking a new step, making a small change, and believing things can be different. Taking a chance on the possibility that is beautiful, potential-filled you.

37

THE SIGNATURE OF HOPE

"Hope is like the sun, which, as we journey toward it, casts the shadow of our burden behind us. Hope lies in dreams, in imagination, and in the courage of those who dare to make dreams into reality."
—Aristotle

Cultivating a steady sense of hope isn't found in the specific outcome of a situation; hope is always found when we let our mind's eye take in the whole and believe that the creative mysteries are leading us to growth.

Some of the feeling states we can experience in life can be hopeless places, and sometimes, we have to fight to reclaim the good. Fight for joy, possibilities, dreams, gratitude, and a bigger perspective of the whole.

We can learn to find beauty, even when the mudslides of life pool in messy masses around our feet and threaten to take us under. We can learn to dig down and in, instead of wallow in the why, and find the diamonds that form under duress. We can learn to reach high and wide and bring starlight into deep midnight, so we always have something to set our compass by.

Hope can become the signature penned upon our hearts, holding us steady and reminding us that even when life tips over, the universe's innate intelligence and love will help us absorb the tip and find the gifts in falling sideways.

It is human nature to hope for better things, but we can open our perspective and have a more encompassing view of those better things.

Maybe better things are found every time we choose dreams over despair, stepping more fully into our infinite selves by believing in the invisible and inexorable heartbeat of love surrounding and infusing this place.

Maybe better things are a refusal to give up on hope, even when the world feels hopeless, because we know the stars are still guiding us and the sun will still rise, and if there's a rise, there is hope.

Maybe better things are found in unnoticed places. And the moment we take the time to notice them, we realize how rich life is with betterment. In that place, we can search for hope and find its existence— hope is only a signature away.

38

DEEP SEA DIVING

If you are waiting for somebody to give you permission to live with more audacity and courage and follow your dreams, that permission might never come.

If you are waiting for someone to come along and make it easier, or show you exactly how to undertake the process, or give you a blueprint for growing your hopes and dreams— you might be waiting a while.

It's not that help isn't available, and it's not that life won't send us signs, helpful people, and supportive circumstances to help us build our dreams; it's just that those things usually don't come until we've already taken the first few steps towards them.

Only we can realize the truth of a dream. The visions in our hearts, the inspirations that fly into our minds and move us, the tiny urges to simply create more opportunities for pleasure, adventure, and joy in our lives— these are all facets of our hopes and dreams.

Inspiration can be found all around us: go to nature if you need courage; nature is teeming with creativity, resilience, and courage. Read a book or watch a show that inspires you not to give up on your dreams. Pull up any social media site and type in hashtags like #MotivationalMonday or #TransformationTuesday, and you'll find a smorgasbord of uplifting words and curated quotes that all aim to inspire growth and dreams.

Ultimately, you are the originator of everything. Your dreams will move with you and through you, so life will pause with you until you move toward your hopes and dreams.

Don't wait for somebody else to do it for you. Step into it instead. Give yourself permission to become more, to claim your space, to speak your truth, to use your voice, to flex your limbs, and to take up the space you've been given.

Be your permission-giver, light-bringer, change-maker, and things-shaker. Allow it to unfold in its messy, elegant splendor, embrace the call within, and dive in.

39
Thickets and Wild Roses

There is so much room for growth, change, and authenticity in our lives. Sometimes, we feel trapped in a place, a job, a relationship, a routine, or a mindset. But we are never really stuck or trapped; we are just scared.

Scared because the territory of the known, no matter how stagnant it feels, is more comfortable than the dark territory of the unknown. Scared because it may not work out. Scared because change can be uncomfortable, and we don't have control over the process. Scared that we may make a mistake and somehow get it wrong.

We feel caged. Tangled and wrapped up in tricky thorns and brambles that keep us stuck, even as we struggle against them and feel even more stuck through our struggles.

Change *can* be scary. Jumping off the cliff of what has been familiar into the wide-open space of the undiscovered can feel downright terrifying.

But there is joy in that journey, too, and I think what's even scarier is not giving voice to your desires and dreams. It smothers your real self. It robs us of opportunities to be the you that you were meant to be.

The beautiful news is that our fears might make us feel small, but we are built for possibilities and growth. More importantly, we are not alone in this process, and we will find that the essence of life is neither narrow nor small.

We will expand into a greater possibility of self and never wonder what life might have been had we taken the road less traveled.

What once felt stuck begins to loosen, and we see our lives through a bigger scope.

Realize that when we take a deep breath and dare to move, we find ourselves on the other side of the brambles. We discover that what we thought was an impenetrable thicket of thorns was the ingredients needed to create a whole field of wild roses that simply needed our faith and belief to grow into their colorful, carefree, joyful possibility.

40

Bigger Dreams

If you don't dare to dream, nothing will ever change, including you.

Maybe— even if we aren't always in a place in life that allows us to pursue our change immediately— it's still worth it to envision the dream because what if it's the dream itself that begins to change us?

What if it's planting the seed of the dream and allowing it to take root inside us that helps us consider a bigger possibility of self?

What if imagining a bigger scope for our lives opens our hearts to a more expanded vision of who we could be?

What if the manifestation of the dream is less important than taking the risk of opening to its genesis?

Maybe the genesis is exactly what we need to stand a little taller, walk a little braver, and believe in ourselves a little bit harder so we find the courage we need to move forward in our lives with faith, fortitude, and love.

Whether or not our dreams manifest in the form of our initial vision, dreaming allows us to see wider, reach higher, and believe we are worthy of more.

Over time, our hopes and beliefs begin to add up, creating the path needed to live with conviction and dare to dream even bigger dreams.

41

On the Nature of Wings

"Run my dear from anything that may not strengthen your precious budding wings."

—Hafez

As you free your wings, you help others free their wings. As you learn to soar, you help others learn to soar. As you live by the light within, you help others learn to do the same. Not through anything you do, but through the ripple effect created by your very act of being.

There will always be those who aren't ready to fly and who fear their wings— don't let them bind yours.

There will always be those who are fearful of soaring and who want to hold you back or keep you small— don't let them make you forget who you are.

There will always be those who are invested in keeping their light dull so they won't understand yours— don't dim to fit in.

For, you've sewn new wings. Wings of transformation and growth. Wings of faith and love. Wings grown over many moon cycles and dark times and finding the ingredients you needed to access what is numinous within yourself.

Ah, see? You're really soaring now. Above your older ways of being and into greater authenticity.

So, trust your flight. Trust your light. Trust that you have been given wings for a reason at this time. Learn to use them well and give yourself permission to keep moving towards the light.

42
Protect the Seed of Your Dreams

Our dreams are not for everyone's perusal and eyes. They are for us to nourish and nurture and bring to fruition. We get to share the eventual fruition as we choose, but the origins of growth are vulnerable.

Other's careless words, negative energy, and naysaying can damage us and drain the energy needed to create the dream. This is why it's very important not to let somebody else's relationship with life become yours. Don't take on their lack of belief, fear of failure, doubts, and clouded vision.

Especially don't expect them to see your authentic heart if they are not invested in seeing their own authentic heart. We must take the visions of our hearts and the voices of our souls seriously enough to guard them with sacred care and only allow in what nourishes them.

Protect the seeds of your dreams. Water them with clear intent and purpose. Root out weeds often. Feed them with joy. Know that nobody else can nurture them but you, so don't expect them to. However, do know that the right people will come along, smile sunshine on you, and support your truth.

Remember, if you've got a dream, it's because it's been given to you to create and crystallize. It wouldn't be in your heart to hope, yearn, and grow if it wasn't yours to actualize.

43
The Gift of Transformative Possibilities

One of the magical things about life and love is that sometimes they surprise you in the best of ways. The unexpected happens. A rose blooms in winter. Sunlight breaks through the shadows. Things seemed to be heading south, but they suddenly made a U-turn and found a way to climb upwards into a better trajectory.

This isn't always the case.

Sometimes, we see something bad coming, and we can't do much to divert it. Or we hope for the best, and then life serves us a triple scoop of the worst. These things happen. They are part of the ebbs and flows of humanity's ecosystem. They are part of the greater process of life.

However, I love the possibility that happy twists of fate and circumstance can occur as well. Somebody finds their better nature, and a conflict eases into a peaceable path forward. We can't find our way through a tight spot, and then we happen to look up and realize there is a ladder waiting for us to climb up into a more expanded space.

When these moments come, our job isn't necessarily to attach to them and fall into the trap of thinking that everything is now going to be "better." Our job is to learn to accept them for the gift of grace they offer and the reminder that there isn't an ultimate magical fix to things— life is not quite as easy as that. But a fix of magic can happen that helps us tap into life's penultimate grace.

People and situations can sometimes surprise us in a good way. We can surprise ourselves with a burst of energy or stirring insight.

A clean breeze of fresh air can rustle through a stagnant space and leave a new energy of invigoration in its wake.

While it's terribly important to learn to sit with life and stay with our process, I also think it's vitally important to cultivate space for the gift of hope— the gift of positive change— the gift of transformative possibilities, where we are reminded that life is not a zero-sum game and grace can happen when we least expect it.

44

Hope's Hum

I like to tilt my gaze towards the sunlight as often as I can. Sometimes, it's not always easy, but I've learned the sun always shines, even when we can't see it through the clouds.

And that belief is where hope intersects in my life, playing a steady hum of beauty, prosperity, and faith in the unseen.

What brings you hope?

Whatever it is, wrap it in blankets to keep it safe and warm— even as you release it on feathered wings to fly to the sky and grow your dreams.

Make a hope chest and tuck little treasures, sacred objects, and scraps of inspirational words into it.

Make it a point to look for where hope is happening. Notice the good in the world. Notice where kindness, connection, and generosity exist. We need hope's medicine to nourish our hearts and uplift.

Let hope sing and help you march to the beat of your own probability. Strum your banjo of sunshine and opportunity. Believe in your seeds of self and sow them far and freely.

Know— and it shall be so— you're growing in the direction of your highest possibility.

45
THE MAKING OF A DREAM BEGINS WITH YOU

It's easy to talk about our dreams and making big changes in our lives.

Sometimes, these are just ideas passing through— thoughts and imaginings that allow us to contemplate new possibilities and then take that energy back into our lives to try to live with more openness, adventure, and whimsy.

But sometimes, we dream of big change, and it gets a grip on our hearts. We feel drawn to it. Intuitively and inexplicably, something deeper within us keeps urging us to move, even if we're afraid of making the leap.

Our inner voice keeps nudging us and inviting us into a more expanded reality if we can find the courage to believe and follow the light in our hearts.

Usually, when we get gripped by a dream of change, when those feelings don't leave us, and we feel called into a new way of being, it's because we ARE being called into a bigger being.

When that happens, I would tell anybody who dreams of life change: do it. Find a way. Start making a plan. Put your intention out there and ask life to come along and support you.

If you're waiting for the perfect time, that time might never come. Maybe YOU are the perfect time, and the rest will work itself out through each step of courage, faith, and change.

Know it will be messy and imperfect. Know most of it won't go as expected. Know that's okay. Know that you'll spend more time not knowing than you will knowing.

Through that process, you might just come to discover how much you like living in the wild unknown. Following the guidance in your heart and trusting in life's intelligent, creative force.

46

The Expansion of Possibility

When we live life from a place of fear, we restrict our opportunities to have an abundant life filled with the good things our hearts desire.

Fear of failure, fear of getting hurt, fear of lack, fear of looking foolish, fear of making mistakes— fear becomes a self-imposed prison that binds our freedom, shackles our hearts, and creates a wall between us and the rest of the world.

Nothing good will ever get in if you keep the best parts of yourself hidden behind that barricade.

Living from a place of love tears down walls and opens us up to receive the gifts life offers for ourselves, love for this beautiful world and the people in it, love for the people closest to our hearts, and love for life.

When we learn to love what's in our immediate circles, the world becomes infinitely more beautiful. We find more love and begin to expand the circle of our own possibility.

Begin with focusing on what's noble and beautiful: the gift of breath in your lungs, the intelligence of your heart, and the possibilities for your life as vast as the sky hanging overhead, reminding us to pause, breathe, expand, and look up.

47

Red Doors

"Once upon a time, in one of my former lives, I had a front door that was painted red. A beautiful uplifting red, cheery and inviting. Just a door. Just some paint. Yet so much more. A true symbol of what made me happy. Of what allowed me to dream and imagine and explore my existence.
That red door signified a welcoming warmth and safety in my inner haven, a daring sass and grit out in the world. Exactly the way I wanted to be."

—April M. Lee

We all have our Red Doors in life. Gateways that ask us to step into something brighter and bigger. We discover thresholds—some tangible, some intangible— that invite us through, reminding us there is a great life waiting on the other side.

Our Red Doors ask us to dream higher, reach further, and find the extraordinary in the ordinary span of our day.

Sometimes, these are simple things: the tulips you buy yourself for no reason other than you love fresh, pink flowers; hanging artwork of faraway places with a vision and intention to travel; and deciding never again to save sequins or fancy dishes for something special when Tuesday and every day and This Moment Right Now are waiting to be celebrated.

Sometimes, our doors are grander. Bold leaps of faith. A change of address or change of name. Identity shifts that lead to a change of self. We leave, we arrive, we revolve, we evolve through our doors stepping into the full of who we are.

It doesn't have to look a certain way— our possibility of being. Possibilities just ask to be realized, actualized, and experienced in our sacred ways. Possibilities are the gift of life. The gift of being. The gift of choice. And as long as we are *here*, in the space of right now, we always have opportunities for better, for more, for growth, for change, for new possibilities.

For new red doors inviting us into a higher expression of self.

48
Rose Gardens in the Stars

Whatever it is that you're dreaming about— dream bigger.

Don't waste time thinking about how it's going to happen, whether it's possible, or how you will get there— just start by dreaming. Allow yourself to imagine something beyond what you have previously imagined. Start with the seed of a rose and imagine planting an entire garden.

Imagine a rose garden blooming in the stars.

Allow your mind to expand and grow: the only way to free ourselves from limitations and invite MORE into our lives is to keep pushing through our previous limitations. Be open and stay curious, feed your heart with what tastes good to your heart. Remember leaps of faith start with pointing our internal compass towards our wishes, hopes, and dreams.

We take flight by making one small step after another as we keep building momentum in our dream's direction.

Our lives will only be as big as our dreams allow. That must begin inside— within our mind and our heart and our spirit— before the universe can respond to our intent, will, energy, and desire and help bring opportunities into our path to help us build and create our dreams.

This is what co-creativity is all about— a continuous dance with the cosmos as we dream big and keep putting ourselves and our dreams out there, then create with the ingredients life brings us. We become bigger through each act of dreaming as we keep growing our gardens towards the stars.

49

WITH HOPE

There are two ways we can go through life: with hope or without hope.

I figure it's just a bit easier to make our way along this crazy, winding path with hope as a companion. I know sometimes it seems hard to find, but it's really very simple. The clouds may part, and the light shines down, and you've been told to keep your faith.

A bird flies across your path, singing along, and you've been reminded to find joy. The sky changes in tone and shade, and you remember, so it is with life; no season lasts forever. Outside of us, or within us.

Our realities can be marked by dreams or despair, and they become what we choose to make of them. Perspective is a choice that lies in the eyes of the one perceiving.

As for me, I decided long ago this world already has too much that has abandoned hope and is in a place of despondency, and I will make no further contributions to that.

As long as I am given a choice as to who I keep as companions, I will choose to walk through this world with the perspective of belief and the glow of hope by my side.

50
A Shero's Point of View

Living an inspired life isn't about hopping from one giant aha moment to the next. It's not about keeping the momentum going all the time. It's not about never having crashes, burns, and false starts.

True inspiration is about showing up. It's about taking small, measurable steps that move you toward your dreams. It's about acknowledging those steps for what they are— you, doing you, and being your dream-shaker and change-maker.

Each of us is living out our story of inspiration if we can learn to see ourselves through the right lens.

We have to learn to see ourselves as the heroes and sheros in our own stories. Even if we're the unlikely protagonist or the dark horse story, we must learn to see the perseverance, grace, and diligence it's taken to get this far.

We have to see ourselves through a bigger scope of possibility and keep rescripting our narratives to honor the courage, heart, and kindness it requires to take this human journey and engage with life from a whole-hearted space. To heal our wounds, uncover our traumas, grow in wisdom, and do the good work of soul becoming.

Even in our dark stories, we can find ways to see our resilience, to cover the story with grace, to forgive ourselves for what we didn't know or do, to notice our strengths, to look for the buried light of hope, and to see ourselves through a shero's point of view.

We can learn that inspiration isn't always a glorious flame but can be a quiet spark we nourish with persistent affirmation, fortitude, and fervent belief in our possibility.

51

DREAM YOUR WORLD

Impossible, though they may seem, do not let the challenges in life rob you of your dreams or your ability to dream your world into being.

Maybe the time is not quite ripe for them to unfold, maybe the universe has more work to do in your life to prepare you for that unfolding, or maybe their fruition looks different than what you expected.

Sometimes, the bigger the dream, the bigger the challenges, not because life isn't supporting you in your dreams but because it is giving you the growth opportunities that will be required to truly stay the course to walk the dreams in your heart.

And if you don't dream them or breathe them into being through your energy, positive thinking, action, and courageous heart, then who will?

Dreams are a gift. There is a reason certain things light different people up; it's because the things that light us up individually represent the map to our treasure chest of dreams— dreams that exist in the space of our hearts and the inspirations that keep hummingbird through our minds, tugging us toward a grander vision.

Don't give up on your dreams, even when life reroutes you, or they seem far away. Even when you feel tested or challenged or are working on finding patience for the creative process. Dreams can take many forms, and we never know when they might materialize unexpectedly in miraculous or inventive ways.

52
THAT'S HOPE

It is difficult to find a sense of hope that transcends circumstances. This world can be a cruel and callous place, and it's easy to fall into despair and hopelessness. Yet there is more good than bad, more beauty than ugly, more light than dark— we just don't always see the hope that's there. But it is there.

Every time cruelty happens, and you let your heart feel, break, and reform, you create an energetic act of reparation, mending, and restoration in the spaces where hearts are closed in this world. And that's hope.

Every time you ask yourself, "What can I possibly do?" And you do something through the act of writing, speaking, praying, calling, thinking, creating, awakening, talking, sharing, singing, transforming, or any other act that keeps you open and caring instead of numb— that's hope.

Every time you try to right a wrong, your effort is seen and valued by unseen eyes and carries a ripple effect of goodness. Every time your efforts feel like they don't matter, don't make a difference, or don't have the consequence you expected, and you choose to return to a space of love? That's hope.

Every time you choose compassion over hate. Every time you refine your rage over injustice into informed action. Every time you sink your heels into the gritty mud of love, and you refuse to accept despair as your set point? That's hope.

It's easy to maintain hope when things go right, but it is hard, hard when they don't— when you hurt, when something breaks, when you see intentional apathy, when your stomach plummets sick, and your heart cracks wide over calculated cruelty.

If you are struggling with hopelessness, remember you're not alone. There is a whole world of people taking a stand for something better, speaking up when they feel something is wrong, praying in quiet hours, doing things behind the scenes that receive no recognition yet whose impact carries far, and sending mindful intentions of love out into the ether so good intentions sprinkle down and land where light is most needed.

There is an entire world of people who are being love's hands and heart by reaching up, out, down, and over, across, and far as they bring love into the spaces they touch.

And that's hope.

53

THE RESTORATION OF WONDER

It can be challenging to restore a sense of innocence to our beings when we've lost our sense of wonder. Sometimes, life's stress chips away at us, and we lose our sense of faith, hope, and awe; it happens to all of us.

The conditions of this life can be like the Wild West— unregulated, chaotic, and unjust. We crack against life's hard edges and begin to garner hardness where a softer space of joy once lived, so sometimes fighting for our right to have joy becomes necessary. To stake our claim in the ground and declare— "No matter what you bring me, life, I still insist on wonder."

Begin small. Begin with the little things. Begin by noticing nature and imagining what a gift it would be if you didn't have access to clean air, a changing sky, or the many elements of trees, seas, flora, and fauna that define our various geographies.

Begin with yourself. List your talents and strengths. Try to see yourself through a compassionate gaze.

Make a list of everything good in the world. Stand under an open sky and look up. Ask life to restore a hardened heart and to help you rediscover curiosity and amazement.

Cultivate this space. Be patient. Sometimes, it takes time to recover this part of ourselves. Whatever you do, don't give up on your desire to awaken to awe and joy again. Don't give up on miracles, magic, and wonder— they are happening all around us when we can take the jaded shades off our eyes and relearn to see from a space of purity.

Most of all, don't give up on yourself because you, dear soul, yes you— you are magical. You are beautiful. You are stronger than you think. You are capable of bright and beautiful things. YOU are wonder.

54

ON UNDERDOGS AND FINDING INSPIRATION IN QUIET WAYS

As inspiring as it is to see someone accomplish fabulous feats, I've learned that inspiration's true origins are humble and often happen in ordinary ways behind the scenes.

That's why underdog movies pull us in. We relate to the humble, unlikely individual who somehow manages to exceed their seeming limitations. Underdogs are all about showing up, taking incremental steps, and not giving up. While the big moment might be the culmination of their efforts, the true inspiration comes before the culmination in their willingness to try.

Each of us are underdogs in our own way, and though others might not always see the moments we choose to grow over giving up, we can learn to see these moments and become a fan of our own underdog story.

So, if you need inspiration in your life, then try asking yourself the following:

What have you been trying at in your life? Can you learn to see the hard, gorgeous effort in that? Can you learn to give yourself exquisite credit for whatever it is you're moving towards?

If you're not moving, can you learn to give yourself gentle credit for how hard it is to just show up and breathe on the days we feel lost, stuck, and overwhelmed?

Can you acknowledge how far you've come and how you keep putting one foot in front of the other and going? Can you learn to trust the process, even if you can't always see the way?

Can you learn to be inspired by your ongoing willingness to be beautifully, imperfectly human?

If you can answer yes to any of those— even if your yes is just a faint spark— I would tell you to grab onto that spark, breathe gratitude and appreciation over it, kindle it with a daily dose of heart-light and self-compassion, invite life into the mix and ask it to help your spark grow:

Then, see what you create from the deepest tinder of your soul.

55

THE THINGS DREAMS HAVE TO TEACH US

"Dreams pass into the reality of action. From the actions stems the dream again; and this interdependence produces the highest form of living."

—Anais Nin

If you stay with a dream long enough, you will begin to find that there is an incredible difference between contemplating a dream and actually living the dream.

Like anything else, dreams often look very different in the living than in the dreaming. So, like any truth we find in dream time, they require a bit of shape-shifting and adaptability in order to make sense of them.

They require a great deal of surrender, trust, and flexibility. They ask the dreamer to hold onto the essence of the dream while continually letting go of exactly how the dream will shape itself and what the final product will look like.

They require faith and fortitude, as well as continually coming back to a still space inside of ourselves and checking to make sure that our dream still feels authentic to our current understanding of ourselves. Often, we are asked to release a fantasy of how we thought something might materialize so we can embrace what is presenting itself to us and find the ingredients for our dreams within the scope of our lives.

Big dreams are not for those who shy away, or turn back, or give up easily. They are for the wild-hearted and those who dare to adventure into soul terrain and keep the faith when the path goes rocky and dark.

Our dreams are vital. They move, inspire, and spur us to push beyond how we imagined ourselves. Though some dreams are grand and inspire us to lofty ideals, dreams don't have to be grand to change an individual's life. Sometimes, they are humble in origin: a space to call our own, more joy in our lives, a heart that feels more uncluttered and free.

A dream will dance with you and not always reveal its full self to you when you begin to follow its threads, but I have found that over time, if we allow ourselves to become part of the interweaving of our dreams, they have a way of taking on a life of their own and create something brighter and better than even we could have imagined.

These are the lessons we begin to learn when we dare to make the leap from dreaming our dreams to choosing to live and become our dreams.

56
LESSONS IN LIFE FROM THE GIRL WITH THE CURIOUS HEART

This is the thing that is so sublime: a whole day is stretched before you, filled with the boundless promise of unending possibilities.

So, if you woke up this morning and took a breath, then break out the fancy dishes, put on your best dress, toast the universe, and celebrate, for you have been gifted with another day filled with new possibilities, new thoughts, new beginnings, new chances, and new heartbeats.

There are new passages of poetry to read, new sights to witness, new sounds in nature to hear, new things to learn about ourselves and each other, and new curiosities and discoveries to see.

There are possibilities for growth, possibilities that something wonderful might happen in the next instant, possibilities that you create that wonderful in the next instant, possibilities for learning something new that enriches your mind, possibilities for seeing beauty in the day that makes your spirit sing, possibilities for discovering something new within yourself you haven't met before.

At the end of the day, you can go to bed more than you were when you got up as you let the new colors, tinctures, and drops of experience from today alchemize with the evolving palette that is You.

Really, what more does one need to celebrate the art of living well than the gift of such glorious possibilities? How splendid is the gift of a simple day when we have the eyes to see, the heart to feel, and a perspective of curiosity and discovery.

57

Dreams Are a Living Thing

Dreams have timings of their own. We are asked to take responsibility for the origins of the dream, but sometimes, it takes a while to fully understand the nature of the dream, and our vision remains clouded.

I have found that you can't force a vision to come into fullness before it's time. It is the act of sorting and grappling with our questions that helps clear our minds and hearts to set the stage for when the bigger picture is ready to come into the light.

If we are seeking a life of juicy intuition, wild expansion, and the creative freedom to fully express and live the dreams in our hearts, then we are going to have to learn to find peace in the middle of flux and flow.

After all, the dreams in our hearts are a living thing because they are our deepest truth, and truth is alive in love. This means our dreams want to come to life. They are seeking us as much as we are seeking them.

They want to emerge, breathe, and grow into material form, and the more we let go of how we think things should look, the more the universe can assist us in creating them.

We just have to keep listening to our hearts, taking steps as we feel called to step, and knowing that following our dreams is how we dream the world our heart yearns for into being.

58

LEAP

There will come a time when you're going to be asked to leap.

It's going to feel so scary your insides will jelly into liquid-lava pools, and your heart will drum into fiery-flight frenzy, and your mind will freeze in suspended disbelief because what you're feeling called towards feels so indelibly BIG.

And you're going to do it anyway. You're going to do it, because some core part of you knows it's the right thing for you to do.

You're going to do it, because the voice of your soul will hold you to it, insisting this brave, big leap will be the genesis for a braver, bigger you.

You're going to do it, because despite your heart's thumpings and pumpings, it has been yearning for this moment, this rich opportunity, and waiting for its chance to break through and break out.

You're going to do it, because you've learned how to show up for you. And you've learned, through showing up for you, that spirit will always meet you in that space and help grow something beautiful and revolutionary.

Mostly, you're going to do it because it's who you are, and you never back down from who you are.

But just in case you're reading this, and you need a nudge in the right direction, just in case you've been asking for a sign or confirmation or message from the universe, here it is:

I believe in you. You are brave, and you can do it.

Now, please go take your leap.

59

THIS WORLD NEEDS YOUR LIGHT

In a world so big and busy, sometimes it's easy to feel your efforts don't matter. Everything can feel so overwhelming and insurmountable, and we, as individuals, can feel underwhelmed and small. And yet, when you think about it, what does that really have to do with you shining your light?

After all, even the smallest flame becomes a beacon of hope in a darkened room.

In a world filled with followers and likes, headlines, bylines, and fitting inside the lines, it's easy to feel lost and alone in the crowd. Yet, when you think about it, what does the crowd have to do with you shining your light?

After all, a solitary lighthouse standing on a hill can be seen for miles and miles. And it is a gorgeous beacon of guidance for those who need a light.

In a world that can be sensational in its dispensation of validation, it's easy to feel unheard and unseen. As if the only ones who count are the ones who make the loudest splash. And yet, when you think about it, what does that have to do with you shining your light?

After all, a mermaid can swim through the water with effortless ease, quiet in her grace; yet, she is utterly desirable and captivating to those who seek the mystery and magic she brings.

In a world filled with critics, the worst of whom is usually the one inside, it's easy to get downhearted and discouraged and believe you are too flawed, broken, or cracked to make a meaningful contribution.

Yet, when you think about it, what does that have to do with you shining your light? After all, just ask a piece of stained glass, a kintsugi bowl, or a colorful mosaic, and they will tell you how their shards and fragments became the ingredients that turned something jagged into a brilliant piece of art.

In a world so full, so big, so loud, everything that makes you feel cut down, quieted down, reduced, minimized, marginalized, ostracized, outside and looking in, it is easy to feel your contribution doesn't matter. And yet, when you think about it, what does that have to do with you shining your light?

After all, the energy of your very act of being has a ripple effect. The love, kindness, and good you cast out into the world continue in waves upon waves— many times in waves and ways you can't even begin to guess or see.

So don't discount yourself. Or doubt that you're here for a reason. Or dismiss your authority and voice. Or think your gifts aren't bountiful or abundant. Or talk yourself out of it because somebody else is already doing it. Or mistake results— as judged and defined by people— as the truth of your soul.

Because the truth of your soul IS light.

60
Mantra of My 2013 Self

I am not here to figure out the easiest, most comfortable, least possibility-of-experiencing-heartache way to get through life. If I wanted to do that, I would take the road more traveled, surround myself with sameness, and never have any adventures at all.

I am here to stand on my tiptoes at the precipice of the unknown and shout into the distance, listening to the unsung songs echo back.

I am here to push the limits of love so hard that I push past the barriers of illusion and fear until they fall, exposing glorious uncharted territory lying in wait.

I am here to walk the road of possibilities and dance along the fringe. I am not here for easy. I am here to change my corner of the world.

61

START, JUST START

Each day is yours to take and make. I know it doesn't always feel this way. I know it's hard sometimes. I know the struggle is real. I struggle, too.

Yet I also know there is so much beauty when we take the time to put on our rose-colored glasses and notice all the places our world is painted in color.

There is good happening when we cultivate good by finding the joy that exists. There is poetry, music, art, and color. Tree tones, river rhythms, sun's red rises and saffron sets. There is strange beauty in grief, which can teach us how hard we loved.

There is strange peace in chaos, which can teach us to find our center in life's mess. There is strange wisdom in not knowing, which can teach us to reach and grow into bigger perspective.

It is there waiting in life's buried treasures and hidden moments and grains of sand, which grist pearls out of life's rub. We must learn to become like the pearl and not the sand. To shine our solar light, even in dark skies. To allow our unknowing to compass us into new terrain of soulful being.

To never forget we are endless beings of love having a human experience and allow that divine truth to anchor us in the light. To work with our shadows constructively by witnessing, allowing and finding grace for anything within us that has not reconciled to the truth of love.

We can do this work— I know we can. We must do this work to become bigger. We must flip the script on life's hardships and use our intentions, words, and voices to write a new narrative on being.

Start with yourself. Start with this day. Start with who you want to be and how you want to experience yourself. Start with joy. Start with light. Start with authenticity.

Start with vulnerability. Start with real. Start with wholeness, which accepts all feeling states. Start with peace. Start with love. Start with seeing the best in yourself. Start. Just start. Go make something wonderful out of your day.

Pearls of Wisdom on Growth, Transformation, and Becoming

62
On Caterpillars and the Essence of Growth

"I embrace emerging experience. I participate in discovery. I am a butterfly. I am not a butterfly collector. I want the experience of the butterfly."

—William Stafford

If you've ever had the pleasure of watching a fuzzy caterpillar crawl along and do its caterpillar thing, you might have had a flash of thought that this little creature has no idea what lies in store for them. It has no idea that at some point, they'll go through a crazy transformation process, which might feel confusing, dark, and difficult, yet result in bright and beautiful things.

That's the thing with any transformation process where we, as humans, take the metaphorical journey of caterpillar to cocoon to butterfly— it usually feels confusing, dark, and difficult, but it also results in bright and beautiful things.

We can't often see when we're amid change that beautiful things can come from things that seem horrible. How new wings are grown out of the old. How it's okay to be like the caterpillar and not know what the future holds: we don't know what we don't know.

We grow new wings repeatedly, every time we let go, every time we move into a new cycle, and every time we release our grip on what was to open our palms to what might be. From Caterpillar to Chrysalis to Butterfly to Ending to Beginning— we grow our wingspan each time we shed who we no longer are, so we can keep freeing ourselves to become who we're meant to be.

Wherever you're at on the cycle today, it's perfect for you. Stay with yourself: that is the essence of growth. Stay with your process, trust the timing of your wings, and allow the energies of patience, struggle, and overcoming to alchemize and support your ongoing growth and discovery.

In the midst of such change or any kind of uncertainty, I find it incredibly helpful to keep referring back to the things I do know: Humanity is resilient, change is constant, nature soothes, the universe is abundant, art is vital to the soul, kindness matters, laughter heals, and love reveals what's best in us.

63

THE GIFT OF YOU

You are the only one who knows who and what you are about. Therefore, you are the only one with the true agency to discover your self-knowledge, claim your own story, and live an empowered life.

There will always be somebody out there willing to define you for you. To tell you who or what you are, or that you are doing it wrong, or that you are not enough, or that you're making too many mistakes, or that you don't fit the mold they think you should.

If you're not careful, it is easy to cloak yourself in these words, carrying them with you wherever you go, giving them power over you as you walk around in a constant state of apology, trying to prove something to someone.

A person could easily get trapped in this prison of self-imposed atonement without ever realizing they have always held the keys to their release, and that release is found through allowing yourself to awaken and embrace a bigger reality.

Release is found when you allow for expansion and let life's disruptions catalyze growth and change. You become bigger in this process and, in so doing, continually leave behind who you no longer are so you can embrace a more authentic, aware self.

Growth is an ongoing process, and personal evolution occurs through all stages in our timelines. We discover ourselves by listening to our inner voice and giving ourselves permission to change when we realize a way of being no longer feels right for us or we've become trapped in someone else's image of who they think we should be, and it's hindering us from becoming who we truly are.

You are not here to offer yourself as a sacrifice to the altar of apology. You are here to inhabit and embody the gift that is your life and, with great gratitude and reverence, become the you that you are meant to be. Allowing yourself to change, release, shed, grow, and change shape as often as needed in accordance with your requirements of growth.

64

BREAKING OUT

It can be hard to break your own mold. We get stuck in shapes that no longer suit us, but we've held them so long we don't know how to break away from our old version of self. We create pockets and parcels where we try to make space for something new to come out, but sometimes, there is still not enough space.

Sometimes, something drastic is needed because, despite our best intentions of trying to pop ourselves out, we fall back into the cookie-cutter shapes we have imposed upon ourselves and the ones others have come to expect of us.

But most molds are meant to be broken after a time. They are only useful for holding us in stasis and space so long as we find their shapes useful and in congruence with the shape we feel called to be in this world. Sometimes, our shape changes and our mold doesn't.

So, we must make a new one. Become the shaker, changer, and breaker of our shape, no matter how messy, difficult, or tiring. No matter, no matter. Because when our soul calls for growth, we must learn to break out of the old so we can free ourselves and find the space we need to begin to create the new.

65

Reidentification

Identity can be something both fixed and fluid. We are often called to grow beyond who we've previously been, yet it is up to us whether we choose to answer that call.

We might feel that something is out of sorts within us, and yet it can be difficult to give ourselves permission to follow that feeling through. We are tempted to try to press reset to make everything go back to how it was. Sometimes, following a feeling to the end of a maze will lead us to an outcome we didn't expect.

When we shift our sense of self, we might feel we've fallen between worlds, especially if we've undergone a big life transition. We find ourselves trying to step into a new identity— though it might feel disorienting and lonely, there are also gifts in this in-between place.

There is space to sort through our pieces and figure out what we still identify with and what we don't, what aspects of ourselves we want to keep, and which ones we want to leave behind. We are afforded the opportunity for self-evaluation, introspection, and reflection to better live an aligned life that reflects our understanding of ourselves.

During these identity shifts, it's important to find ways to anchor into what still holds true and do small acts of grounding that are good for our hearts and souls. Go be in nature. Seek out small moments of gratitude. Remember, it's a beautiful thing not to know who and where you are, as it is only in that vulnerable, amorphous space that we can learn to take on a new shape; we can't change our shape if we're entrenched in the boundaries of an old identity.

In those moments of deepest unknowing, we can try and practice patience. Remind ourselves that the soul has a timing all its own, that life has a way of moving towards wellness, and that just living life will help sort the contents out. In the meantime, even if we don't know where we quite fit or belong, we can always come back to a sacred space within and know:

We always belong to ourselves.

66
I'm Just Not Myself

We are not meant to stay the same person for the entirety of our lives. Hard as they may seem, emotional growth and spiritual change are exactly what we came here for.

It's difficult when we've left behind one way of being and haven't quite stepped into another. We find ourselves in a blackout of sorts. We can't see the bigger picture but feel the amorphous shifts within this undefinable space.

It's easy to fear these shifts and the unfamiliar. Sometimes, we feel we must live up to some status quo of self and return to a core set point if we lose our equilibrium. *I'm sorry, I'm just not myself,* we might say, as if this is something terrible that must be remedied immediately.

However, I've learned that the words— *I'm just not myself*— are always an invitation for life to grow into a new set point of self and leave the old status quo behind.

Sometimes, we must breathe the change and our answers to life by experiencing and living the questions, let ourselves be out of sorts for a bit, learn to turn each time the winds of change blow in, sift through the pieces that no longer belong, and find a new set point along the way.

In this space, we embrace self-evolution and the metamorphosis of soul. With grace and gratitude in our hearts, not quite the person we once were, not quite the person we're yet to be— we can find the courage to embrace uncertainty.

We might even find ourselves whispering with conviction, "I'm just not myself, and that's a beautiful thing."

67

New Moons

Deep breath, dear one. Yes, it's hard to change before your very eyes, sometimes becoming aches. The murmurings in your heart might not yet make sense, so you feel stuck in mid-dream, uncertain as to what tomorrow might bring.

However, that's the beautiful thing about life— there are always new moons, new seasons, new starts, new cycles, new possibilities, new chapters, new dawns, new dreams, and new tomorrows.

We are never stuck, static, or stagnant. If life feels static, there is never any time like the present to embrace your courage and take the first few steps down a new path, even if you don't know what that path will look like.

Begin by acknowledging your change to yourself. Ask for help from life to help you understand the nature of your metamorphosis. Set an intention on the new moon to illuminate what feels dark over the next cycle.

Trust in the time of your awakening, and when in doubt, take a cue from our lunar guide and allow for your own darkness. Trust that when the time is right, you too will phase into full, and come back to a space of light.

68

You Are the Reason

"Anything that is of value in life only multiplies when it is given."
—Deepak Chopra

Change can be hard. Change can be scary.

When it comes down to it, there may seem to be dozens of reasons not to, but here's one very good reason why—

You.

You.

You.

You are worth your change. You are worth your effort. You are worth a beautiful life. You are of value and a needed facet of light.

The more you learn to value yourself and ask more for your life, the more you invest in and give of that value by daring to become a higher expression of self—

The more you multiply in value. Then the more your gifts, warmth, kindness, presence, talents, awareness, impact, and unique essence grows.

You are worth your change, brave soul. You are reason enough. You are raison d'ê·tre. **You** are the reason.

69

NEW EYES

There are times when change is necessary. When it's time to change something in our outer world and make a big shake-up or move, sometimes changes in circumstances are good, healthy, and necessary.

But sometimes, big change is not available to us. Maybe our external circumstances don't allow for it, or we're at a time in our lives when the relationships, situations, and responsibilities around us don't necessarily allow for the freedom to radically shake things up.

Or we might just find that regardless of our circumstances, we chronically think the grass is greener on the other side. That if we only had this or that or the other, life would somehow be better.

Ultimately, we are the only ones who can truly ascertain what we need and how to best create new space in our lives. Sometimes, though, all we need is new eyes to see the old so it can be looked at anew.

We can find a fresh perspective that brings a sense of rewilding and reordering to our days. We can take a deep breath and remember that we have limitless choices when we tap into our heart's wisdom and remember the scope of our capability.

We can look at our lives and see each tiny gift and small wonder for what it is— a reflection of the miracle that is this brief, glorious wisp of riotous life.

70

BIGGER BEINGS OF LIGHT

When we live life from a place of fear, we put up walls to keep experiences out that we could potentially let in. We close our hearts to the beauty of the tiny miracles unfolding before us each day and the opportunities for magic, connection, and curiosity.

What a small way to live life, and while it is inevitable on our human journey that we will experience times where we feel let down by others or see the ugliness in the face of this world instead of its beauty, there is also so much joy and warmth to be found when we can keep our hearts open.

Freedom, truth, joy, beauty, connection, and miracles can be found when we operate from a place of love. It takes courage to live like this. But an open heart is stronger than a fortress of fear, and it knows that it's big enough to keep evolving, healing, and growing stronger through life's experiences.

More importantly, an open heart is a heart that grabs onto the experience of life and savors the good, the bad, and the in-between because it knows there is transformative alchemy in that mix. Each time we find a way to find the growth in a situation, we are actively choosing to become more.

Our growth might be reflecting on what we've learned from something. Maybe we choose to create meaning from our circumstances and seek whatever gems of insight and wisdom can be gleaned. Maybe we choose to find a way to bring love into the situation by practicing self-love and self-grace.

There is no right, wrong, or exact way to choose to grow; it just matters that we choose it. When we do so, we also transcend old programs and patterns, grow beyond our old confines of self, and liberate ourselves. We leave behind the confines of fear, expand into greater potential, and open our hearts to everyday miracles.

In this process, we become bigger beings of light.

71

BECAUSE YOU CAN

Strive for better. Be better. Do better. Not because you must, not because anyone is watching, not because anyone is keeping track, but simply because you can.

Simply because you are the only one who can choose to step into your potential. If you don't push through your barriers of self, how else will you create new space to reach higher and see what's beyond the limits you previously knew?

You and life can equate to one powerful partnership when we learn to work with the greater flow instead of always trying to fight the tide.

Life will always find a way to grow us, so instead of fighting it, we could give it a helping hand, collaborate with it, and see our circumstances as an invitation to learn to bend and flex our hearts. As we grow stronger, we can learn to grow upwards and keep setting our trajectory for the stars.

72

Unpacking the Backpack

Sometimes, we hang onto the past, the negative, and how things used to be because it is familiar, comfortable, and habitual.

Growth can hurt. It requires us to release and sacrifice our attachments to the past, which have sometimes become so ingrained into our being, our thought process, and our worldviews that we don't even realize we are carrying around a backpack that has been slowly weighed down with baggage that was never ours to carry in the first place.

Our metaphorical backpacks can carry many things. Old resentments, bitterness, and hurts over situations and relationships that didn't work out. Stories we've repeated to ourselves that keep ourselves small and oppressed. Ancient traumas, and dramas, and pains.

Sometimes, it's not our choosing that we've had to carry the burden of old wounds because of the hurts in our lives, and we're trying to heal our wounds and struggling to do so— please be gentle with yourselves if you're in this space.

But also know we're not meant to stay in the wound forever. We're not meant to carry that heavy weight until it becomes a part of who we are; we're meant to lay it down at some point and find what we need to undergo the good work of growth, healing, and change.

We're meant to learn to release, forgive, heal, let go, rethink our old notions, and not give up on believing in something better for ourselves. We're meant to challenge the accumulated weight of the past and find out who we might become if we laid that weight down and stepped into greater freedom.

We're meant to mindfully unpack the backpack.

Just because something feels comfortable doesn't mean it's how things must be or that it makes us happy. Real change requires self-examination, and self-examination leads to action. Action leads to healing, and healing always leads us deeper into our authentic selves.

73
Who We Wish to Be in This World

Change is inevitable, but growth is a choice.

While we can't stop change from entering our lives— life just kind of happens, and most of the time, we aren't expecting any of it— we do have a choice about how we choose to receive those changes.

When life is changing, we can resist it by reaching for the reigns of control, repression, avoidance, denial, and easy fixes that try and fit something back into a box it no longer fits, sweep it under the carpet, pretending it's not there, or lose ourselves in any number of addictive processes that will keep us so busy we never bother to look up and deal with what's right in front of us.

Or we can stay present and emotionally available to ourselves and allow the change process to help shape us, add to us, affect us, and make us more than we were before.

That is growth— becoming more than what you were before. And it can be messy, chaotic, emotional, and confusing. It can be very scary at times; in fact, allowing that space for growth may be the hardest thing you'll ever do, but there is no other way to expand your heart, soul, and mind except to choose a path of growth.

We are not here to stay static lest we repeat the same lessons repeatedly. We are here to become. Life constantly provides us with the necessary ingredients for change; it is up to us to choose what to do with it and own our rightful say on who we wish to be in this world.

74
Spiral of Becoming

Learn something new about yourself today. Recognize that each brand-new day starts with a bunch of unlived moments that we get to realize and live.

Know that all experiences and shades of being have value, so even the seemingly "bad" days will still teach us something about ourselves.

Know that if we dip deeper, beneath the surface of "seemingly bad," we will often find unnoticed treasures and hidden lights, which become the catalyst for more profound transformation later.

Remember, becoming isn't linear; it's more like a twisty spiral bringing us closer to our truth. There are a lot of nutty bumps, confusing moments, and goofy tumbles along the way. They're all a beautiful part of our bigger collection of self when we learn to embrace all our shades.

75

This Process Called Life

We're not supposed to have it all figured out in life. Everybody goes through seasons of feeling like they have things together and feeling like things are falling apart, seasons of rest and seasons of change, seasons of knowing and seasons of unknowing.

During the times when things are falling apart, people seem to judge themselves most harshly as if they somehow should have known better or done differently. Here's the deal, though: the only way you are going to grow is to go through seasons where things fall apart so you can learn about who you are, learn how to put yourself back together, and become something different than you were before.

It is only in the times of unknowing that we have the ingredients we need to soul-search, to work on ourselves, and to listen to our heart so we can find new knowing.

Becoming is hard. So is authenticity. So is letting yourself break so you can grow.

What's even harder is going through life pretending to be someone you're not, pretending to have it all together, pretending you're in control. There is no quicker way to suffocate the authentic self that is trying to get through inside.

Life is a process. It is okay to trust it.

76

Divergence and Displacement

There is often a gap between what was and what will be. It is a space filled with disquiet wonder, unraveling identity, and who we are unbecoming— the face of an unrealized self, peers out through the divergence in between.

When we experience major changes in our lives— grief, crisis of self, break-ups, divorces, relocations, endings, and other major changes— we feel ourselves diverging from what was and subsequently feel displaced. We might feel torn and caught between worlds.

Psychologically, displacement is a terribly confusing place to be. It can leave us feeling like we lost our place in line, and we're not quite sure where we now fit. Our old map of self no longer works, and we don't know how to chart a new one.

It is almost impossible to experience major life changes without feeling displaced. Our circumstances demand that we attend to their immediacy; any corresponding grief, pain, heartache, and stress preoccupies our attention and stretches our coping skills. We are busy dealing with the changes in our lives, and we begin to change right before our eyes.

We often don't even have words to express the strange shifts and feels inside. This can be jolting— we've changed in invisible ways that others can't see, and we've barely begun to grasp. Those changes can leave us feeling disenfranchised and uncertain about where we fit, who we are, and how to find a new rhythm.

We miss our old familiar self, even as we can't force ourselves to crawl back into that space. Displacement chafes and leaves us searching for a new sense of belonging, wandering outside our old lines, seeking what lies beyond what we once knew.

This process takes time and requires a great deal of patience and self-grace. We'll be asked to make a temporary home in the nebula of the in-between as we try and remember— for everything unforming, something new is reforming, gestation is a process, and incubation is sometimes necessary for something inside ourselves to grow.

Compassion helps, too, smoothing over the discomfort of this space and helping us see that sometimes discomfort is a necessity for comfort is enticing and often hard to release. We would never find the motivation to change and expand if not pushed past the comfortable limits of who we used to be.

77
IN THE DARKNESS

There will be times when you must learn to sit with the darkness. Sit in the discomfort of your change process and explore the black box where cessation slowly fertilizes the soils of new origination.

Perhaps the darkness comes in the small hours of the morning when we wake and worry and wonder; the shadow dancers come out to visit us and taunt us with every fear we have over when, if, and how things will work out. Sometimes, darkness happens in the broad light of day, and we show up, do life, and put on the best face we can, while inside, we feel the out-of-sorts schisms happening within us as we grapple and struggle with our unanswered questions of self.

It never feels good to be in the darkness. We might find our minds spinning, our stomachs knotting, and our chests tightening with fear. We might wonder about what feels unsolvable and unknowable. Maybe we wonder how we got ourselves into this mess, what we're going to do, or how we will figure out an exit plan.

When we find ourselves in this place, it's human nature to want to do all we can to avoid it, but it's a necessary part of transformation. This is the cocoon where we shed and release and sift and evaluate, where we come face to face with our fears and doubts and the voices of the anxiety in our mind.

This is the necessary process of dying to an old way of being, and it hurts. *Oh yes, it hurts.* I've been there many a time. I hate it even as I keep learning to embrace it, and here is what I've learned:

When you find yourself in this space, take a deep breath. You are safe in this moment. I promise you are, even if it doesn't feel like it. Don't forget that you have a strong mind and a stout heart. You can figure this out. You can change and grow and make different choices. You have resources, capabilities, and cleverness you've yet to tap.

Most importantly, you are never alone; you can ask for help and know that help is on the way. Terrestrial help, celestial help, energetic help, nature help, life help, love help, light help, even shadow dancer help— help in all sorts of forms that you won't see coming, but it will show up and meet you in your need and support your becoming process.

Over time, you'll look around and realize the darkness has begun to fade. You'll begin to discover the gifts of the darkness as you notice a sliver of hope waits on a new horizon.

78

New Wings

It's easy to talk about being the change, but to truly change is a different thing entirely. In part because the work of change is arduous, aching, and decidedly unglamorous.

There is little initial appeal in emptying the contents of one's life for scrutiny. All you have is a sense of conviction that you've had enough of the old ways and are willing to take responsibility for new ways. And when you have such a conviction. Listen to it.

The process of real change is day-to-day— time in the trenches, challenging your behaviors, thought life, habits, relational patterns, and emotions. It's the release of pretending you got it all under control.

It's a commitment to doing things differently and then doing the work. And nobody can do this work for you. It is your decision, your accountability to hold yourself to better standards, and your responsibility to oversee your work. Work that is lacking in glory because it occurs inside, and there is little validation initially for such tiresome, internal tasks.

But if you stick with it, the validation will come— possibly from others, but by that time, it really won't matter. For you will have found that in the process of changing your life, you have fallen in love with your own life and vision. You will have claimed your life with such beautiful embodiment that you will never go back to the way things were before.

You cannot shove a butterfly who is flying free back into its cocoon.

If you're stuck in the middle of the work today and can't see the forest through your trees, just keep going. Try again tomorrow. It may be hard, but it's worth it. You will find your change, and your new wings will soon come.

79
Tending to Our Inner Gardens

Life has very little room to bring us the green of new growth when our space is already cluttered with physical, emotional, mental, and relational weeds.

The dandelion grows through the cracks of the sidewalk. The ivy creeps up the side of a building. It tells us that life continues to grow and will find a way despite whatever tries to block it. But it is much easier to help life along and give it fertile space to grow into a beautiful garden. Instead of making it push its dandelions through our cement.

Sometimes a good pruning and cleaning of the weeds is what we most need to create open ground for expansion. So, we can invite in new life and create space for it to grow. Journal your feelings. Do some release work. Mindfully speak into the universe what you're working on letting go.

Forgive or at least work on forgiveness. Write about what you've learned from your current soul cycle. Buy yourself a new plant, or cacti, or a bouquet of flowers to represent your invitation to new growth. These are all ways we can tend to our weeds: by showing up, staying present, and choosing to do the work of letting go, clearing out, and setting an intention for growth.

We are in a constant state of transformation and creation. The energies of decay and release are balanced out by new seeds and growth. We can't stop this process from happening. We can learn to trade resistance for acceptance and tend to our inner gardens of self with vigilance, care, and faith.

80

SHAPES

We sometimes forget that part of our personal growth and evolution is not just our ability to metamorphosis and change shapes but our need for those things.

This is a need we don't always understand— particularly if we believe our life path is meant to be fixed and that we should have ourselves "figured out" or have things more well-ordered, organized, and tidy.

Sometimes, we get scared when we begin to question our path, and yet if we don't allow ourselves the space to question, how can we discover more about ourselves and learn to listen to our intuition and soul's urgings for growth?

A person could live in a square hole their entire life and never realize they were meant to be round, expansive, and growing upwards in gentle spirals of light. Even as they do the inner work of spiraling downwards into self-discovery, healing inner wounds and old patterns that no longer serve who they are becoming.

Our questions are clues. Our discontent is an invitation to sit with ourselves and reflect. Our urgings and yearnings are opportunities to seek new meaning and engage with the self with curiosity.

We are meant to change. Built for change. Constantly changing. So, we best learn how to better embrace change and work with our growth with constructive determination and curiosity.

When we feel stuck, rigid, or trapped in our lives, we can take a deep breath and allow for the possibility that we are trying to change forms and know ourselves in a new way.

We can seek support from those who have walked the path before and allow space for our questions to flow.

We can try to trust that through our process of living, we will gradually find the answers to ourselves— in a non-linear, imperfect doodle of geometry, heart, and alchemy. We, too, will eventually evolve into a new shape.

81

THE COURAGE TO SURPRISE YOURSELF

It doesn't matter how well you think you know yourself; the day you stop surprising yourself is the day when you stop growing. Be curious, be open, and allow yourself to be unexpectedly moved.

You might surprise yourself with new thoughts, new perceptions, or new revelations that suddenly come through. You might surprise yourself with your own audacity of what you dare to dream or think. You might surprise yourself with a new way of being or seeing.

Life loves a good surprise, and part of our growth is to always allow for the ever-unfolding mystery of ourselves. If you need a little inspiration, do something differently.

Read poetry. Make art. Try out a new place you've always wanted to go. Learn a new scientific fact about the world around you. Watch a documentary on wildlife. Go to nature and take the time to notice something you've not noticed before.

Start each day with a curious heart and the questions, "I wonder what adventures in living this day might bring?" and "I wonder what new things I might learn about myself today?"

Sometimes, surprise is a matter of shifting perspective, and other times, life sneaks up on us, taps us on the shoulder, and brings something new into the mix in the most surprising of ways.

82

Metamorphosis

There are times in our lives when change happens suddenly. A lightning bolt moment will crack us wide open, and we never see it coming. But more often than not, change happens in degrees, gradations, and tones.

Life's ocean slowly erodes and reshapes our soul-shore. We respond with subtle variations of intention and thought that gradually lead to new patterns and shades in our palette. After a while, those shades become a part of us, and we realize we've integrated new ways of being, and in so doing, we've created space for more change.

So, don't be discouraged if you feel like you're not moving as fast as you think you should. Or you've been trying to transform and find the nature of your metamorphosis has taken place throughout many seasons instead of one swift swoop. Or if you feel like you should have healed or empowered or improved yesterday, and you don't think you're far enough along today.

Just offer yourself up to the waters of life and trust your heart-terrain is exactly where it needs to be in the change. Then, think of one small tangible thing you can do to support your personal palette of growth and move in that direction.

83
Upside Down and In-Between

Being human can be a very disorganized and disorienting experience. We can get lost in ourselves and get in our own way, or we can stay too long in a space and not be able to figure out how to get ourselves out. At times, we get stuck in the mud, and we feel like we're moving through life upside down underwater.

When we feel stuck, no matter where we find ourselves, we can always do what we can with what we already have, release the bigger pictures, and focus on finding our way day to day.

We can set small goals and map out simple tasks for ourselves. We can shake things up: take a class, find a hobby, or try something different. We can focus on finding joy in the moment by making a gratitude list of everything that makes us smile or writing down ten things we like about ourselves.

We can color, doodle, or sketch. Read a story, or better yet, write a story. Say a prayer of love. Say a prayer of peace. Offer up a loving kindness meditation.

We can be in nature. Take a hike. Go sit by water. Go listen to a tree. Look up at the sky and breathe. Create presence in our immediate circles of connections.

It doesn't matter what we do, but it helps us learn to work constructively with the upside down and in-between times in our lives. Sometimes, the simple things help us the most, encourage us to stay on our course and wait until the energy shifts. Sometimes, the simple things help us build a path to greater movement. We see the bigger picture we've been seeking and feel more assured of our next step.

When life feels stuck, and you're not sure where you are in the process, remember that being human is a messy collection of experiences, feelings, and states. It's not about perfection. Growth isn't linear; change is chaotic, and it happens in small shifts and giant leaps with a lot of waiting around in-between.

In those in-between times do what you can to find perspective and just stay busy with the simple act of engaging in the perspective of you.

84

Breaking Ourselves Awake

Some of the best gifts in life come from things that can't be fixed—things that are broken, falling apart, and in tatters. These things force us to dig deep into our well of self and seek the building blocks of resilience, reinvention, and realization of our capability to make it through.

This becomes a realization of self we would never have realized if things had stayed together in the first place.

It's hard to become. Sometimes, it aches and chafes. It's difficult to break, fragment, and unravel. But the cracks create new space, where new grace and insight can enter, so we can see something beyond what we've previously known and become something more than we were before.

Even the most splintering things in life seem to come with their own strange medicine of transformation. When we begin to step back from the need to control and fix, instead letting the work of change become more present in our lives, we might begin to see that sometimes, it is only through life's fissures that we find a higher path of regeneration, redemption, and growth.

85

Deconstruction

We can't begin a new life without letting go of an old one. If we try to skip that process, we will often find our old life follows us into the new, still trying to finish itself.

Anyone who has ever been through a major life transition knows about deconstruction. Sometimes, we deconstruct a place we've lived, a relationship we were recommitted to, a period in our lives that has ended. Sometimes deconstruction happens internally and may eventually lead to external change, but the dismantling begins within our inner foundations.

Both forms require a lot of packing, unpacking, dissolution, questioning, evaluating, shifting, planning, laboring, grieving, releasing, hoping, wondering, and figuring out our next step. Taking something apart is psychologically dissonant and difficult. It can make us feel like we don't know where we belong, yet deconstruction is often necessary for completion and closure.

It is only in deconstructing the foundation of what has been that we will find the space and the ability to reconstruct something new. When you find yourself in this space, go gently on yourself. Letting go takes time. Shedding takes time.

You might feel uncertain and caught between worlds for a while. Find the small things that help ground you. Remind yourself often, "I am going to be okay." Take deep breaths. Know that you may be so busy showing up for the change that you will do retroactive griefwork— when you can better access and allow for the sorrow of what has passed— after the fact.

But if your heart can grab onto soft rays of hope and light, then, also allow for the possibility of what may come. All endings lead to new beginnings. When something dies, something else is reborn.

It may take time, but if you stay with yourself, there is a new life waiting on the other side. You might not see it right now, but it's coming, and there will be new gifts and beauty. I promise, dear soul.

86

No Longer Willing

It takes bravery to be the person you are meant to be. To stand up and place loving boundaries around your life that welcome and nurture you and minimize what hurts your soul.

To cast off others' interpretations and judgments about who you are. Refusing to let them hold that kind of power over you so you can live and claim your truth, even if nobody else understands that truth.

Arguing in favor of your innate expansiveness and ability to carry forth your dreams, instead of arguing in favor of staying small by defending your limitations. Giving yourself permission to be the divine love that you are, realizing that love begins inside yourself.

Sometimes, bravery looks big and bold, sweeping through our lives, uprooting the familiar in exchange for radical change, rearranging everything in its path, taking us on exciting adventures, and ushering us into new territory.

But, often, before reaching that bold sweeping state, the origins of bravery begin with the faintest of a flicker. A simple spark, set into motion when we find the courage to speak the words—

I am no longer willing.

87

THE BUTTERFLY EFFECT

Definition: a property of chaotic systems (such as the atmosphere) by which small changes in initial conditions can lead to large-scale and unpredictable variation in the future state of the system
—Merriam Webster Dictionary

It starts with a "yes."

The yes is usually said in a quiet space, on a lonely night, when you're listening deeply, and you decide you can no longer ignore the insistence of the voice within.

You whisper your "yes" out into the stars and wonder if anyone is listening. Even though you may be terrified of what your "yes" may mean, you feel your heart nod in resounding accord.

You begin to allow yourself the possibility of more. The possibility of your possibility, and what might happen if you let go and surrender into unfolding. Slowly, perhaps quickly, things begin to shift. You begin to see space and movement where you perceived none before.

The more space you find, the more you allow yourself to unfold and let go as you feel and grow into your possibility. You might even have to shake up your life to do so. Releasing, recanting, resetting, relocating— your heart thrums stronger with each brave shake.

Except the path doesn't look as you expect. You thought you were heading right, then the universe gives you a left. You thought you were heading up, when instead you wind up falling down.

You thought you were walking forward, then you find yourself, seemingly, stepping back.

You keep on saying "yes." Moving slowly, moving sideways, still moving towards.

What you may or may not realize is that when you gave your "yes" in that quiet space long ago, your "yes" became an answer of YES to life. YES, to your heart. YES, to your potential. YES, you will open yourself to the change process allowing you to become your most authentic expression of self.

Your YES sets into motion a cycle of events like the butterfly effect. Each one cascades into the next, impacting, tipping, and affecting the entire ecosystem that is you, offering you the exact ingredients you need to become a more authentic expression.

The ingredients aren't what you expected. Some of them are tricksters— things disguised as seemingly bad so they can trick you into new learning and growth.

But as you begin to look back, over the rocky road you've walked, crawled and swam to make it this far— you begin to see when you mix the ingredients together, you've been given exactly what you needed to experience, expand and know.

Your YES created the butterfly effect, in which your heart and life conspired to bring into material form whatever you needed for the highest growth.

As you step forward on the path you created, each new step is courage. You realize how far you've traveled from what you knew to what you now know. You are doing it. You are staking claim to your life. Your heart and your dreams embody a fuller expression of your soul.

88

The Bold Stroke of Reinvention

The concept of reinvention sometimes sounds a little more glamorous in theory than it feels when we live it. It sounds like an invitation to live life in glorious technicolor. We admire the ideas and imaginings that reinvention's brave, bright colors evoke and notice we feel inspired to dream bigger dreams when we contemplate reinvention.

But what we might not know or understand about the process of reinvention is the gritty inner work and emotions that occur behind the scenes to create those brave, bright colors of alignment and change.

The inner work of reinvention will teach us that shifting an identity is hard because it requires the leave-taking— and often griefwork— that comes from letting go of older ways of being and older concepts of self. All while we retain enough of a sense of original self to tap into our inner compass and stay our course.

Reinvention continually invites us to let go of the pain of the past so we can move forward with the integrated wisdom of our experience.

We are asked to lose old ways of being and old ways of understanding ourselves, even as we hold onto enough of our essence and allow the wisdoms, lessons, and love we've previously experienced to help us hold onto the truth of who we are. This is hard, brave work that often leads to a sense of uncertainty and loss of identity.

This is the strange dance of tension between growing ourselves forward and being content where we are now; trying to make our dreams happen and receiving our dreams as they happen; and being an agent of change and creator of our lives and ceding to the bigger process when we realize our lives are better lived in surrender.

There is no perfect balance to this. Equilibrium is unobtainable. The sweet spot between what we can control and what we can't is where our biggest lessons and brightest faith are found.

We learn to reinvent ourselves through the tensions of creating and receiving, unbecoming and becoming, experiencing and integrating. We slowly give ourselves permission to keep redefining and reinventing ourselves with each bold, brave stroke.

89
CREATURES OF THE DEEP

I have found that it's usually not very helpful to ask, "Why?" There are a lot of whys in this world; such is life.

We live in a beautiful world, but there are rips and tears in its fabric that any of us can get caught in. And, of course, when you get snagged, have it out with life if you need. Have it out with your higher self. Have it out with the universe. Have it out with the forces that be. Have it with God, the fates, the destinies, and the what-could-have-beens.

Have it out as much as you need for as long as you need. Just know that for some things, the question of "why" will only take you down a dead-end road that leads to little except resentment, bitterness, and self-pity. If this is where you need to be for a bit to experience these emotions, then by all means, be where you need to be. We deserve to feel what we feel— and sometimes need to feel it long, fast, and hard— before we are ready to move on and feel other things.

But at some point— for our wellness, our healing, our moving through and mending of hearts— I have found it helpful to accept that life happens. Things will come to pass in this place. Sometimes, it's wonderful and good. Sometimes, it's tragic and sad. And a better question than "why?" is how we choose to navigate it.

Do we do something destructive or choose to construct something new?

Do we stay open to life or close ourselves off to the world?

Do we remain in the broken place of what was or try to move into the space of what may be?

We don't have a say about the things that break us; we can only say what we'll do with our pieces. No matter how fractured and shattered those pieces may be, we are all equipped with the glue of love— each of us finding it in our individual ways and forms, and it is up to us to find a way to mend those pieces back together.

Make them into something more nuanced than they were before. Bigger. Deeper. More authentic. So, we can keep growing into these beautiful, numinous creatures of the deep, who always figure out a way, even in the dark, to find the light.

90
The Destination is the Path

The purpose of any truth is to learn to live it, embody it, and own it. Let its veracity become the key to liberating our hearts and beings on a deeper level.

After all, obtaining wisdom, truth, and knowledge doesn't do any good if we don't integrate it into our being. Without integration, it's mind candy— something sweet that our brain sucks on for a while, which does nothing to sustain us because we haven't found ways to make it nourishing and substantive in our lives.

And that's why we're here— to learn to integrate and then live our truth. The only way I know to do that is by opening our hearts, listening to the voice of the deeper self, and finding the courage to live our truth and become.

Becoming doesn't happen all at once. It's about continually taking small steps that keep moving us toward our true north because there are no shortcuts along the path— the destination IS the path.

We keep unbecoming who we no longer are to step into a more authentic expression of self. There are no shortcuts to our dreams, no shortcuts to leveling up and becoming a bigger person, and no shortcuts to living our heart's truth.

There's just dialing in, listening, and then taking small steps daily that move us toward our true north. There is trusting, allowing, and receiving. Knowing that if we find ways to live what our heart tells us, we will be fully supported on the path. Because that's what embodying our truth is all about trusting, allowing, and living our hearts out loud.

91

Mud or Stars

Spirit has its own timing for each of us. We sometimes want to be "there already" and somewhere other than where we are at. "Level up" without the work of going down into the tunnel of the soul so we can dig for our truth and find the gems within.

The more you undergo this process, the more you realize there is no end when it comes to the soul. We are bottomless, and so there is always a deeper level to unravel; it is how we transcend our prior gateways of self and expand our awareness into the infinite.

We get tripped up, because we think we've already done the work. We've already dug to our deepest level. We've already squished around in our mud and returned with the golden lotus. Yet, that's often not how it works— there are always deeper truths we are invited to realize.

If you identify as a lightworker, if you identify as a healer, if you identify as a sacred space holder, if you identify as somebody who is here to change the world for the better, then most likely, you've had to dig. And dig. And keep digging. And every time life plunges you back into the mud, you wonder why you're there, if you're doing it wrong, or if you missed the mark somehow.

Yet, I would say you are right on target with your own soul growth. Anything falling apart is there so that new space is created in your life. It's possible that the new space may be even greater than what you've already imagined and is in perfect accordance with your soul's higher plans for you.

Don't forget, we live on a planet of creative evolution. A planet that is always moving towards life and wellness, which means sometimes the planet itself has to purge, cleanse, dig, and erupt in order to create space to align itself with new life. Since we've been given a place on this planet, we, too, are tied into its creative process and are each involved in a creative evolution of self, which moves us toward new space, new life, and new alignment.

This means that whether you find yourself in the mud or the stars, you can always trust that you are moving in the direction of wellness.

Pearls of Wisdom on Self-Love, Self-Belief, and Self-Trust

92
Canvases of Grace

Self-love is not self-centered; it's self-caring. It's not about self-gratification and self-interest but self-acceptance and self-compassion. Self-love has nothing to do with selfishness and everything to do with treating ourselves with kindness, care, openness, and warmth.

When we learn to treat ourselves with exquisite tenderness and begin to learn to love ourselves with abiding affection, we start to become gentler, softer, and kinder. We become more accepting of our nuanced shades and embrace our myriad parts. The compassion we come to know inside can't help but change who we are outside, so everything we touch becomes gentler, softer, and kinder.

Like all the best paradoxes, we will find that love doesn't diminish the more we love ourselves but increases. So, it can't help but flow outward, making us better able to love others. The difference is that we love from a place of choice, not obligation.

We are no longer emptying our wells dry to fill others up or give them the words of warmth and kindness we also need to hear. We are making space to gift those things to ourselves. It is not self-serving to do this integral work of loving ourselves; it is necessary so we can live with greater authenticity, compassion, and freedom.

We grow fierce with courage in matters of love, and that energy radiates from us. Then, wherever we go, we become these beautiful, walking canvases of grace whose love spills out upon the thirsty ground.

93
Shine Bright for Yourself

It is our sacred responsibility to find ways to discover the light within ourselves, or as I like to say— learn to make our own sunshine.

We can share our light with others and glean inspiration from each other if our light is feeling low and someone else is shining a little extra bright. We can learn from what others are doing to help encourage the creation of light within ourselves.

What we can't do is be another's perpetual light if they are unwilling to find their shine. We can't drain ourselves to light another up. We can't keep our heart light shining bright as we try and ignite the heart light of another.

We can't dim ourselves to make another shine brighter without beginning to lose our shine. No matter how large the scope of our inner light is or how great our ability to generate warmth, belief, hope, and light, we slowly collapse when we try to lift another with our light who refuses to do the work for themselves.

Be an inspiration, a guide, a lighthouse, a candle, bright and beautiful— whatever you wish to do with your light. Gift your light wisely to others, and know that it is our sacred responsibility and sovereign right to find and live our path of light.

In the words of my younger self—

"It took me a long time to realize I am not here for others. I am here for me. And when I am here for me, I can better be there for others in the ways I was meant to be. This life's great paradox: I shine most bright for others when I shine most bright for me."
—Heliotrope Nights

Shine bright for yourself, first and always.

94

Don't Abandon Yourself

We fear abandonment from others, yet how often do we first abandon ourselves? Our truth, our voice, our thoughts, our opinions, our wishes, our desires, our perspectives, our fears, our individuality.

Many of us have lain down our rights to claim ourselves, letting others define and dictate the terms of the relationship or letting the world shape who we become instead of listening to the information in our hearts so we can inform the world who we choose to be.

When we do this, we abandon what is most essential inside of ourselves. Sometimes, we don't even recognize that it's happening, and our unwitting neglect of self becomes a slow drift. Over time, we begin to feel out of sorts and have a loose sense of self, and yet we can't pinpoint the cause of our unease and why we feel so thin and vapor-like.

The good news is that reclamation is as simple as choosing not to give up on ourselves. It's making the choice to return to the compass of our hearts and return to ourselves through small steps and giant acts of courage and faith. We can learn to tune into what's inside of us. We can learn the landscape of our inner world.

We can start with a journal entry or do something that brings us joy and lightness of heart. We can travel to a new space, a new land, a new coffee shop— we can always work with what we have and create adventures to meet ourselves. We can search for our missing pieces and trust that our hearts will intuitively guide us to find our clues to ourselves.

We can listen to our hearts, get in touch with our wisdom, and ask ourselves what we need. We can be patient with our process— good things take time, and the good work of replacing and reclaiming ourselves is a process we live out through many cycles and seasons.

But we can begin this work and take up the sacred flame of self. We can learn not to abandon ourselves each time we show up, listen to what our heart has to say, and then find one way— no matter how tiny or tall— to honor our truth of self.

95

TO LEARN SELF-TRUST

Why is it so difficult to trust our experience of self when that same experience is often the key that holds the answer to our questions?

Why is it so difficult to trust our experience of self when our soul feels wrong, our core feels cold, and our heart feels stuck, yet the world says this is the path we "should" take, so we keep on walking it instead of finding what we need to heed our own voice?

Why is it so difficult to trust our experience of self when there is nobody else capable of telling us about that experience except ourselves?

What if we live in such a way that we become our own experts? What if we treat our matter of soul as if there is no greater matter? What if we realize to love is to know the divine and, in so doing, find the divine within ourselves?

How would things look different? Where would we allow ourselves space to grow? Most of all, if we embraced that deep felt-sense of innate soul trust, who might we become?

If we really learned to trust ourselves and believed deep down in our ability to make it through and be okay— no matter what happens— then we would have so little to fear because we would know that at any given point in time, we are standing at our crossroads of change gently beckoning to the unmet self as if to say:

Come on out, my friend, just walk with me— we've got this.

96

To Live at the Pace of Love

What does it mean to live at a self-honoring pace?

I've been exploring that question for years, and I've come to see that living at a self-honoring pace is deeply tied to trusting our intuitive self and our experience.

We can't be self-honoring if we constantly judge, doubt, criticize, or feel wrong about our way of being in the world.

Being self-honoring means being self-loving and learning to live at the pace of love by listening to our hearts, trusting our internal rhythms, and validating our experience of self, even when others and the collective voices of society don't understand.

The way of the heart is ALL about finding our answers through the act of living and staying open to what life brings us. Learning to live at the pace of self-love reminds us that we don't have all the answers, but we can stay open to the process of finding out and learn to trust deeply in our inner voice.

Start by listening to your soul cycles. Ride the wave of energy and take inspired action when you feel nudged. When you feel called, step out of the stream of life and rest for a bit. Allow yourself space to process, grapple, and think.

Seek out wisdom when it speaks to you. Reflect on your wants and needs. Know you don't have all the answers and be relieved—you don't have to have all the answers. You just have to keep showing up for yourself and trying to live a self-honoring path.

Become an expert on YOU: your contractions and expansions, your ebbs and flows, your shifts and growth. Refuse to give up on creating a life that profoundly honors the truth of your soul. This is what it means to live at the pace of self-love.

97

CULTIVATING SELF-LOVE: A FEW HOW TO'S

What do we do if we struggle to find the voice of love inside ourselves? Sometimes, we haven't had loving role models in our lives, and the voices of criticism, disparagement, or cruelty have torn us down, so we never learned how to develop a space of compassion and warmth inside ourselves.

The good news is that we can change this and learn greater self-love. Our minds are wired to create new pathways and patterns of being, and our hearts innately know how to love. That wisdom resides inside each of us, so even if this world has done its very best to make us forget how to love ourselves, our hearts still remember, our minds can learn, and we can cultivate our relationship with self-love.

Don't know what self-love even means? Aim for the ballpark of developing the qualities of inner warmth, compassion, and acceptance, and you'll be headed in the right direction.

If you seek to discover a more loving voice inside of yourself, then think of it like pulling on and building a new skill. We can draw on external resources to instill a pathway for self-love. If you need a few ideas, try these:

What color is self-love? Or try these variations: what color is compassion? What color is grace? What color is kindness? Take 30 seconds and imagine that color is gently swirling through your heart.

Draw on archetypes of unconditionally loving figures, such as the proverbial fairy godmother, the goodly oracle, or the wise woman who always knows just what to say. Find the characters in books, films, stories, or real-life role models who represent the qualities of kindness, warmth, and wisdom to you. Imagine that they are part of your inner circle of support, teaching you how to be gracious and warm towards yourself.

Tune into nature. Notice how the earth manages to make space for all of us and compassionately grant us space on her land. She embodies acceptance, and we can learn to cultivate a greater sense of acceptance by paying attention to what the trees, the seas, the plants, the sky, the moon, and any other natural element have to teach us.

Last, never forget that you are a powerful agent of change. If you set an intention to learn to love yourself, then you can absolutely trust that your heart will begin to draw into you the right resources, solutions, supports, ideas, and inspirations to help you create a pathway into learning to love yourself, exactly where you're at.

98
Sacred Circles

There are certain truths in our lives that we will keep spiraling back to. Like a constant reawakening where the shells fall from our eyes, and we suddenly see more clearly. We continue to lose our shells as we arrive at deeper levels and meanings of our truth. Our work is never done; self-discovery is our life's work.

We tend to think we should be finished with something—learn the lesson, have an insight, be "over" it. But the truth they don't tell you is that life isn't about being over anything. Life is about learning to be all things, embracing all experiences, all aspects of self, and all shades of our full.

And so, we form sacred circles back around ourselves. Sometimes wounds we thought were healed, old memories we believed laid to rest, and past pains we thought retired get re-churned up, and we wonder why they've come knocking again.

They've come knocking again, so we can keep learning. Keep meeting unrealized aspects of self. Keep realizing and actualizing who we are. Keep releasing old wounds, thought patterns, and ways of being on deeper and deeper levels.

Until one day, we will have spiraled so deep into the truth of our core that we will see that it all comes back to love; every moment and each lesson is an opportunity to learn love is the force that's been drawing us inward all along. Because discovering the self is an act of love. Knowing yourself down to your deepest level is an act of love.

Honoring your truth and finding the courage to live it? This is the essence of what it means to fully embody self-love.

99
BUILDING OUR INNER HOME

If home is where the heart is, I continue to build my home where my heart resides— inside myself. There is plenty of space for others to come and go and even pull up a chair, grab a drink, and stay awhile. But at the end of the day, when it's just me, I want my heart light to burn still, high and bright.

This is why I believe it's vital to find the things that light us up and spend regular time returning to our inner home.

Nature. Colors. Animals. Things that help us connect to love. Small comfort rituals and tiny acts of presence. Brie cheese on a picnic blanket with a favorite show in the living room. Fairy lights and fluffy blankets. The gift of a cherished book who has become an old friend. Time spent connecting with the heart through meditation, contemplation, journaling, music, and art.

It doesn't matter what we do; it matters that it fills us up and nourishes our inner sanctum.

Loving others starts with loving ourselves, and when we love someone, we want to spend time with them, cultivating that relationship, creating a sense of warmth and flow, and this includes our relationship with ourselves.

If we want to build a home inside ourselves so we can always find a space of safety and be a boon friend to ourselves, then time with ourselves becomes a necessity and our subsequent gateway to creating a well-trod path to help return us home.

100

THE WAY OF THE HEART

It's increasingly easy to feel lost in the shuffle of this world. The language the world speaks is not always the language of compassion or connection. There's often a false sense that others are doing better in life than we are.

It's as if there are invisible rules and standards that we're each trying to live up to, and when we fall short of our own expectations, we feel like a failure. We expect to know things nobody taught us, be well-organized, have it all figured out, and be fixed in identity. Yet these expectations are the opposite of the true journey of being human.

We're not supposed to know; we're supposed to make mistakes to learn the nature of this world and gain experiential wisdom. Life is meant to be fluid and often chaotic. It has its own ebbs and flows, and we do better when we learn to lean into its cycles instead of resisting them.

We often must break to awake. Disruptions of consciousness are the only way to create space for change and new perspectives. In this space, we are invited to step into a bigger version of ourselves, and we can better connect with the call of our soul and live life from a heart-centered place.

Being ourselves, doing our inner work, and paying attention to the language of our hearts is how we connect with our purpose. We live life moving forward while learning to turn inwards, and where the two intersect creates the way of the heart. The wisdom of the heart becomes our salvation in a world often out of sync with authenticity and soul.

Our heart wisdom will beckon us into a deeper relationship with ourselves, and when we listen to it, we begin to make a shift: instead of this world giving us information on who we are, we allow our hearts to give us that information, and in so doing, our hearts inform our world.

101

Mosaic

Don't ever be sorry for putting your whole heart into something. The best of your heart— regardless of the results— and the growth that comes from going all out, far surpasses our perceived sense of success or failure.

You will learn so much about your passions, hopes, desires, dreams, and what you are made of in your whole-hearted process that you will have found a greater gift: your truth.

This gift will continue to carry you and inspire you on your journey. Instead of living halfheartedly in an inauthentic world, you will live wholeheartedly and create your authentic world. When we engage wholeheartedly, we begin to see the gifts in all things.

If the outcome of something doesn't seemingly work out, it doesn't mean it's because we failed or made a mistake or life is out to get us. And it doesn't mean we shouldn't have opened our hearts so deep and tried.

It's just a learning lesson, a new soul expression, a chance to grow. It's a new experience to add to our collection of humanity, divinity, and being. It's an opportunity to take that love we poured into something or somebody else and pour it back into ourselves— in spades.

Every experience is valid; every part of you is real, and good, and true. When you are going through life with that big, beautiful love-light wide open, then no matter what happens, you can know you have now become a masterpiece of art:

Your very life is a living mosaic of soul and heart.

102
Let Your Smile Be Your Guide

Let your smile be your guide today. Find the things that tug its corners up and focus on them. Notice what makes you laugh, even if it's just finding the absurd humor in yourself and this corkscrew process of life.

Set a goal this week that your biggest goal is to find greater grace and acceptance for yourself, then notice how that supports you in finding grace and acceptance for others.

Remember, a perspective shift is always found by looking at something from a different angle. Mentally list three things you appreciate, then see if you can add to that list throughout the day.

If the day tilts downwards, and it's hard to find the good, place your hand on your heart and breathe in something bigger than yourself. Remember, you are so much more than the sum of a day. Ask the stars to send you a smile.

103
Your Beat of Purpose

Sometimes healing and being with yourself begins with a single realization: you were never damaged to begin with. Not in your soul where it counts the most.

Once you begin to understand your inherent state of wholeness, you will begin to love yourself with fuller acceptance— no matter where you are.

Fuller acceptance is found through showing up for ourselves, learning to be present, listening to ourselves, and having the courage to believe and heed our words.

We softly turn the light on inside rooms within us that once felt dark and explore unmet parts of our psyche and soul. We begin to hold our hands through hard times and difficult feeling states and learn to tolerate ambiguity and discomfort. Each time we stay our course, we grow stronger and more assured of our wholeness, being, and power.

We begin to realize that self-love is not just feeling good about ourselves but learning to love over the darkness inside of us— the wounds, pains, fears, and traumas, and all our shades of self.

We are not afraid of what is within us, because we know we can find a way to sit in the cave of our hearts and witness ourselves.

We learn to carry our fullness in greater ways and hold a torch of hope so high for ourselves that we can't help but embody our true selves, not some image of who we think we should be for others.

This is how we learn to be our brightest selves, put our hands on our hearts, feel our beat of purpose, and stay in our center with reverence and awe.

104

Don't Drink the Poison

If negative thoughts and words could take on the physical appearance of a big black cloud, then maybe everyone would see that when we tell ourselves hurtful things and focus on the negative, we poison ourselves. After a while, that poison corrodes our self-esteem, self-worth, and the most vulnerable parts of ourselves.

Ouch, my dear ones, ouch. Perhaps if we're stuck in this place, we can find a little more self-compassion. Perhaps we can gently and fiercely choose to challenge these messages.

Perhaps we can begin to insist on a new vocabulary of self, heart, and soul, where we become students of the language of self-kindness that we are learning to speak with fervent fluency.

Perhaps we can learn to actively challenge the poison that holds us back, choose not to drink the poison, and begin to shift our focus to more nourishing things.

We can focus on finding kinder words. We can imagine a more self-loving version of ourselves. We can make a gratitude list of the small things that bring us a sense of warmth and appreciation.

We can list twenty words that evoke a feeling of peace with us. We can think of ten simple dreams we'd like to create in the next week. We can count our little successes and small victories in life and give ourselves gold stars.

There are hundreds of ways to shift our focus away from the poison, and when we do this, we tune into a more peaceful, accepting space. Our nervous system will thank us, our heart will thank us, our mind will thank us, and we will thank ourselves for doing this good work of soulful nourishment.

We can tell ourselves how proud we are of ourselves. Acknowledge the courage that it takes to show up for the human journey and stay present, open, and brave as we seek the heart's way.

105
Got Comparison? Try This.

Comparison, negative self-talk, self-pity, and focusing on what others are thinking are all things likely to make us feel fairly horrible about ourselves.

It can be hard to pull ourselves out of these feeling states and find a better way. Sometimes, it takes a lot of practice, learning, and relearning. However, it is worth learning to do this because there is no peace of heart or contentment to be found there.

Peace and contentment can only be found by focusing on our path and learning to accept and appreciate our unique journey. So, instead of comparison and the negative spiral of berating and shame, try this:

Be affirming of you. You are the only you there is, and as such, your journey is your own and incomparable to others. You deserve to claim yourself.

Be kind to you. The words you feed yourself will either build you up with positive thoughts or tear you down with negative abuse. You deserve good words.

Stand tall in you. You are beautiful, wonderful, and strong enough to face life's challenges. Nobody has time for self-pity when so much life is waiting to be lived. You deserve a life well lived, and you deserve to fall in love with the life you have.

When in doubt, just look to nature. A tree doesn't run around wishing to be a river, nor a mountain wishing to be the sea. Vast big sky beauty does not compare itself to the luminescence of the moon, nor a resilient blade of grass to the grace of a cat.

Each of us has a place, purpose, and unique beauty within this greater ecosystem.

So, keep coming back to your space. You are the only thing you can control, so instead of worrying about others, use that tremendous energy to create a beautiful heart, a curious mind, a delightful spirit, and a life of your design.

You deserve to embody and embrace your essence of nature and the gift of your life, and there is no comparison when it comes to that and the unique beauty only you can create.

106
Self-Love Affirmation for Difficult Times

Whenever I'm in a place that feels dark. A place that feels like I can't get out, or the walls are closing in, or like life is no longer on my side—

These are the things I say to myself:

"You are strong. You are brave. You are clever. You've come this far, and you will not give up on yourself now."

Then, I have found that it can feel very comforting to hold one's own hand and, with kindness, say these following words:

"I am here for you. I will not abandon you. I've got you. And I believe in us."

107

Canon in Trust

I keep finding as I go that developing our relationship with self-trust is vital to creating a healthy foundation of self. We must learn to trust our experience of self and know that what we intuit, perceive, sense, and feel is valid and deserves our attention, care, and acceptance.

Sometimes, we encounter new emotions and feeling states inside of ourselves. They can be incredibly ungrounding and overwhelming, like finger paint smeared everywhere we try to make sense of the picture.

During these times, we can learn to practice mad self-love skills and remember that judgment and the ego are slippery little tricksters that make us doubt our process and question the things we feel. Yet when it comes to living open-heartedly and staying with our process, the best we can do is to continually give ourselves permission to be exactly where we are at.

Our experience of ourselves will be the experience that informs us the most. So, we must learn to trust those flashes of intuition, sparks of knowing, and intuitive urges and nudges of soul that guide us on the path. We must learn to trust our griefs and our joys, that which moves us to action and that which deposits us into inertia, our sense of purpose and the meaning we make, and our perceptual sensitivities and unique frameworks for looking at life.

We can remain open and teachable while still fundamentally returning to an informed core space, where we sit with our own sense of wisdom and examine what holds right and true for us. We are the only ones who can learn to find peace inside of ourselves and honor our experience of living in a way that satisfies our personal requirements of soul.

For that, we need trust. Big trust. Self-trust. Heart trust. Soul trust. Each of us exploring ourselves. Learning about ourselves. Doing the work of self to find growth where we need, roots where we sink, mending where we bleed. A loving of self, so deep, the obfuscation of this world can give way to a clearer heart-seeing.

108

Manifesto of Belief: a letter to my younger self

I know it's been tangled and hard, but my dear girl, let me tell you what you're going to do— you're going to trust yourself. Against the odds. Against what lies unseen.

You're going to trust the questions that sit unanswered in your heart. You're going to trust yourself in the debris. In the breaking. In your grief. In the deconstruction of self and the unknown pieces of your psyche's submergence. You will trust yourself and hold your hand through your fall from who you once were.

You're going to forget about the instant success-ers and mind over matter manifest-ers and "positive vibes only" tribes, which disconnect you from the most integral pieces of yourself: the darkness within, which exists to guide you through the tunnels in life where the soul goes quiet as it prepares for rebirth.

You're going to trust yourself when it looks like everybody else is winning and you're losing. You're going to trust that some days, your wins will be getting out of bed and moving forward.

Maybe your purpose here is to be the most human you can possibly be, to embody every inch of your humanity, and to shine with your faith that our inherent love, beauty, and goodness still exist within this human space.

You're going to trust that human space. Trust the trail of being a true human. Trust the trail of real in all its gritty splendor and glossy mess.

You're going to trust your brokenness, your chipped parts, and all the times you strive and fail. You're going to trust that failure is success in its own form and that life is moving your experiences together and revealing the bigger picture of you in its own time.

You're going to trust your imperfections and tribulations, and you're going to become an expert on emotional reincarnation. For you will resurrect, rebirth, and reinvent yourself many times over.

So, you're going to trust your feelings and see they are all part of the same tangled ball of red yarn leading you deeper into yourself, deeper into your heart, deeper into the truth that is you.

109
Cartwheels and Spirals

Take soft and gentle moments for yourself as often as you need. There are many things that will blow you off course in this world, so you have to learn how to find a safe harbor: safe being in those spaces where acceptance, comfort, and grounding prevail.

Know what you are about, even as you give yourself room to not know and grow. There is a tension between knowing and unknowing, whose threads weave new colors and patterns into the synapses of our tapestry.

Make a little space for those times when life becomes circumvoluted and the bigger picture spirals. Life is not linear, so sometimes the best we can do is cartwheel in the air and find levity and perspicacity when we look at the world sideways, trusting we'll find new footing once we land.

Don't mistake others' opinions for truth or anything other than a reflection of their inner world. You'll find the more well-organized the heart, the less the judgment, and the more space for grace.

Above all else, just keep being present for yourself. Show up, listen up, love up: learn to embody you. For only in your fullness and richness of self, will you find what you need to hold your own hand, stay on your path, see yourself through, and keep on walking your truth.

110

QUESTIONS OF SELF AND FEELING STATES

On this journey, we are constantly invited to live the answers to our questions of self, and through learning to stay with ourselves and live the answers, we find our resolution.

Stay with yourself. Learn to tolerate intolerable feeling states. Feelings are fluid and never last forever.

Learn how to constructively work with difficult feelings like angst, restlessness, and discontent. Develop perspectives that help you feel bigger than a feeling state and connect to a higher perspective.

Teach yourself to breathe through your struggle. Experiment with when to sit still and when to move so you find what works for you. There is no right or wrong to this, though our choices can lead us to be destructive or constructive, and it's good to aim for constructive.

But even on the worst of days, when we self-destruct, self-sabotage, or fall into a canyon of darkness within ourselves, we can still find grace waiting there; we can still find a way to love ourselves in the dark and find our way out through breath and new intention.

All this is to say— you are doing okay, fellow human. Keep mapping the territory of you and trusting your questions of self will be discovered in their own time.

Move towards what helps, and stay away from what doesn't. And always remember, if you feel you've fallen off track, that change for the better is always available. There is no reason why we can't say to ourselves, with wry humor and heart humility:

"Now that I've had THAT experience, I think I'll choose differently for myself today."

111

Truth-Living and Truth-Speaking

Diminishing yourself to make others happy by appearing softer, quieter, smaller, and less *you* do absolutely nothing but rob you of the precious ingredients of yourself. One of the best ways to show gratitude in our lives is to inhabit them to the fullest capacity.

Shine bright, be strong, be humble and brave, grow and use your voice, stretch your wings as far as they go, and be you to your highest extent. Changing to appease others by being less than who you are only shrinks you and shows a lack of gratitude for the gift of your life.

We honor our lives by mining them for all they are worth, living authentically, developing heartfelt gifts, and learning to live and speak our truth.

This is never about bad-mouthing somebody else or making another's journey wrong to build ourselves up. Instead, truth-living and truth-speaking are always about taking responsibility for our thoughts and feelings and how we relate to the world around us.

Truth frees us— because truth is alive in love. Truth grows hearts. It doesn't tear them down, and the only way to grow your heart— and this is so achingly simple, yet at times so difficult to put into practice— is to continue to fully embody yourself and learn to live your truth.

112
Core of Self-Honesty

Our ability to be honest with others is only as strong as our ability to be honest with ourselves.

If we lie to ourselves and develop an inner dialogue steeped in distraction, justification, blaming, rationalization, and avoiding self-examination, then we create patterns of behavior that prevent us from facing our deeper truths and communicating our truth with accountability and clarity.

The only way to get to that deeper truth is to take the time to do the work of self. To look at oneself with a gaze of kind scrutiny that doesn't shy away from internal truth, no matter how difficult or inconvenient.

To learn that self-acceptance does not equate to self-indulgence or allowing things to continue unchecked. Instead, it is a necessary step that allows us to accept how things are so we can allow for the possibility of how things could be and begin a process of change.

The only way to outwardly speak and live our truth is through the doorway of the inner self. This is found when we take time for self-reflection. We accept and see how things are so we can work through them. We move forward and arrive at the uncharted territory of new possibilities and a new clarity of self.

That is the core of self-honesty: learning to listen, sit in peace with what is, and see who we are. In all our imperfect, uncertain, ambiguous, work-in-progress, fluid, colorful, lovely humanity.

113

EXCESS BAGGAGE

"Self-love is an ocean and your heart is a vessel. Make it full, and any excess will spill over into the lives of the people you hold dear. But you must come first."
—Beau Taplin

If you are tired of carrying it, lay it down for a while.

You will probably not solve it or fix it at this moment. So, it doesn't need to be carried. Its excess baggage is weighing you down and keeping you from looking up.

If you are carrying all of it, lay it down for a time. You are not meant to carry the whole day, or year, or world in each given moment. You are meant to carry the moment and find your joy. Moment by moment, minute by minute, day by day— we are not meant to carry more.

If you are carrying it for someone else, go ahead and lay it down for a bit. You cannot carry yours and theirs indefinitely without collapsing inward as you find your health, mind, heart, hopes, and dreams paying a heavy price and costing you the most beautiful parts of yourself.

Especially lay it down if you are carrying it for another able-bodied, resource-laden, capable being whose seeds of potential you have watered with your energy, heart force, and tears.

If you realize that after all this time, those seeds you've been busy tending in another still have not taken root or grown, lay them down and walk away. Your seeds and malnourished soil need your energy, tears, and heart force to tend to them.

If you are tired of carrying it, lay it down for a while. You may just like how much better you feel without it as you begin to notice— now you have space to carry the whole of you.

114

JUST SAY "YES"

People are not entitled to our light, our time, our energy, our feedback, our support, or any part of ourselves. We give those things out of freedom and love. When we realize we are not giving of ourselves out of freedom and love, then it's time to step back and evaluate our boundaries.

When you have a giant open heart, you want to give, but there is a difference between giving on our terms versus another's terms. It is the difference between inviting somebody to come into our inner well, and we freely share a cup of our water with them. Compared to having somebody come along and take a cup without our permission because they feel entitled to it.

We were never meant to carry another; only they can do that for themselves. The more we free ourselves to walk around without the energetic weight of others' expectations and baggage, the more we find newfound liberation. We don't want to return to being a sherpa of other people's expectations and stuff.

"No" is a holy word. It is meant to be intelligently used in the service of love toward others and ourselves so we can keep freeing ourselves to embody our authentic being. But I think even more important than the word "no" is the word "yes." When we choose to express it towards ourselves and remember—

Our boundaries are much easier to set and maintain. We realize their purpose is less about saying "no" to others and more about saying "yes" to something inside ourselves.

115
In Wholes, Not Halves

Love supports the whole person. Not just our shiny and beautiful parts, but our gritty, challenging, and in-between parts. In other words, The Whole.

The entire entity of a person encompasses our need to breathe, grow, evolve, fall backward, fall forward, fly for a while, trip a bit and get back up, try on a new size, find the words to our song, stretch and expand into the role of our essence— our need to become.

Love is filled with grace, space, and a foundation of respect that can survive conflict, strife, and change because the fundamental core of compassionate acceptance remains intact.

The kinds of relationships and people you deserve in your innermost circle are the ones who will nourish your spirit and support you in your growth and becoming.

Anything less than this will cage you and slowly stifle your growth and expansion. You deserve to love and be loved in wholes, not halves. And, of course, the best place to begin to find that love is through your relationship with you.

116

COMPASS OF LOVE

Get busy being yourself, doing the things you love, and learning to love in the best way you know how.

It doesn't matter if others don't get what you're about; your journey is yours to understand, and the right ones will come beside you and give you the space to discover yourself.

It doesn't matter if you're producing anything; love is about healing, reconciling, and becoming, not production.

It doesn't matter if what you love and how you love can be quantified, counted, or measured because the best, most important things in this world cannot be quantified, counted, or measured.

What matters is that you find the courage to make the journey of authenticity and love so that your heart can be who it needs to be.

True worth cannot be measured by numbers, labels, or possessions that only serve to tie us down and keep us small. Freedom is found when we can learn to see beyond quantification and realize those values are determined by something, someone, or some system other than ourselves.

It is so easy to stand in the middle of the fray and forget: WE are the determiners of our own value, and that which matters most cannot be calculated or ordered or timed.

Our value lies somewhere in love's infinity, only found beyond the bounds, and if our hearts are learning to align themselves with the compass of love, everything else will follow.

117
SELF-TRUST REQUIRES CONTINUAL SURRENDER

Trusting ourselves is not a one-time linear deal; it is a continuous surrender. Surrendering control of the smallness of our egos requires knowing and ceding to the bigger wisdom of our wiser selves.

I learned this truth the hard way. During a difficult season in my life, I finally realized that even though I thought I was working on surrender, I was still hanging on. I was trying to control how I thought things should look. I didn't trust myself enough to be in an unknown space and figure it out.

Another way of putting it is: when we don't trust ourselves, we are betting against ourselves, and why would we do that? Why wouldn't we bet on ourselves and believe that we have the cleverness, resourcefulness, and heart knowledge to find our way through?

If we embrace the idea that mistakes are part of the journey— and we could even reframe the word "mistakes" as growth experiences since that's all they really are— then we might also embrace the idea that our growth experiences are necessary for helping us find the ingredients we need to transform along the path of the heart.

Those experiences allow us to move into our hearts, abide more deeply within ourselves, and cultivate greater belief, spirituality, faith, perseverance, grit, and courage in our lives. As unorthodox and wild as it may seem, we can trust our experiences. We can trust ourselves. We can trust our mistakes, our growth, and our unknowing.

We can trust that we've been on the right path all along, and any unknowing was simply there as a tool to lead us into deeper knowing. And we can absolutely trust that our future selves will figure it out because some way, somehow, our future selves always figure it out.

We can continue to let go of our need to go and stop betting against ourselves. Instead, we engage with fierce self-belief and the wisdom to know when to surrender the weight of control. And pick up the wings of radial self-trust instead. Then, we'll see how it feels to give ourselves permission to transcend worry in light of belief.

118

Success Can Be Found in Sitting Still

There will always be something that tells us we're moving too slowly, too fast, or not quite right.

Often, this "something" is us and our mental chatter, which internalizes external messages and comes up with some kind of expectation for what we should be doing or how we should be structuring our time.

Sometimes, it is very good to allow ourselves to ride the tide instead of trying to carry or turn the tide, including the tide of ourselves, our soul cycles, and our change process.

We are where we are for a reason. And at any given moment, it's the perfect place to be because it's all just part of our process.

If we can just be self-honoring and permit ourselves to be where we are without having to judge it, worry about it, dissect it, or make ourselves wrong, we'll find that taking time to be in our flow makes us feel so much better equipped when it's time to dip back into life's bigger stream.

Stay with yourself. Rest when you need to, move when you feel called, and take the steps you know to take. Gather information and stay patient when you feel stuck and don't know what to do—sometimes success can be found in sitting still.

Take a big breath, try and find the love in the situation, and learn to be a good friend to yourself. Speak healing words into your narrative and rewrite your story through a lens of patience, joy, and grace.

You are moving at your own pace, and that is a beautiful thing.

119

IT IS ALL SACRED

Our relationship with ourselves, in all its shapes and forms and moods, is sacred. When we are our better selves— our loving, kinder, gentler, more patient selves— we tend to feel like we are being good, the best version of ourselves, more presentable and acceptable, and more spiritual.

While it is good and noble to keep learning how to access our better selves and find a higher way, we lose so much that is authentic, real, and raw; we lose so many opportunities to practice self-love and, in return, learn to love others better when we invalidate the experiences of self that feel ugly, dark, and less.

Self-love is the fundamental footstep to the sacred path. It is a path that we are all on, whether we are aware of it or not— all of us trying to return to a space of love, all of us seeking love to help heal the wounds in our lives.

The only way we can learn to find self-love is to embrace all our moments— the beautiful ones, the ambivalent ones, the ones where we are sitting at the back of life's class angry, churlish, and scowling.

These moments all mean we are HERE. Here in the beautiful, difficult, finite, possible space of this place— it means we have chances, choices, and possibilities. Regardless of what we choose to do with them.

Chances, choices, and possibilities are inherent gifts. Inherently holy, hallowed, precious, cherished, prayerful, revered, sublime, and divine, and all the words that usually get relegated to religion but really shouldn't because they are simply adjectives that describe the gift of being HERE and the opportunities that are our lives.

It is all spiritual and sacred when we have eyes to see. We can learn not to judge our experiences as better or worse, more valid or less valid, more spiritual or dark when we begin to see that the gift itself is the whole of being utterly human.

We were never wrong. We were never bad. And even in our darkest of places, there is always something divine to be found. It is all spiritual. All sacred. All a chance to love.

120

SELF-CARE ON A SATURDAY NIGHT

Listen to your intuition. Pay attention to the whispers of your heart, for they contain great wisdom. Embrace change, be ready to welcome it in, and adapt when it comes knocking at your door.

Grab a cup of cocoa or tea and imbibe coziness. Give the dog a bath for cleaner and fluffier cuddle time. Change the sheets because you deserve to be kind to the skin that you're in. Grab a book and read about a philosophy, an adventure, a story, a world very different than your own. Better yet, read poetry and see the soul of another mirroring aspects of the soul in you.

Clear space to nurture your inner garden lest it wilt and diminish. Speak your truth even when it's hard. Learn to love yourself seamlessly, in a way where even on your worst of days, you recognize you are fundamentally enough and have always been okay, even when things aren't okay.

Fall in love with yourself in these moments and be in a love relationship with life itself. The more you appreciate and value your life, the more your life will appreciate and value you. Keep returning to the basics of tending a happy heart and a happy life. Relax into an even deeper level of patience with wherever you find yourself. Keep developing a gaze of thoughtful joy and fairytale wonder.

Make sure you've stocked up on scented candles, good books, and chocolate chip cookies for those moments when you need a little extra care.

121
Self-Love is an Ongoing Journey

Self-love is not a destination but an ongoing journey where we learn to see ourselves— our true selves— with grace and acceptance.

Self-love evolves over the course of our lifetime. It is the continuous act of maintaining authenticity and courage. It begins with a relationship with ourselves.

Self-love continually challenges us to learn to incorporate more loving kindness into our concept of self each time we uncover parts of ourselves that feel unlovable, broken, and out of harmony with our whole.

Self-love is learning to believe and trust in our experience of self and stay open to our experience with curiosity and kindness so we can better understand the map of ourselves and be a good steward of our unique wisdom, experience, and truth.

Self-love is a gift we continue to give to ourselves each time we choose to bring more forgiveness and compassion into our thoughts, beliefs, and inner world.

Self-love expands every time we create opportunities for kindness for ourselves and choose to replace an old story of negativity and doubt with a new story of grace and belief.

Self-love is the ongoing act of learning, never forgetting how to hold our own hand and walk alongside ourselves throughout the journey of our lives.

Self-love is an amazing, evolving art installation filled with color, mixed media, and poetry. We keep adding to it, modifying it, and growing it throughout our timelines.

Self-love then becomes a continual work of art; we, the creators. Our life is the canvas, and each day, we are given an opportunity to add a new experience of love.

122

MY DEAR ONE, I BELIEVE IN YOU

We are the only ones who can know who we are on the inside. We are the only ones who can learn to embody our truth and walk a path where our internal world is in alignment with our external world.

Being yourself in this world is the most beautiful and the most difficult. It requires so much personal integrity to do your work and to create a life that is most coherent with your highest truth.

It's a process. One we are all unfolding into. Perfection is unobtainable, and from my perspective, undesirable because how else will you learn and grow and get bigger?

Progress is marked through the simple act of continuing to show up as best we know how, root out our honest, and deal with what comes up. Then, let life support and create with us to become wiser, more authentic, more loving beings.

Be brave. Keep showing up for you. Know that many will not get it— and that's totally okay, as it's not their path. But the right ones will show up and walk beside you and lend encouragement on the way.

Always remember to keep working on being your own biggest encourager, as there is nothing more powerful than saying out loud to yourself: *My dear one, I believe in you.*

Pearls of Wisdom on Being, Receiving, and Patience in the Process

123

Come Together

Life is not a controlled environment. It is an ever-fluctuating terrain governed by a constant rule of change with millions of variables and unpredictable outcomes. We lay the groundwork for our best plans, and sometimes they work out, but often things turn out much different than expected.

We are left trying to navigate the unexpected and often feel frustrated, uncertain, and confused. Learning to surrender to an alchemy greater than ourselves and how to become part of the greater flow when we feel caught up in its streams and need to allow our path to unfold instead of trying to shape our path.

During these times, we learn a great deal about patience in change, and we often forget that as much as we often say we don't like change, we are built for change. We are built with the capacity to develop, grow, evolve, and adapt— to change habits, thoughts, perspectives, patterns, love, lose, and learn to let go.

We are built with the capacity to create something out of whatever resources we've been given— remembering that all the goodbyes, all the voids, all the chaos, and everything that falls apart in our lives are simply part of the ingredients we need for new creation.

Life is in a constant state of creation, and whether we realize it, we are in a relationship with life and, therefore, part of its creation. Best then to release the reigns of control, learn to trust the process, and give life a little space to do its thing.

You never know what the two of you may create when you come together.

124
On the Value of Being and Receptivity

Sometimes, the journey doesn't look how we expected, and we can't see our next step. Things might feel cloudy or stagnant, or we might be forced to slow down and realize that our timetable is not life's timetable.

We realize we can't move things forward from our current vantage point, so we must learn to wait for things to shift and make the best of where we are at.

These moments can be hard on many of us; waiting on life's timing does not offer instant gratification or immediate results, but there are potential gifts that we can find in this space, which hold great value if we can learn to embrace them.

The gift of self-discovery, introspection, and time to pay attention and learn from the vast library of wisdom in our emotions, feelings, and inner world.

The gift of cultivating a sense of inner peace and acceptance that transcends our circumstances.

The gift of learning to release expectations, develop a newfound appreciation for life's greater rhythms and cycles, and develop more peace, trust, and patience with the process.

The gift of learning to understand and subsequently engage more intelligently and creatively with the seasons in our lives so we can live more fluidly and in flow.

The gift of exploring our interconnection with life, listening to the voices of nature, noticing the signs and synchronicities all around us, and being in a bigger relationship with life, our hearts, and the numinous.

The one thing that all these gifts have in common is that they are gifts of being and receiving. They are gifts that we only truly discover when we can shift from always doing, moving, and pouring energy out and open to being, contemplating, receiving, and allowing energy to pour in.

The path of true discovery begins with stillness. It begins with opening to receiving from life's wisdom and paying attention to the subtle nuances and rich gifts found in a slow-down space, which can only be accessed when we learn how to sit with life, listen, breathe, be, and receive.

125

IN FLOW

"Rivers know this: there is no hurry. We shall get there some day."
—A.A. Milne

Living in flow isn't about things always going right; it's about learning to work with energy intelligently and lean in the directions that life curves. Flow is about listening to our inner cycles, honoring our wisdom, and intuitively working with the ingredients that life gives us to stay centered and on track.

For example, we learn to bend and catch sideways when life gives us curve balls. Unplanned incidents are a beautiful time to say to life, "Help me move through this with as much ease and peace as possible," instead of spinning out and making things worse.

In this space, we learn to relinquish our expectations of how things should be and choose to work with life on its own terms, allowing the path to unfold and engaging with the path with curiosity and adaptability.

Flow is a mindset shift that begins in the heart when we release the illusion that we control life and instead choose to empower ourselves to control how we work with life and the energy of the day.

When we are in flow with the greater process of life, we learn the value of being, receiving, and acting from a space of quiet trust and belief. Our energy shifts, our attitude shifts, and we move from a space where we don't waste our efforts on what we cannot force or control but instead focus on what we can.

We learn to become more like the water when we are in flow: fluid, malleable, and quietly confident, trusting our ebbs and flows, knowing our currents will shift in tandem with the greater cycles of life, trusting we will get there when we get there.

126

On Cycles and Process Living

Life is not linear. It is a cyclical, winding, and often seemingly chaotic process, which doesn't mean it's not moving in an intelligent direction. Our relationship to our growth, change, and becoming is also a process. We heal in waves and cycles; we grieve in waves and cycles; we live and learn in waves and cycles— continually contracting, expanding, and changing.

No matter how well we know ourselves, we will always surprise ourselves with our process. We can predict how we think we'll react, but it's not until we're in the mix that we gain experience and deeper self-knowledge.

We are asked to stay open to our process, not trying to over-interpret what we're feeling when we don't have the full picture but allowing our soul to help puzzle-piece together the bigger picture. It helps a great deal to remember that we are working with multiple processes at once.

The greater cosmic and karmic cycles, the moon's phases, nature's seasons, and earth's shifts; the cycles in our external lives that encompass everything from our circumstances, dreams, goals, projects, and relationships to others; and the cycles in our inner world, which can include our healing, growth, self-awareness, spirituality, intuition, and heart wisdom.

That's a lot of cycles within cycles! When we look at it from that perspective, it's no wonder life continually invites us to cultivate the art of surrender and trust and gives us opportunities to learn more grace, reverence, and patience in the process.

In this space, we find more wisdom and understanding of what we can control and what we must keep surrendering. We learn to tune into the simple gifts of the day and realize that the moon, the seasons, and the small changes in the natural world are all teaching us how to live with more ease and being.

We see ourselves as part of a greater whole and allow for space for each other, ourselves, and life's endless dance of shadow and light. That's what cyclical, process-oriented living is all about: we allow ourselves the space to shift and grow as we go, trusting in our journey of self within the greater processes of life.

127

SACRED SPACES

"Your sacred space is where you can find yourself again and again."
—Joseph Campbell

We have to learn to create sacred spaces for ourselves and take the time to nourish those spaces.

Sacred could be beneath a favorite tree, that spot by the sea, or a comfy chair and quiet corner in your home. Or maybe it's just a place in your mind and heart where you allow yourself to go when the world feels unkind, and you seek solace.

What makes a space sacred is not so much location but intent. Intent to approach our sacred space with the idea of finding quiet, turning inwards, and allowing our minds to calm so we can better receive.

Receive from life, our hearts, our inner voice, our truth. Receive fresh inspiration, imagination, and muse. Receive stillness, reflection, and rest. Receive, breathe, and be.

Receive whatever you need to connect with in the heartbeat of that moment and whatever layers of knowledge your deeper self seeks.

Or maybe the only thing you need is simply to try to calm the mental chatter and interrupt and slow down the constant stream of energy flow that seems to compose so many of our days.

You realize as you take a deep breath and try to ease into your peace that this is what you seek: these small moments when you take the time to sit with life and drink in whatever your thirsty heart needs.

128

Equilibrium

There is a balance between yin and yang, movement and flow, making magic happen and allowing magic to happen.

Nature, in its seasons, intelligently and intuitively knows when to push, rest, force, and yield. When to adapt, change, and evolve, and when creative growth is required. When to move, roam, and migrate when a space no longer fits or has become uninhabitable.

We find our sense of harmony and equilibrium by experimenting with our sense of balance.

Learning to relax and receive when energetic effort isn't producing results.

Learning to gather our momentum and point it in the right direction when going with the flow isn't taking us in a direction that feels good for us.

Learning to show up and reach when we realize we've hibernated long enough.

Learning to sink into hibernation if all we do is labor and push growth.

The beautiful part of this equation is that just like the multitude of beings in the natural world— who all have their own rhythms, rhymes, and seasons— so do we.

We find our sense of equilibrium by tapping our sense of timing, our inner tools, and our personal rhythm to find the seam between movement and stability. We learn to trust our innate intelligence and intuition to guide us to keep contracting and then expand into the soulful being we are called to be.

129
NATURE'S TEACHERS

"There is something infinitely healing in the repeated refrains of nature— the assurance that dawn comes after night, and spring after the winter."
—Rachel Carson

You can't stop a river from flowing; it will press on somehow.

You can't stop the daylight, the twilight, or the endless phases and faces of the moon; each follows an innately cyclical rhythm, dancing in harmony with something much bigger than us.

You can't stop a dandelion from growing. They are golden messengers of resilience that find a way to push through life's cracks, assuring us that no matter the obstacle, life will always find a way.

Each of these natural teachers helps us remember this vital truth: life is composed of many forces bigger than us, and we can't stop it from happening. We can't control, cajole, or force. We can't outplay, outwit, or outlast.

The best we can do is keep an open mind, an honest heart, and a sense of humor and learn to meet life on its terms— not where we think it should be but exactly where it's at.

130

Great Expectations

It's difficult to relinquish expectations. We all have them; we all have a notion of what we'd like to see happen or how things should go.

Often, we superimpose our ideas of how we think things should happen on top of life, and then we're left floundering and shaken when life goes in a different direction. We bump into a lot of messy things that are very different than expected.

It's hard not to expect. It's in our human nature to attach an expectation of outcome. Yet when we expect an outcome to look a certain way, we automatically give up some of our power, agency, and peace by sending ourselves the message, "I can't be happy/content/okay/etc. unless x happens."

Placing expectations on life is akin to getting into a power struggle with life. Life will always win, and we can get pretty tossed about when we fight the current and demand things look a certain way. Except we are not promised things will look a certain way; we are just promised today because we are not here on our terms; we are here on life's terms.

If we make our inner peace contingent on things working out, then we will not know peace. If we center our sense of happiness around things needing to feel secure and stable and say— "I can't be happy until I know how it will all work out," then we likely won't be happy either.

We don't have the reassurance of how our circumstances will look. We lay our best plans and see how life responds, knowing that life tends to take us on twists and turns we can't always imagine;

sometimes, we are better off not knowing what's waiting around the bend.

This is where the magic is, though, in this space of the wild unknown. This is what living open-heartedly will require: staying open, exploring, going into uncharted territory, and observing and learning the lay of the land. We fall down only to discover a side trail we wouldn't have seen had we not fallen.

We learn to allow it to be what it is instead of trying to shape it. Releasing expectations and conditions as we learn in completely new ways what it truly means to trust the process.

131

To Bring Balance

If life feels ungrounded, confusing, spinning out of control, like you're just trying too hard— slow down, stand still, breathe. Listen as you let life unfold and come to you.

If life feels stagnant, inert, or stuck on repeat— get moving, try something new, and introduce fresh energy. Take a few steps forward to gain momentum.

Look for where you're feeling out of sorts and see if you can find a way to bring balance into your whole. This is a necessary part of growth and gaining wisdom on the path.

To learn to step as we can, rest when needed, work with the dichotomous energies of our feeling states, emotions, and fluctuating energies, and keep finding ways to care for ourselves with more harmony and love.

This is how we create inner peace within our ecosystem of selves and intelligently work with the cycles in our lives, not resisting or insisting, but gracefully persisting by doing what we can and knowing when to rest and let go.

132
The Gifts of a Free and Clear Heart

To be yourself and not your image, to find peace where you are standing, to live in love and not fear, to remain open to life and receive the gifts each day holds, to learn to let go and not control, to become malleable to change, to love where you are planted: this is the beauty of a free and clear heart.

How do we clear our hearts and receive this beauty?

We learn to sit in silence with ourselves. We carve out space and find the value of introspection and reflection. We create opportunities for experiences, spend time in nature, and learn to trust our intuitive flows.

We do release work and practice forgiveness until it begins to stick. We teach ourselves how to stay present during times of uncertainty, when life feels stagnant and stuck, and when we think we've missed the path.

We keep returning to the space of ourselves, reflecting, evaluating, sifting, processing, and bringing in as much grace and compassion as we can.

We learn to sit in silence, hand on our hearts, and focus on turning into the frequencies of love, joy, and peace, which recalibrate our nervous systems and create space for ease.

We allow ourselves the gift of the moment and learn the art of being, realizing that sometimes, glorious living happens when we just sit still and breathe.

133

ON THE MOUNTAINSIDE

Patience with the process is challenging. There are times on our journeys when we want to be there already— on top of some metaphorical mountain we've been climbing— enjoying the views.

Instead, we find ourselves halfway up, unsure of the path forward, and we feel tired and weary. We're no longer at the exciting origins of the beginning; we've lost our enthusiasm and perhaps our sense of vision. Nor do we have the glorious outcome of meeting our goal and feeling we've arrived and reached the top.

We're stuck on the mountainside, hanging out in the middle. The top feels far away, and the bottom has long since passed. We are tired, dirty, hungry, and uncertain as to why we thought it was such a great idea to climb the mountain in the first place.

It's hard to be in an in-between space, no longer in the newness of a cycle, yet far away from whatever destination we've set our sights on. We wonder when and how we'll get there, who we're becoming, and if we made a mistake following our current path.

What we often don't realize in the moment is that this, too, is a valuable part of our journey. If we pay attention, we find that life brings us gifts when we're on the mountainside that we would have missed otherwise.

Maybe the clouds dance overhead, enchanting us and sparking a new inspiration within; we would have missed the moment had we been busy climbing. Perhaps we get resourceful, go foraging, and find a patch of the juiciest, yummiest wild berries. We might discover a peaceful meadow of brilliant wildflowers, take sanctuary, and eventually return to the journey fortified and rejuvenated from our respite.

Sometimes, life can't be forced, nor can our paths. We learn to wait in these moments, discover the gifts, and find goodness there. We learn how to appreciate the progress we have already made and trust that if we just stay open, things will eventually shift, and we will see our next step with greater clarity.

Perhaps we even move forward with more resources, strengths, and treasures, wiser and lighter in spirit, because of our time on the mountainside.

134

On Stillness

There are gifts in stillness and learning to slow down.

It's unnatural to many of us, especially in today's busy world, but if we keep our lives cluttered with busyness, obligations, and constant stimulation, we never have time to go within and learn to listen to our voice, our truth, and the words written on our hearts.

Words that help us connect with our authentic selves, words that help us discover the light within, words that connect us to our true north— our inner compass that helps us connect to what holds value for us, our sense of purpose, and the unique brand of inner wisdom each of us carries.

This is the beginning of the spiritual path. This moment of stillness in our hearts helps open us to a deeper awareness and transcendent relationship with the intangible.

One can spend one's entire life in an unsatisfactory quest for fulfillment when, all along, the holy grail of peace, ease, and well-being exists inside oneself.

First, we learn to go within and listen. Then, we learn to act, step, and move. This is what it is to live heart-centric and authentic in what can often feel like a distracted and inauthentic world.

Be still and know, my friend, that receptivity is golden and a gateway to your deeper truth.

135

SEA SURFERS AND BEACHCOMBERS

Emotions are a beautiful Universal Language. We learn to feel before we learn to talk. No matter where you live, everybody knows what it's like to feel things like love, anger, fear, joy, hurt, grief, humor, sadness, and contentment.

To isolate yourself from that is to isolate a basic component of what it means to be a human being. As uncomfortable as some emotions are, how will we ever be our authentic selves if we don't let ourselves feel?

We must learn to surf our emotional seas and swim in our inner waters by learning how to tolerate feeling states, feel our feelings, stay in the moment, and understand our emotion's vast intelligence.

We tap into the language of our emotions through many things: stories, books, and poetry that speak to us; music and art that move us; safe talking spaces that reveal us; nature that wilds us; introspection and journal reflections that allow us to express and create a vocabulary for our emotional truth.

If we stay with our feelings, we learn that feeling states are fluid and don't last forever. We'll learn about the nature of our emotional waters and become more adept at surfing our inner seas. We can learn to ride our emotions like a wave, stay afloat, cope, regroup, and reapproach if we wash out.

We might even discover that as life shifts and we return to a calmer, grounded space, our tides have churned up treasures we wouldn't have discovered otherwise.

In the process, we become beachcombers of self, collecting new truths, insights, and self-knowledge. Realizing certain truths of self can only be accessed through learning to dive into our inner oceans and surf the wisdom of our seas.

136

Bruises and Pearls

Some days are so tender we feel bruised by the very act of waking up. Grief hits, trauma rears, sadness or badness or grayness sneaks in, blinking rapidly— sometimes humaning is hard.

Vulnerability has the capacity to sink us or swim us; often, it does both. After dropping into the ocean's darker depths, we find enough of a push to move toward the light and find a breakthrough.

Remember, those hard days are not a measure of anything other than being real, being here, and grappling with the full scope of self. They are part of being human, part of living in a hardened world, and part of undoing the hardness and exposing our layers piece by piece as we get closer to our softness and deepest heart truth.

Sometimes, we bruise in the process.

Take a cue from water on those days and just be. No more or no less than your most broken piece. Feelings are mutable and require room to breathe.

Our brightest pearls are only found when we dare to swim in the sea's deep. Healing comes when we allow our whole selves the space to release and be free.

137

LIFE CYCLES OF GRIEF AND LOVE

I always say that love wears a million faces. But so do other things: grief and sorrow, compassion and kindness, beauty, holiness, grace, faith, and hope. Love is just the tie that binds and wraps around it all.

We can think we have our emotional territory navigated and figured out, and it can shock and surprise us when we find ourselves tripping, floundering, and feeling lost and disoriented in a space we thought we knew.

The thing about our life journey is that we don't pass through the same territory twice. Just because we thought we knew sorrow because of a previous experience doesn't mean sorrow will feel the same as the new sorrows that may enter our lives.

Just because we thought we knew grief because we've already undertaken a grief passage doesn't mean grief won't knock us sideways and teach us new gifts when it shows up in new form.

Just because we thought we knew what love was doesn't mean love won't have new ways of sneaking up, surprising us, and teaching us more about its faces. Teaching us new psalms, lamentations, transformations, and revelations. Teaching us how love truly is the core underlying all, so it can always be found anywhere. No matter the emotional territory.

Emotions and life experiences are fluid, so we continually have learning opportunities. Like the moon, the sun, and the seasons, we go through multiple cycles throughout our lives.

It is how we grow, deepen, evolve, and expand our hearts as we travel closer to the truth of our souls in a constant dance of ebb and flow.

138

A Blessing of Peace

Sometimes, we have those days with a lot of twists and turns where words fall into convoluted cracks, and our small spaces of stillness and silence become extremely golden.

That's life, sometimes, isn't it? Twisted and turned with cracks in between, we learn to anchor ourselves in the pauses. Cradle our moments of solitude, find the tiny anchors and things that center us, and help us remember that sanctuary can be a place we build inside our hearts.

We find ourselves again in those spaces. Tap into sacred laughter and gentler ways of being. Allow our ego-states to fall away as we drop into deeper truths that bring us back to the light within and allow us to reconnect and rekindle.

If you've had one of those weeks, I wish you ease.

If you're feeling fatigued, I wish you rest.

If you're feeling grieved, I wish your heart the comfort of 1,000 peace songs.

And if you need joy, I offer you this wisdom: Go find something that makes you laugh. When we can find levity in gravity, all the heavens smile with us.

Be good to you, and cherish your soul. It holds the truth of who you are.

139

JUST TAKE CLASS

It is a beautiful gift when we discover our agency and empower ourselves to change and actualize. And yet, like any other gift, we can lose our sense of balance if we use it too much and do the same thing repeatedly.

We keep trying to make things happen and steer our ship. Maybe we give the universe a little room to do its work, but we get upset when our expectations and timelines don't gel with the universe's timeline. It can take a while to figure out that perhaps the universe isn't the problem; perhaps we are.

A seasoned dancer knows there is an easy and hard way of doing things. Years of practice in training your muscles and teaching your body to stay in alignment with itself will produce effortless turns, leaps, and moves. Stop practicing or get something out of whack, and it will throw your balance off. Sometimes, the harder you force it, the worse it gets.

Some things just need patience, relaxation, and breath before you find your flow.

Our relationship with the universe is not so very different. The more we align with ourselves, our truth, and our spirit, the more things tend to flow. The more we fight the process, get lazy, try to keep things the same, and don't give ourselves or life space to become whatever it needs to be, the harder, more arduous, and effort-filled it is.

I once learned from my dance teacher that you are never too good or too advanced to just show up and take class, no matter what the level. I have found this to be true of being a student of life as well.

We can always take class, no matter how "advanced" we think we are.

We can study life, remember the lesson of how to embrace, remember the lesson of how to let go, and practice steps we thought we knew but have been reminded— you're never too good to practice, train those muscles, and work on old and new skills alike as your heart learns new levels of alignment.

There is a certain pattern and direction to things. Sometimes, we must trust in it, stay with its rhythm, and believe that when the time is right, we'll find that effortless flow.

140

THE DIRECTION OF WATER

Have patience, my friend. Life has a natural rhythm and pattern, and each thing comes in its own time.

The more we stress and try to control our lives, the more we miss the joy of living in the present. We end up restricting opportunities that may come our way because of the walls we've erected out of fear.

Breathe easy with the knowledge that there will always be ups and downs, ebbs and flows, chaos and quiet, for such is life. The things that are meant to happen will indeed happen in their own time.

In the meantime, occupy your time by learning to love yourself better and love others, and gently watch your life unfold. Life is like water: constantly flowing and circulating and following a meandering intelligence all its own.

You can't miss the good things meant for you; some things just cannot be changed despite our best efforts.

Do what you can and keep learning to let go. Even when we feel lost and can't see beyond the bend, it is comforting to remember that the river always finds its way, and water always moves in the direction of flow.

141

Under the Surface

We unravel who we were in a pile of messy colors so we can change tone and hue. In this space, we find that the soul has its own process; we often need to sit with the mysteries within us and submerge ourselves into our inner seas.

We do a lot of work in this space that's hard to put into shape or words. We integrate. We change shape. Our dreams, intuitions, and feelings might be hard at work, putting integral pieces of soul and psyche into place. When we pay attention, we can consciously work with the pieces we can sense and see.

We might have old emotional residue rise from our deep that we're invited to clear out through journaling, movement, art, ritual, or anything that allows us to take a psychic shower, tune into our inner world, and clear out another layer of emotional residue.

We open greater space to receive each time we shed, unravel, release, and let go. Integration takes time, and a lot happens under the surface. Things feel silent— and still up top, yet new life is alchemizing deep in the sea. Our heart, soul, psyche, and consciousness layers are all busy working together to help bring new movement when the time is right.

We have a lot of questions when we're in the middle of an integration process. Sometimes, it feels like we are making progress; other times, it feels like we are standing still or moving backward. Integration takes time, and in this space, we are invited to be, receive from life, and simply say—

I trust I'll have what I need for this day.

I trust in my process of self, which is slowly integrating who I was and who I am becoming.

I trust all will unfold exactly as it should, even though I have no notion as to how it will unfold.

I trust. I trust. I trust.

142

My Serenity Prayer

There are many words one can find to help bring them to a place of relinquishing control:

No. Just breathe. Go with the flow. Trust the process.
Allow. Peace. Receive.
Yes. Stay present. Just keep swimming. All will be well.
Amen. Namaste. Blessed be.

But lately, beneath a frost-laced sky and the dark of winter's sheath, I am finding that out of all the beautiful words that circle around me— offering their soothing advice on finding liberation and release— there is a simple phrase that offers release.

With palms open wide, ready to redeem and surrender all but the most cherished parts of me, I'll say, "I no longer choose to manage this."

143
WATER WISDOM

Lighten up. Play. Be like water today, for the river doesn't move—it just flows.

Water teaches us to be less attached and move through our lives with less stickiness and more ease. Clear and pure, not allowing ourselves to get sucked in and stuck on things that aren't worth our life force, but instead, finding ways to meander along, using the least among of effort, so we don't waste our energy.

Carving out our path with our life force instead of forcing our life force to fit a pre-set path. Allowing life to move with and through us, as we learn to put in less effort, allow more, and become increasingly adaptive.

Knowing there are seasons for rushing tides and rapid streams, and seasons for gentle pools and softer laps and easy ebbs. Knowing these seasons can happen multiple times within the same month, the same week, the same day, and the same breath.

Trusting that the ones who are meant to share in our streams will draw near, see the beauty our waters offer, and release all others to seek water elsewhere. Remembering the vital importance of tending to our own wellsprings and keeping them clean and clear.

Water offers endless wisdom when we realize it is a living, breathing life force on our planet that is constantly modeling, guiding, cleansing, purifying, and supporting us.

Teaching us how to be more malleable, liquid, and fluid and find greater peace and surrender in our flows.

144

Balance: an ongoing renegotiation

One of the tricks to learning to be at peace with life is learning how to be at peace with our ebbs and flows.

Learning when to act, move, and push ourselves to show up and create, endeavor, or produce. Learning when to be still and receive and rest instead of a step.

We are constantly invited to keep learning how to interpret our moods, emotional states, and life's ups and downs in a way that supports our expansion and compassion and keeps us growing on the journey of self-love.

Finding balance in our lives is often fleeting because life's change is constant. When we think we have it figured out, or everything juggled, or have created a new equilibrium of steadfast circumstance, then something is bound to change, and we will find ourselves renegotiating our relationship with the energies in our lives.

This requires a lot of shifting and fluidity. Learning to step when we feel called. Slowing down and resting when there is nothing else to do— giving ourselves permission not to know and finding a new rhythm of motion and receptivity.

Asking ourselves, how can I best love myself in this season? What do I need to do to support myself right now? What's my best course of action or conscious receptivity in this moment? Then, we do our best to listen to what comes through and stay with our process of self.

145

KEYS

There are those days where you just have to be. Be with your own restless stillness and your own half-formed knowing. Be in the rain and the breeze and sink into the soft rhythms of nature, which never rush their own process of change, instead changing exactly when it is time in small increments and then giant bursts of blooming seed.

Yesterday is behind us, and tomorrow is still out of reach. What we have is this present moment of being in our own mysteries. We are learning to recognize the keys to unlocking the self, which life brings into our path when it's time for greater clarity.

Keys don't always arrive in grand ways; often, they come in small clues and cues— bits and pieces of feelings, scraps of words, soft signs and subtle nudges, slight erosion, and quiet reshaping.

The constancy of nightfall and the break of each new day reminds us life moves towards perpetual motion, growth, change, and prosperity. A deepening vocabulary of self that gradually helps us better understand our truth.

If you are in the abyss, have fallen between the cracks, or would like to know the answers but can't see the path, allow yourself to pause and breathe. Know it simply isn't time for clearer seeing.

You'll see when you see— no sooner and no later. In the meantime, tread gently. Practice self-kindness. Hold a warm mug of amenity. Nestle into comfort rituals. Stay close to the trees and listen to their songs of wholeness.

Give yourself this space and time. Quit trying to be the shaper. Become the shaped.

Most of all, just be. You are learning about receptivity and allowance and how to open your heart to life's myriad keys. Knowing that when the time is right, the answers you seek will unlock and become seen.

146
INTO THE WOODS

We need to go into the woods of our soul often. Exploring the heart of our own forest and finding our soul's secret gifts. We have worlds within worlds inside of ourselves waiting to reveal their holy mysteries when we carve out space to go within.

Going inward is how we learn to listen better; it helps us slow down and be intentional about our relationship with ourselves. It is a mindful act where we can explore the flora and fauna of the self. The more we do this, the more we notice our shifts, witness our changes, and begin to learn the language of our soul's cycles, ebbs, and flows.

If we are seeking to live life from an authentic, intuitive space, then our experience of self is going to be the experience most helpful to us. Being in touch with our experience of self requires a great deal of self-awareness gained through reflecting, listening, observing, discovering, exploring, and learning our personal heart language.

Only through knowing ourselves can we develop discernment and wisdom regarding our process. When we go inside, we begin to see our inner world is crackling with information and saturated with intelligence. Going within helps us tap into our soul wisdom and find the essence of our life force, which sustains, grows, and nourishes us.

The more we learn to spend time with and within ourselves, the more we grow our relationship with our inner earth. We learn the nuances of our soil, notice the way our seasonal patterns play out, and pay attention to the ebbs and flows within and how those interplay with the exterior world.

We find our natural rhythms, see our intuitive cycle, learn to listen, and gain a deeper awareness of our truth.

This is what living soulfully is all about: trusting the world within, letting our voice be our guide, and leading heart-based lives of believing in our deeper soul process, which is invisible but utterly real.

147

PARACHUTES

The closer we travel to and with the heart of the universe, the more we will be asked to keep surrendering. We will be asked to trust the process in bigger and bigger ways, and though we may feel we are free falling through the cosmos, I have learned through experience—

The more we learn to trust the process, the more we realize we have a parachute on our back guiding us safely into new terrain. All we must do is pull the cord. We pull the cord every time we stop focusing on the feeling that we are free-falling through air and instead choose to turn inwards and focus on trusting our hearts.

The journey through unknown space is our gateway to knowledge and our initiation to understanding the numinous inside of ourselves and our unique relationship with the magic of the mysteries. Through that understanding, we are driven to create, build, and manifest change in our material world that aligns with the truth of our soul.

In an effort-oriented, results-focused, product-driven society, I am coming to see we have it all backward: First, we receive the vision and new knowledge through undergoing the process, and then we create aligned change from this space of new knowledge.

In-between the space of inception and aligned action, is where we think we're free-falling when we're simply traveling through the heart of space. Being asked to trust the void space. Being asked to find patience for the process. Being asked to lean in and surrender our efforts to the greater universal flow.

We think we are spiraling in this space, and our doubts, worries, and questions of self, make us feel we are spinning and spinning, and yet we are always held. We're just being given enough space to learn. To learn how to trust in greater ways and find peace in the change.

What might life look like if we always knew we were carried? What might life look like if we focused on the parachute, not the fall? What might life look like if we allowed ourselves to be breathed through uncertain waters?

I think a lot more space would open up for each of us— space to trust, be curious, recognize the subtle ways we try to control the outcome, and cede our need to know for a more magical, soul-quenching life of mystery and wonder.

148

Ecosystem

What if when things go wrong, they are still going right? What if the things we like least about ourselves have the most to teach us? What if the pieces of ourselves we think we are missing are inside us all along, slowly coming up and crystallizing so we can realize them?

What if our soul knows exactly what it's doing, and it's just interfacing with this world in a topsy-turvy way, because we don't always understand its methods?

What if we turn our hierarchies upside down and learn to see the value and wisdom from whatever we deem as on the bottom? What if we trade our hierarchies for circles, where everything has a place in the whole of our ecosystem?

What if vulnerability becomes our fiercest strength, and owning "I don't know" is exactly what we need to find our knowing?

What if we start where we are at each day, believe we're enough, and know whatever aspects of self that emerge have purpose and contribution to our greater whole?

What if our personal evolution becomes a revolution of radical acceptance and love? Knowing each of us will be whoever we are meant to be; we don't have to try so hard. Knowing we will fulfill whatever purpose we are called to fulfill; the universe is ripe and abundant and will not withhold all the good and beautiful things promised to each.

Knowing we ARE embodying our soul path through the simple act of living—we don't have to be anyone or anything special; we just have to be ourselves. When we're doing this (even if we don't quite know who, what, or where we are at times), we cannot lose our way.

We can rest in the knowledge that all of it— all the twists, turns, detours, and losing then finding ourselves— is just a part of our path. And I believe we are each already walking the path beautifully, my brave fellow souls.

149
IN NATURE, WE REMEMBER OURSELVES

We remember who we are when we go to nature because nature understands what can be so hard for us to remember— our innate sense of belonging. If you pay attention, you will begin to see that everything has a place, a time, a purpose, and we, the gentle gusts of our lives, are counted among the pattern.

We find new truths in the musk of the woods, the olive sponge of the tundra, the rings within rings upon the trunks of strong trees. They are old and wise and never doubt that their purpose is to watch over us with vigilant tenderness, standing tall, and taking their place in this space and time.

The flowers create symphonies of color and bloom cheerfully in their time, not shying away from being their brightest selves. When their season ends, they let go and fade peacefully, trusting they will someday bloom anew. They teach us how to be our most riotous color and trust in our bud, growth, decay, and reseed process.

The birds teach us to look up and transcend our confines of self. They sing and find flight with joyful assurance, sweeping the air as they've been called to do. They constantly realize their wings in blithe patterns of descent and ascension and teach us to do the same.

We can tilt and fall and lose ourselves fifty times in one day, only to watch a lackadaisical cloud drift over a slope of blue, reminding us that we, too, can learn to form and reform multiple times along our path.

When we go to nature, she will always reveal something new to us, but no matter what lesson she has to teach, she will never fail to put her arm around us, remind us that we each have a place in life's ecosystem, and sing us her reassuring song:

We belong, we belong, we belong.

150

THE BEAUTY WAY

Go in gentleness.

Trust in times of challenge.

Keep your heart centered and full by going into it often.

And if others start to pull you from your path, release them in love and say:

"May you be supported, may you be guided, may you find the light you need. May I be supported, may I be guided, may I find the light I need. May we be supported, may we be guided, may we find the light we need."

Then keep focusing on your light and walk the beauty way in peace.

151
TO SEE AND RECEIVE THE ANSWERS

So often, it's not that our meditations, good intentions, warm thoughts, prayers, and deepest hopes are not answered; it's that we don't know how to see and receive the answers.

We attach expectations to how something should look while missing out on what's right in front of us, reminding us how deeply connected we are to the world around us and that no hope of the heart has ever gone unheard.

Do you see the snow softly fall? You have been offered cleansing.

Do you see the daylight break, each day still and new? You have been offered beginnings.

Do you see the friend, fur, flora, or fauna— companionship is found in many forms of life— reaching out, nearby, in your time of need? You have been offered comfort.

Do you hear the thoughts churning through your mind? You have the ability to figure out a solution.

Do you see the bare tree hibernating until the budding rush of spring? You are reminded that everything happens in its own time, and you will have new seasons.

Do you see the faded scar on your arm? You carry a story that tells you that the deepest wounds may always leave a faint mark, but they can heal and leave you all the stronger for your resilience.

Do you feel the hopes and dreams for contribution, evolution, and revolution placed deep in your heart? You have the ingredients for growth and change.

You see, it's often not that the answers aren't there; it's that we fail to recognize what is sitting right in front of us. We ask for a sign when there are signs everywhere.

Sometimes, we only need to cast our intentions to the winds, let them be carried into the sky above, then simply look up, pay attention, and receive.

152

WE ARE GOLDEN

*"I've now realized that I was thinking about it all backward.
I expected my work to shape and define me and help create the next step I was meant to take. I thought somehow what I was doing would inform my being, and the path would flow from there.
What I have learned since is that I wasn't called here to do something first. I was called here to learn bigger and deeper ways of being.
Be in a relationship with myself. Be in a relationship with the island. Be in a relationship with the universe.
Trust. Surrender. Release the plan. Release the how and the what. Focus on my why: To be a bright light and hold space for the light and, in so doing, awaken the light in others.
I am learning that my soul's purpose isn't something I will do; it is who I am called to BE. When I bring myself back to my heart and let whatever I create flow from my center—when I focus on my light— I'm golden."*

—Revelations of The Sky

I wrote those words back in 2019, right around the time I was figuring out this life-changing lesson:

Our true purpose isn't found in what we do but in who we are. Our very act of being helps us step into our purpose, and then the good things we will organically feel called to do will flow from this radiant space.

But those good things will begin to feel empty if they are not fulfilling and in alignment with our hearts. This is the gift found in our being— this light, wisdom, and innate sense of belonging to our hearts and ourselves.

When we realize our purpose isn't what we do but who we are, we begin to invest in and value becoming and being the light we wish to see. We can't help but begin to shine and allow all else to flow from this inner essence.

When we do that? You are golden. I am golden. We are golden.

153

NOMADS IN TIME

Sometimes, our paths are lucent; we have a clear sense of purpose and vision about which way to go; circumstances line up to lead us there. Sometimes, it's misty veiled where the fog obscures, but we still see the outline of shapes to help us navigate forward.

And sometimes, it feels like a black void where we're lost and directionless and must become like the mouse, sensing our way in the darkness, relying on other senses to guide us when vision fails.

In this black space, we stand to learn so many gems of wisdom about being human, allowing ourselves room to grow and surrender to the process of life. Because we all lose our way from time to time, it is part of the journey.

We become like nomads wandering a deserted path, trying to figure out which way to go next, hoping that the obfuscation of the dark unknown will give way to the illuminating clarity of the light so we can see our way again. We are not always meant to see or know or have a concrete sense of what's waiting around the corner.

It is only through the unknowing— of blindly feeling our way along the dark path—that we are forced to stretch and grow, to sense and trust, to bump into something and realize we're headed in the wrong direction. We learn to regroup and navigate by the wisdom of the stars, gain new soul experiences, and step outside of what is certain to make space for the uncertain.

Any dreamer or risk taker or visionary who defied "No, you can't" with "Yes I will," anybody who is living life bravely, openly, and authentically by trying to follow the path of the heart will tell you—

It is not about getting lost; it's about finding the courage to stay on the path, to keep walking forward in faith— even when you can't see what's next— and trust that you are being led in the exact direction you need to go.

Pearls of Wisdom on Relationships, Connection, and Love

154
How We Wish to Be Loved

"We accept the love we think we deserve."
—Stephen Chbosky

I have come to believe that it is up to us to take responsibility for creating an atmosphere where we can receive the kind of love we deserve. This means we must create an atmosphere where we treat ourselves how we wish to be loved.

If we want to learn to love ourselves more unconditionally and find people who can love us with more freedom and grace, we must first learn to set boundaries, say "no," and sometimes even let go of the people who are unhealthy for us.

Keeping relationships that make us feel bad, continuing to let people take from us who don't give in return, and feeling like someone only wants pieces of us and not the whole person are not reflections of relationships based on unconditional love. They reflect relationships based on a pale imitation of love and include heavy overtones of guilt, obligation, co-dependency, fear of loneliness, and an inability to love ourselves enough to choose ourselves.

Please be kind to yourself if you find yourself in this space. It can take time to figure out what love is and isn't and then find the courage to insist on more love in our lives and make positive changes that create opportunities for receiving love. Please know, though, that unconditional love flows from a free, pure, and honest space, and each of us deserves to find this kind of love.

Don't know where to start? Begin here:

Focus on self-love and work on making choices in your life that reflect your ability to be healthy and love yourself. Then, you will find that the light inside of you will grow so bright that you can't help but love other people this way as well. Loving relationships filled with love always begin with you.

155
The Work of Change, Growth, and Love

We are meant for connection, for acts of kindness towards one another, for support and help along the way. We are definitely meant to love one another.

What we are not meant for is to chronically carry the burden of change for someone else, caring more about their life than they do and expending massive amounts of energy fixating on the pieces they need to change as they do the same behaviors over and over.

Healthy relationships are reciprocal, free-flowing, and balanced between give and take. Unhealthy relationships feel lopsided, with one person doing the bulk of the work, holding the other's wound in their hands, and trying to heal something that isn't theirs to heal.

When love becomes a constant taking on the burden of responsibility for someone else's life path, it quickly becomes toxic.

We can love one another, but we can't change one another. All we can do is work on changing ourselves and loving others in the ways we feel called, and remember that the work of change, growth, and love is always an inside job.

156
Compassionate Detachment

Don't assume other people are broken, need to be fixed, want to be fixed, or that you know what's right or best for their lives.

The only fair assumption is that as fellow human beings, they have their soul path, and they are walking that path as best they know how. They are subject to mistakes and learning by trial and error, getting lost and wandering in the wilderness, falling into holes, getting back up, and rising, redirecting, and renavigating—just as you are.

Learning to compassionately detach and make space to let another go their own way is one of the more challenging lessons we must learn. Yet, it makes all the difference when it comes to our peace of mind and peace of heart. We can choose to get sucked into another's story and drama, or we can choose to free ourselves and trust life to help them work it out.

Sometimes, the best gift you can give yourself is to practice releasing somebody with loving-kindness: "May you be safe, may you be well, and may life guide you as you need."

Then turn that beautiful blessing back around on yourself: "May I be safe, may I be well, and may life guide me as I need."

Then remember, even when our physical paths diverge, we are still connected at the source where it counts. Life is big enough to know our hearts and meet each of us exactly where we are at: "May we be safe, may we be well, and may life guide us as we need."

157

Score-Defying

Life is not a competition, and no one is keeping score. There is plenty of room for everyone to find their place. There is plenty of room for people to shine and be beautiful and inspiring. To be broken, messy, and chaotic. To make mistakes, figure it out, be better, and grow.

There is enough room for each of us to dance with our shadows and light. There is enough good stuff to light each of us up and hard stuff to challenge and grow us. There is plenty of space for people to become even more themselves as they continue to move in the right direction for their hearts.

It doesn't matter what somebody else is doing over there; what matters is what you are doing right here— your hopes, dreams, challenges, growth, path, and vision for yourself. Comparison is toxic. It is a dead-end street that will only seek to deter you from aligning with your authentic self.

If you are preoccupied with everybody else, you will never create space to find and receive your authentic truth, which is your gateway to greater freedom, space, and light. Whenever you realize you're getting caught up in what is happening with someone else, stop and discover your truth. Stay in your lane and redirect the focus back to you.

When it comes to life, there is no right or wrong way to live it. It is not a race, it is not about comparison, and there is no magic scorecard rating our decisions. Life is not that narrow-minded or petty. Through the eyes of life, our being here and finding the courage to take the journey is the success.

So, every time we take a deep breath and refuse to let condemnation be our set point, every time we stop comparing ourselves, every time we suspend judgment and just let people be people and let ourselves be where we are at—

Our heart expands a bit more, and life becomes much more spacious. We start to realize that the only thing worth keeping score on is the exponential, score-defying condition of our heart and our ability to stay open to life and love.

158

You Knowing You

I often hear people say that they can give good advice and help others but can't seem to take their own advice and help themselves. I think this is because we have become very good at operating from an other-centered place while our center is not balanced.

We freely offer our opinions about what we think others should do in their lives as we struggle to tend to ourselves with the same due diligence and care.

The fact that we sometimes struggle to take our own advice tells us how complicated and complex the landscape of life is. It is never as black and white as we like to make it out to be.

Much of the time, our relationships would be far better served by practicing more patience and compassion toward others as we listen to their stories and understand they are sharing the sacred space of their interior world rather than by telling other people what we think they should do.

Relating in this capacity starts with our relationships with ourselves. How will we ever find balance inside if we don't take the time to honor and listen to what we are trying to tell ourselves? If we don't take the time to get in touch with our own untold stories?

Pause, breathe, put on your oxygen mask, pull the speck out of your eye, and get your center back on mark.

We cannot love and relate from a whole place if we ourselves are not first whole. Sooner or later, when we have been living life off-center from our truth, something starts to break down. We spend years exhausting and losing ourselves by shaping our lives around that breakdown. Meanwhile, other parts of us work overtime to prop it up and fix it.

Take a moment for yourself today. Listen to what you have to say. Be kind and loving towards your stories and truth. You are worth this work of the soul, which starts with you knowing you.

159
Move Yourself Forward Instead

You cannot move a relationship forward if the other party isn't willing to do their part of the work. Your work lies within you. Your thoughts, your actions, your hurts, your hopes, your heart, your internal resources— all pieces of you that can be worked on to find greater healing, wellness, and authenticity in your life.

You can't do the work for someone else; you just can't. You can't dive into them and dig around and rearrange stuff in a territory you are not meant to excavate. That's for them to do. Not you. What a relief, right? You've got enough of your stuff to excavate!

This is where so many relationships can get off track. Instead of looking ourselves squarely in the face and figuring out how best to grow ourselves, we get lost in trying to do it for another.

If you find yourself caring more about someone else than they do, working harder at their life than they are, or carrying the excess baggage they refuse to pick up and carry for themselves, this is a really good time to stop.

Just stop.
Lay it down.
Let it be okay where it is.
Let it be okay that things aren't moving forward.
Move yourself forward instead.

Turn all that excellent care and attention to the parts of yourself you have neglected. Focus on the territory that is yours to excavate. Develop a richer relationship with yourself. Trust that life will bring your relationships to where they need to go. You don't have to keep working so hard.

You don't have to carry it all. You just have to find the courage to explore, address, and be the scope of your beautiful, untapped self.

160

THE GREAT RIVER OF LIFE

There will be people in this life who feel like a giant whirlpool whenever your lifestream goes near them. People who will suck you into their swirls until you find yourself wrapped up in their drama, their energy, their issues, their obstacles, and their life force.

You will know them when you find them because there is a sense of being stuck in an eddy. One in which you must force yourself to swim extremely hard to stay afloat, and you often find yourself getting pulled in despite your best intentions.

When you have a respite from the situation, you realize you feel minimized, tired, disoriented, chronically angry, sad, or frustrated, and somehow lessened by the experience. You are left questioning yourself and having conversations with them in your head, which you know will never occur in real life.

Don't let somebody else's whirlpool become the compass by which you set your course. There's no way to fight the force of another who is unwilling to change and has developed a pattern of pulling others into their currents to fill a void within themselves.

You cannot fill this void. EVER. So, the sooner you find your way out of their eddy and learn just to keep moving to your flow, the better off you'll be.

There are lessons we can learn when we've fallen into another's pool. Lessons about who and what is healthy for us. Lessons about why we allowed ourselves to get sucked in in the first place. Lessons about what we need to heal within ourselves, so we don't repeat the pattern.

Ultimately, our job isn't to get sucked into every pool we find; it's to find the wisdom, strength, and self-knowledge to simply say, "This isn't my path," readjust our course and then go on around.

Trusting the Great River of Life has much better waters to help support our hearts, our wholeness, and our flow.

161

DELICIOUS UNMET SIDES

"Really, though, what do I know about what another person is capable of? I still don't have a clue what I'm capable of. I keep surprising even myself."

—Val Emmich

We always have to give the people in our lives space for change and leave them room to surprise us. When we have a fixed notion of who someone is, we are limiting them to an idea that doesn't allow room for the full spectrum of their humanity.

People are fluid, dynamic, and capable of great movement and change. Often, when others' actions don't add up to who we thought someone was, they are simply on their journey, trying to explore an unmet side of themselves.

We are all evolving on our paths, and change happens to us all. Keep giving each other space to grow, learn to become more flexible in our relationships, and be gracious with each other. Be less rigid when someone is exploring a new facet of self and see it for what it is: an adventure in self-discovery.

Just as much as we need to allow others the space to change, we accord ourselves that same space. We all have delicious unmet sides waiting to be discovered. When we allow ourselves space for curiosity and discovery, we can begin to see that our possibilities are beautiful and vast.

162
The Path of Greater Presence

How can we learn to be more present in our relationships?

We must learn to sit with others where they are. To truly see the real them and not who we think they should be or who we want them to be. To be with the whole of them. To create a safe space where they feel able to be their real selves.

Our ability to do those things is only as strong as our ability to do the same for ourselves.

We must learn to sit with ourselves where we are at. To truly see the real self, not who we think we should be. To be with our whole. To create safe spaces where we can engage with authenticity and clear gazing.

We need to allow ourselves the gifts of being, and the space to be still and present with the whole of who we are. When we give ourselves space, we can explore our core selves, listen to ourselves, and learn how to bring nonjudgment, peace, and self-grace into that space.

This is how we increase our true, authentic presence toward others in our lives: first, we excavate the inner self by learning to listen, witness, and acknowledge what is there. Then, we do the work of clearing out, organizing, and learning self-compassion.

As we do these things, we can better show up in our outer world without our attachment to expectations of how others should be. Instead, we learn to entreat with clarity, presence, and compassionate kindness, and we allow ourselves to truly listen, witness, and meet others where they are.

163

Gaze

You can't love another into fullness. You can't make them see something they do not wish to see within themselves. You can't make them see you for the truth of who you are when they cannot see the truth of who they are.

Last, one of the hardest things to learn: you can't expect somebody else to see and love you into wholeness.

The precious mirror of a relationship is one whose reflection can be easily clouded if we do not do the work of our inner world and learn to see ourselves through a clear lens. If we do not learn to recognize our external projections, we cannot deal with our inner introjections. If we do not learn to take massive responsibility for our essence and entity.

Only when we do this self-work do we see things with crystal clarity, compassion, grace, and a clearer gaze. We stop expecting others to be something they are not, and we see ourselves and honor our authenticity in a deeper way.

Living life in a way where we go about the self-work of embodying, believing, and seeing is the only way I know to truly love ourselves into the wholeness of being.

164
SCORE ONE FOR TEAM LOVE

It's very difficult to be open and available for someone else if you are not first open and available for yourself.

When we cannot be open and honest with our needs, feelings, desires, truth, and space of self, we are not operating from a space of authenticity. And if we are not operating from a space of authenticity, how can we expect our relationships to be authentic? The relationships then become about something other than authenticity.

Sometimes, people reject others, so they can't get close enough to reject them, and they are sure they will be rejected since they have already rejected themself.

Or maybe they find themselves over-giving to everyone else to receive back the love, validation, and affirmation they secretly yearn for but deny themselves.

Perhaps they relate to others in patterns of fear, avoidance, denial, and negativity, so nobody has the chance to get to know their true self, because even they don't know their true self.

If we want to strengthen our relationships to reflect more love, we must start with our relationship with ourselves. Peeling back the layers one by one and seeing what's there. We must learn to relate to ourselves with honesty, integrity, respect for needs, forgiveness, and compassion— even for the parts we don't like so much.

An authentic life starts with being present with yourself. Be so real within you that you can't help but be this real with others. You will find that operating from a place of authenticity feels so spacious, so true in your heart, and so good in your soul that you can't bear to fake it with anyone.

Then you just get to be you, and people get to see the real you. You get to be present and available to yourself and the people you encounter. And there is that much more space for the giving and receiving of love in our lives, so everybody wins. Score one for team love.

165
Free to Be You and Me

Continuing to let go of expectations of who we think we should be is one of the most freeing things we can ever do for ourselves. Often, we become so rigid in the shoulds, musts, and have-tos that we suffocate under the burden of them.

We don't leave room to switch directions midstream if we feel called to growth and change. We miss out on the person we could become if we let growth happen organically instead of keeping ourselves in check and cramming ourselves into the box of who we think we should be. We trade a self-imposed dictatorship for the freedom of self.

Nobody is perfect. We will mess up. We will disappoint people. We will make mistakes. We will fail when we try. We will look back and acknowledge we could have handled something better. We will learn to apologize.

We will see our flaws, faults, and growth areas and learn to get over ourselves. Life will continue, and we will be okay if we allow these experiences to shape us and help us grow in our imperfections.

The people embracing life most joyously are not perfect people; they are simply people who've learned to embrace their imperfections. Who allow life to transform their fault lines and reshape their inner worlds. Who remove "should" and "have to" from their vocabulary and let the river take them for a ride.

Toss your "shoulds" out the window today. Examine your expectations of yourself and ask yourself if they are really working for you. Consider whether you are allowing yourself space to grow and flow. Free to be you and me— what a wonderful world that would be.

166

IN THE TRENCHES

Some of our most powerful lessons will come in the form of relationships that hurt us. Relationships where we are forced to dig deep into our trenches of self, psyche, and soul so we can better understand our hurt, grasp what we've experienced, and navigate the dynamics.

The trenches can be brutal. It's where we painfully dig and put in the emotional, mental, and spiritual labor required to examine, sort, and understand. It's where we pose the question, "How much of this is me and how much of this is them, and what the hell happened here?" And do the tricky work of trying to figure out where we need to take responsibility and where we might be blaming ourselves for something another brought to the equation.

This work is particularly hard if the person or people who hurt us appear oblivious to the damage caused or don't seem particularly interested in taking responsibility for what happened, let alone dropping into the trenches to help us dig and sort things out.

As irresolute as this is, we must remember that we can't make others see things from our point of view. We can't make them own a blind spot in their character or admit the areas where we might feel they lie about who they are or see themselves as more virtuous than we experienced.

It's painful when we are left incomplete, unsatisfied, and lacking answers. We need time to do griefwork over the loss of the relationship and the loss of our ideals. We need time to sift through what was and wasn't real. We need time to excavate, mend, and repair our precious interior of self.

As painful as these relationships are, they offer potent lessons. If we can stay with our hearts and do the vital work of grieving, healing, releasing, and changing our old patterns, there is freedom on the other side. Freedom that creates real change, ensuring we won't keep repeating the dynamic. There is healing of familial, ancestral, and karmic wounds. There is newfound wisdom, strength, and grace.

Ultimately, there is love the more we do our healing work. Over time, we will find that we can keep love and carry on, trusting our ever-increasing light to bring in the ones who truly are aligned.

167
Exit Plan Out of the Ghostlands

When we hold onto our resentments, anger, and bitterness over something that happened in the past, those feelings begin to take on a life of their own. We might even build a fortress of hurt and pain inside of ourselves. Life may have long moved on, and we might still be on the defensive.

If we don't relentlessly pursue our right to have a peaceful heart, we will forever live at war with those ghosts. We retrace what happened in our mind and blame ourselves for what we didn't do, or blame somebody else for what they didn't do, or blame the situation itself and the greater forces of life.

We keep scouring the ghostlands of the past, trying to make peace, but we come up empty each time because there is no new life to be found there.

Forgiveness is our exit plan out of the ghostlands. It is the magic door that will instantly transport us into the gifts of the present. Forgiveness helps us write a new ending to our tired old stories into a tale of resilience, compassion, and self-love. It helps us release our ghosts when we realize that every one of us is only human and, as such, is marked by the fallibility of mistakes, imperfections, and imperfect timing.

Forgiveness is a process that takes place across many levels. We can learn to forgive ourselves for all the times in our lives that we didn't get it right and realize that we did what we knew to do then. We each have a right to make mistakes— it is how we experience, learn, gain wisdom, and grow our hearts.

We can learn to forgive others for the times they didn't get it right, and their actions hurt us. This can be tricky when our hearts feel hurt, but over time, it helps if we remember that they, like us, are also making mistakes along the way and may not have known how to do differently at the time, experiencing, learning, and growing as they went.

We can learn to forgive this life for being what it is: imperfect, jagged, beautiful, and flawed. Take all the bruises, callouses, and ugly parts, and see they are part of the palette of what makes us whole. Repurpose them as teachers and growing experiences and do our best to cover them with grace and love.

As we do the work of forgiveness and leave the ghosts of the past in the past, we keep finding that there is joy, too. And that is worth fighting for our right to embrace our life, free ourselves, release our specters, and claim a heart of forgiveness, acceptance, and peace.

168
Respectful Dialogue as an Act of Love

Finding the courage to speak your truth in love is not about running over other people, picking apart their ideas to invalidate them, or making another wrong to make ourselves right.

We all have a right to our perspectives, but what isn't right is tearing others down to make ourselves right. Rage, blame, justification, and defensiveness don't require courage. They just require a quick tongue and a lack of emotional control that leaves a lot of verbal destruction in its wake.

Love requires courage. Speaking your truth in love means taking responsibility for the energy you bring to a space when you speak. Love asks us to find the courage to engage in respectful dialogues where we learn to listen as much as we speak. To truly listen— not pretend to listen, without absorption— but learn to listen with our minds and hearts.

Listening with the mind is simply a matter of stopping and pausing long enough to receive what another has to say. It is a kind of listening that invites us to slow down and pay attention to something or someone outside of ourselves.

Listening with the heart is an entirely different matter because it not only requires us to take the time to hear what someone says, but it also asks that we try and understand it from their perspective instead of filtering it through our own. Understanding how their unique experiences and way of being in the world contribute to their perspective.

This is where many get lost in communication: we filter somebody else's point of view through our life experience and discard, judge, or misunderstand the other person's perspective and process, which usually leaves everybody feeling frustrated and unseen.

Love asks us to remember that no matter how big our differences are, we all share the same thing. We are all on this human journey to learn about authenticity and love. If, in some small way, we can extend a piece of love to one another with respectful dialogues— where we choose to hear and see the person and not just the issue— we all walk away better for it.

Speak in truth and peace within yourself today, and speak in truth and peace to others. Remember that sometimes, one of the most powerful things we will ever do is simply accept somebody else where they are without trying to talk them out of it and extend the same acceptance towards ourselves. Now, that is an act of great love.

169
Lessons on Relationships Learned as an Empath

1. Energetic exchanges in our relationships are invisible but very real; those intuitions, senses, and perceptions we pick up on— even when we're not entirely sure why we feel what we feel— have substance to them and shouldn't be dismissed.

2. Our body's wisdom never lies, nor does our internal experience of a situation. How we feel, what we sense, and how our body reacts all offer us information on the relationship if we can tune in and stay open to listening to these wisdom sources.

3. When we begin to feel tapped, drained, trapped, and taken from by someone, it is time to reevaluate the relationship and notice how it truly makes us feel.

4. We can't walk somebody else's path for them. We can't carry their load. We can't complete the journey necessary for their soul growth. We can only attend to our own.

5. It's okay to renegotiate boundaries created in the past in any relationship to realign them with your life in the present. Just because it once worked doesn't mean it now works.

6. Projection exists for various reasons, but it always results in not seeing a person for who they really are. If you don't feel seen in a relationship, then it's an indicator that you need to take a step back and evaluate that relationship.

7. Instead of putting it on another person to be what we need to fill something inside ourselves, we must learn to seek wholeness within and belong to ourselves.

8. We don't owe our life force, time, or energy to anyone, and though we will find many to whom we willingly give, share, and offer of ourselves— this is our choice, not our obligation, and we always have the freedom to make new choices.

9. Sometimes, the most powerful gift you can give yourself is permission to free yourself from somebody else's ideal of you. Let it shatter. Be your real self. Set the boundary you need, and let the pieces fall where they may.

10. Trust that life will rearrange a relationship if it's meant to last and help close the door on it if it's served its purpose. Those who are meant to stick will allow us to grow, evolve, and change— they'll give us space to be our full expression, and those are the ones worth keeping.

170

The Whole Story

"It was the best of times, it was the worst of times, it was the age of wisdom, it was the age of foolishness, it was the epoch of belief, it was the epoch of incredulity, it was the season of light, it was the season of darkness, it was the spring of hope, it was the winter of despair."
—Charles Dickens, Great Expectations

When Dickens said it was the best of times and the worst of times, his words captured the journey of wholeness: happiness and sadness commingled with every space in between. We are not here to seek happiness only and avoid those experiences we see as lesser. We are here to take all experiences as they come and honor them as the whole of our stories, told from all sides.

We are called to do this work within ourselves and to bring this same wholeness into our relationships. Love doesn't call us to only take the best of times in another and reject the worst, but to recognize the value of the whole person so we can take our experiences of them as they come, take them as they come, and embrace the whole of their story.

Love frees. It doesn't entrap. It is not about controlling one another but accepting each other where we are at. It is about taking personal responsibility for ourselves so we can ensure we bring our best selves to the relationship instead of blaming someone else for our unhappiness.

There is space to move and evolve, allowing the fluidity of relationships to ebb and flow as they need to in response to the seasons in life. It seeks not to cage, manipulate, or hold someone back from being who they are but to shine the light of unconditional love onto another, so they are free to be their best selves.

It is healing, freeing, unconditional, and liberating. It is you. It is me. It is within each of us when we learn to release the reigns of control and stop gripping the handlebars trying to steer another in our direction. Instead, trust that within the thrumming heartbeat of this earth, the evolution of love awaits us all.

Seeking to teach us that when we let go of our need to attach from pain and fear, we become free to simply love ourselves, love another, and love each other. We become free to embrace the whole story and see that all of it— all the jubilation, ache, beauty, grief, shadows, and light— is a love story spinning out and being told from all sides.

171
Questions for Evaluating Relationship Exchange

Are you working harder to help somebody than they themselves are working? Do you care more about another's life at the expense of caring about your own life? Are you directing more energy another's way than you are towards yourself? Do you care more about helping somebody grow and reach their potential than they do?

When we answer "yes" to any of these questions, it's always a good time to pause, do a little gentle self-reflection, and ask ourselves why we are working so hard on someone else's behalf when they are not working equally hard on their own behalf.

We cannot do the work of change for someone else. We cannot meet another's karma, learn a life lesson for them, walk their path, or fix their inner pain. We cannot make them reach and grow to their potential. They must do these things for themselves and take ownership of that process. All we can do is keep taking ownership of our own change and growth process.

When we pour our life energy into someone who is not pouring their life energy into themselves, we run the grave risk of losing ourselves and depleting our inner resources. We start to find that it's not an equitable relationship exchange, that we've lost ourselves in over-giving, and that we're not receiving much to fill ourselves back up.

Ultimately, we are left exhausted. The person still hasn't changed, and we realize we spent the best of ourselves investing in someone who didn't value our efforts and isn't willing to invest in themselves.

It can be hard to find the balance between caring for ourselves and caring for others and to determine what feels right for us. That is up to us to decide for ourselves, and we can go through a lot of trial, error, and learning curves in the process.

However, as a rule of thumb, I find it helpful to remember that if I'm working harder at somebody else's life than they are, if I'm investing in their potential more than they are, if I'm trying to fix, solve, figure out, do the heavy-lifting, emotional labor or otherwise try and manage their life on their behalf— it's a good indicator I need to stop, evaluate and turn my attention back to mine.

Investing in the only heart, soul, and potential I can.

172
Permission to Remap Boundaries

Our boundaries are not immutable. They can be reevaluated, remapped, and realigned when needed. It helps to give ourselves permission to do a little survey work occasionally and make sure the borders and limits we've implemented in our relationships, commitments, and exchanges still hold true.

Sometimes, we get stuck feeling like just because something has always been a certain way, it should stay that way. We've created a pattern with our behavior that everyone is used to, and we worry that we'll disappoint people, or they'll react negatively if we start changing things.

Yet, either we've changed, or life has changed, and something begins to feel off. We start to feel like our old way of doing things is no longer working for us, which usually is a clue that we need to take a step back, evaluate, and reconsider.

It is an important reminder to give yourself permission to evaluate and change your boundaries when you recognize something no longer feels right— whether that's a situation, a relationship, an old thought pattern, an old behavior, or anything else that begins to feel unaligned.

People are not entitled to our light, our time, our energy, our feedback, our support, or any part of ourselves. We give those things out of freedom and love. When we realize we are not giving out of freedom and love, then it's time to step back and evaluate our boundaries.

We have the choice to remap our borders and limits, to rename and reroute how we'd like to claim and direct our precious resources of self, time, energy, money, knowledge, compassion, heart, wisdom, and life force. Freedom is found when we listen to our hearts and honor our need to repattern certain aspects of our lives. When we realize change is needed, we give ourselves permission to change.

173
LOVING KINDNESS MEDITATION FOR CLEARING SPACE

What others say about us is always more of a reflection of who they are than who we are.

What we say about others is always more of a reflection of who we are than who they are.

Any relationship can be a teacher if we can see that it is here to help us grow, to help us shine a light on unmet places inside ourselves, and to help us keep moving toward wholeness.

Sometimes, all we can do is let people be where they are while we accept and do the good work of being where we are.

If we need to create space and clear the emotional and psychic debris from unmet expectations and failure to be what another wanted us to be or what we hoped another would be, we can create energetic space by compassionately saying:

I free myself not to meet your expectations of me. I free you not to meet my expectations of you. May we be safe, loved, and guided towards our highest truth.

174

WITHOUT LIMITS

When we say we love someone, then we spend our time trying to change them through words veiled in criticism, actions intended to manipulate the situation to our favor, and choosing punitive passive-aggressive silence that seeks to lay blame— and we do this all while avowing our love— that's not true love.

It is merely a distant shadow of the liberating light that is love. True love accepts somebody for who they are right now.

Love respects their right to find their path and gently walks beside them, offering a helping hand instead of trying to direct that path. It is rooted in transparent communication that takes ownership of actions and feelings and seeks to forgive, resolve, and grow from differences.

Love accepts the natural ebb and flow of any relationship and knows how to breathe easily through the ups and downs. Love knows that relationships rooted in freedom will organically move toward healing and wellness instead of moving toward fear and control. Love is unconditional, vital, and regenerative as it renews itself repeatedly.

Freedom is at the core of love; it doesn't seek to change, entrap, or bend others to be what we need. Love accepts us where we are and allows us to be what we need to grow and become a higher expression of ourselves.

When we work on embodying love— even with all our human flaws, frailties, and woundedness— love will help us transcend our limitations and teach us how to be without limits. Love is a blessing and a mystery, and when we give it space to shape us and rearrange, love is its own wild force that grows untamed.

175
Rainbow of Shades

When we can be our whole selves with another, we know we have found relationship gold. A precious alchemical compound that allows for the full scope of our being, with space for both contraction and expansion.

When we must hide parts of ourselves for fear of rejection, judgment, misperception, and belittlement, then the relationship ranges from downright unhealthy to simply incomplete— a fragmented exchange of contained selves— where the deepest real of a person is not valued or held in higher regard than the shinier, superficial gleam.

It hurts not to be cherished for all that is most authentic in ourselves. It can be lonely, alienating, and isolating. And yet, others' ability to see their true selves is only as strong as their ability to see their true self and acknowledge what is most real and deep inside them.

Heart wisdom comes when we can open our hearts and minds and see everything from all angles and sides. It comes when we see the interconnections between all things, the interconnections in all parts of another, and the interconnections between all parts of ourselves.

You can't make others see what you wish them to see in you. But you can keep learning to develop your own wise eyes of the heart and learn to look at yourself through the lens of heart wisdom. This is profoundly different from what the mind thinks it knows. After a while, you learn to keep walking your path and simply step around those who can't see your full scope.

And when the ones come along, who do? There, you'll find your pot of gold with plenty of space for the rainbow of all your beautiful shades and whole.

176
A Multidimensional Responsibility and Necessity

It is easy to feel lost and unseen in a world that often houses careless hearts. Some people don't treat their relationships with the reverence that should be given to the fragile gift of another's trust, friendship, and love.

Entrusting part of ourselves to another, in any relationship, is an offering of the gift of self. A glimpse into and sharing the sacred territory of our hearts and souls.

Those who cannot receive those gifts with care (and you know who they are because they are the ones you have struggled to forgive, let go of, and move on from) often lack care toward their true self.

They fail to see the gift of their own life as something to be revered and cherished. They often relate to others the same way they relate to themselves: with a lack of thought, negligence of their inner home, and disconnection. The same patterns are reflected in their relationships.

We are better for others when we learn to revere and cherish who we are. The more we explore and know the interior of our hearts, the better we can share from an authentic space. It creates more room for honesty, trust, and care in our relationships. When things go wrong, we can maintain emotional availability and openness to seek resolution and healing.

This is a process, not an absolute. It's not about perfection— we are delightful works in progress who learn as we go— but about the willingness to learn to love yourself.

Learning to love who we are, embracing ourselves, and having an authentic relationship with the self is not some fluffy, one-dimensional luxury. It is a deep, wonderfully multi-dimensional responsibility and necessity.

177
BEAUTIFUL THINGS

We cannot tear somebody else down without tearing ourselves down. Directing criticism, hate, judgment, and negativity toward others will only erode our foundation and develop those qualities within ourselves.

Whatever seeds you plant within yourself are the seeds you will sow in this world. While we can't always control what is happening, we have acres of space for our choices about what we develop in our hearts, minds, and spirits.

Compassion begets compassion. Peace begets peace. Love begets love. Beautiful ways of being beget more beauty.

Let's create beautiful things and keep adding to that treasure: letting go of the things we cannot change, sowing the seeds of integrity, authenticity, and forgiveness in light in the spaces we can, beginning with ourselves.

178
CHOOSING TO TRAVEL LIGHT

"I have decided to stick to love...Hate is too great a burden to bear."
—Martin Luther King Jr.

I've been thinking lately about this quote and what it means on a deeper level. How it truly feels to go through life carrying around bags of bitterness and pettiness and resentment. Bags filled with old stories of the past. Bags of blame. Bags of fear. Bags of shame.

Those are some heavy bags.

They are dark and sticky and weigh one down until they start to get so stuck they can't see any good in life. Before they know it, they can barely step without the bags, tangling them up, shackling them further to the mess. The light is trying to shine through, but all they can see is the shadows cast by the scope of their baggage.

What a waste. Of life. Of heart. Of possibilities. Of relationships. Of opportunities for healing. Of beautiful self. Of love.

The older I get, the more I am working on trying to feel what I feel and then release it to life so I can be at peace in my own heart space and travel light. Especially if I'm letting go of somebody else's story, script, and life, which was never my responsibility to fix, hold, or contain in the first place.

Then you're just kind of free to meet people where they are and love them for who they are.

Sometimes, with the great ones, you are lucky enough to do that up close. And sometimes, with those who are very hard to love— because they are bound and determined to stay stuck, and you realize you just can't manage an unmanageable— you get to do that at a distance and trust life to work things out.

Either way, we all have choices about who and what we want to be, and it feels a lot better going through life happy, loving, and free. For me, I want to travel light, and so I will keep choosing what I need to free my heart and remember that the only thing any of us truly take with us is the love we have inside and how we choose to live it.

179
Making Broken Things Whole

> *"Break a vase, and the love that reassembles the fragments is stronger than that love which took its symmetry for granted when it was whole."*
>
> —Derek Walcott

Love is a choice— one we make over and over again, one we choose to make within ourselves, and one we choose to make with those we love. Sometimes, we don't see how to make that choice, and we must find our way through the murky mud of doubt, anger, bitterness, resentment, and confusion to find love.

In these moments, we forget that love can be like the humble yet hopeful lotus growing in the mud. The lotus teaches us that something exquisite can come from something dark. The lotus reminds us that sometimes we need the grit of the mud to develop deep roots and, through our struggle, grow something more beautiful out of faith, perseverance, and abidance.

Sometimes, in our relationships, we go through the mud to get the lotus, and love may seem like it's falling apart and breaking. But often, love is just getting a bit gritty and muddy to break down whatever is no longer working. So, love can awaken and arise into a greater form.

In these moments, if two people can meet in a heart space and, despite their differences, see that they are still on the same page, then love will transform a relationship and find a way to evolve it forward. Love will take what seems broken— rebuilding, repairing, mending, and healing— rearranging the pieces and filling the cracks with liquid gold.

Love helps it become more beautiful than before. Taking something broken and making it whole.

180
Happy, Uncluttered, and Free

At some point, it helps to become well-practiced in the art of forgiveness. This might not come easily or automatically, but it is worthwhile because when we learn to forgive, we learn how to free ourselves in brighter ways.

Some people struggle with the word "forgiveness," so if it feels more accessible to you, instead of "forgiveness," try "acceptance, letting go, and releasing."

When we forgive, we do all three: we find a measure of greater acceptance for what has happened. We choose to shift something inside of us, so we begin letting go of our sticky attachments of bitterness, resentment, and hatred. We find a way to create space by releasing the person, situation, or circumstances to life.

When we forgive, we loosen our grip, soften, clean out toxic feelings, and shift those to more neutral feelings of compassionate detachment. We create more space, so we have more room to experience the beautiful things in life; it is hard to revel in life's roses if our inner gardens are clogged with weeds.

Learning to forgive can take a while, but some of the best things we can do for ourselves take time and are worth our investment. Even if it means we keep returning to the same wound and working on bringing more healing into that space each time we realize we're still hanging on to the old story of anger and strife.

When it comes to forgiveness, we can take as much time as we need; forgiveness isn't a race or a destination. It is a tool we can use on our journeys when we realize we're dragging around the baggage of the past and it's time to lighten our load. It's a tool we can use to create space inside, so we have room to experience more authentic expressions of love in our lives.

While the actual inner shift that takes place with true forgiveness can be hard, especially if something or someone has deeply wounded or hurt us and our hearts are struggling to release that pain, the act of practicing forgiveness is quite simple. It doesn't require anything fancy, any big words, or a particular skill. It just requires a heart that is open enough to express some version of this sentiment to the greater forces of life:

"Help me learn to accept, let go, and release. I choose a heart that is happy, uncluttered, and free."

181
LISTENING TO OUR HEARTS IN A DIVIDED WORLD

Note: this piece of writing was given to me during my meditation time on June 3, 2020, when I was grappling with the pain, wounding, and divisions in our country and world. That day, I opened my heart and asked for guidance, wisdom, and how to cut through all the chaos and voices and listen to my heart. The following is what came through.

Doing the right thing for you isn't about making somebody else wrong. Making others wrong doesn't make you right. Throw out the right. Throw out the wrong. Throw out the judgment and the labels. You must learn to see beyond sides.

Ask yourself instead, "Is this loving?" And is this loving? How about this? Then, do that. Do what is loving and move in the direction of love.

This is the only way to create a compass of truth that will help you navigate the troubled waters going on in your world and in your country right now.

If you feel lost, seek and ask love to reveal itself to you. Pause, wait, and call on love. If it's not loving, then it's not coming from a place of truth.

This is how you learn to distinguish the truth: does it make you feel more open? Does it make you feel more connected? Does it make you feel more free— even if being free challenges you to take a hard step?

If it doesn't leave you open, if it doesn't leave you connected to your fellow human beings, if it causes fear and doubt in your heart, then it is not coming from a place of love's truth.

Truth will never enslave you. Truth will never conquer you. Truth will never subjugate you. Truth will not ask you to hate another, for truth is love and love is truth, so when you move toward truth, you are moving toward love. And when you move toward love, you move towards truth.

Once again, do not make others wrong to make yourself right. This is the surest way to give fear a foothold and to create division. Instead, ask yourself: does this feel loving? Does this feel in my heart like the right step to take? Does this feel like it is moving me closer to my fellow humans, closer to the heart of the earth, or does it feel like it is moving me farther away?

Step towards as often as you can. Step towards each other, not away. Learn to see beyond parties and agendas— see the human instead. See the voice. See the story.

The more you see each other in your humanness, your voice, and your stories—the more you will know what is right to do, and what is right to do will always move you toward the direction of love.

182
EVOLUTION OF LOVE

Love, at its core, is peaceful. Like aloe, it awakens and soothes.

There may be times in any of our love relationships when we're not feeling the love because of stress and conflict, being human, and the simple fact that anytime two people— with two different need sets and perspectives on life— are relating, they are bound to bump into one another in the process.

But at its core, love helps people work through those things and brings them back to a steady state of grace and peace, time and time again. Love is the glue that makes things stick.

What love is not is contentious, chaotic, strife-inducing, unstable, demeaning, minimalizing, manipulative, and turbulent. When any of these things occur chronically in a relationship, it is no longer a pattern of love playing out but something else entirely.

The only thing I know to impart to teach people how to learn to distinguish between imitation and the real thing is to become a student of love. Seek it in all its forms. Learn to develop a love relationship with life and see how life begins to unveil new aspects of love to you.

Love can take many forms and many guises. We learn about it in every heartbeat, breath, and moment of the day if we stop and truly see and listen. It will teach us how to transcend old patterns and limiting beliefs, it will teach us how to better belong to ourselves and better belong to others, and most of all, it will teach us how to live with more space in our lives.

Space for grace. Space for possibilities. Space for connection. Space for joy. Space for grief. Space for healing. Space to become a catalyst for a greater expression and evolution of love.

183
Paint the Sky with Stars

We aren't meant to walk somebody else's path for them, which can be a tough truth.

It's not that any of us necessarily want to try to walk somebody else's path— most of us have enough going on with our own. It's more that when we care about people, we want good things for them. We want to see them flourish, grow, and be happy and free. When we want those things for the people we love, and when they make decisions that harm or hurt, it is rough to be the bystander.

That's usually the point we want to jump off our path, hop onto theirs, and try to steer them in the "right" direction. When that happens repeatedly and chronically, we will eventually lose ourselves in our efforts. Lose our own hopes and dreams. Lose where our path ends and theirs begins. Lose our own sense of self.

So, if we can't walk their path, what can we do?

We can pray for others. Send light, hope for healing, and ask that life support them. We can put the intention out into the ether that we desire whatever is for their highest good. We can encourage. We can love— sometimes up close and sometimes from afar— depending on what boundaries necessitate.

We can hold space, keep believing in them, and keep believing life is full of miracles and love can bring about redemptive change. We can release them to the universe if we recognize we're no longer meant to be a space holder for them and know that the universe is absolutely big enough to support them.

We can work on ourselves. Work on our path. Get busy cultivating what we see on that path. Pruning the trees, planting roses, learning the language of bunnies, clouds, and grass so we receive nature's healing qualities and learn to go deeper within.

We can look for places where our path feels dark and work on painting the sky with stars so we always have something to navigate by. We can stand exactly where we are and send love backward and forward on our own timeline, trusting it to reach our younger self and future self, bringing hope, mending, and integration.

We can work on nourishing what is inside of us: our hearts, our thoughts, our breath, our feelings, our gratitude, and our stories. We can do the work of self. We can trust that if we do this, we will be so full of life and love; we can stay on our path and shine our love light so bright that it casts a glow onto others, encouraging them to find what they need to meet their requirements of soul.

184

STRUT ON MY FRIEND

Just because somebody is doing life a little differently than the way we do it doesn't mean it's bad or wrong. Sometimes, people need to wander outside the lines they've previously drawn for themselves to expand, be more authentic, and actualize a part of themselves that has previously gone unexplored.

We can be so quick to judge what we don't understand. We can quickly attribute negative characteristics and unfavorable evaluations to others' actions when, in fact, we know very little about where that person is truly at and know nothing about what that person needs for their heart, self, and soul requirements.

We can't expect other people to do things as we do. They are not us, and we are not them. We are all living life on our terms, figuring it out as best we know how, and growing in the directions each of us needs to grow.

What a kinder place it would be if we could find some compassion and grace instead of judging what we don't understand in another. Then, we could wish another well on their journey and say—

"You over there, my fellow human, you're doing an amazing job trying to figure all this out. Keep up the good work and strut on, my friend."

Pearls of Wisdom on Compassion, Sensitivity, Courage, and Grace

185
What Courage Is and Isn't

Courage doesn't mean you go through life calm and collected, never letting anyone see you tear up or sweat. It doesn't mean that you put on a good front and keep a stiff upper lip, never appearing fragile, vulnerable, or unknowing.

Courage doesn't mean that when you finally try to speak your truth, it will come out easily and crystal clear instead of garbled, or shaky, or different from the way you rehearsed it in your head.

Courage doesn't mean perfection and image and success, never falling or disappointing people or screwing stuff up. Courage doesn't mean you charge straight up a mountain, never tiring and needing to stop and rest for a bit because some days it feels so high up and too hard to climb.

Courage doesn't mean you always feel strong, confident, and prepared, never weak or tired, and like you can't keep going. It certainly doesn't mean there won't be times you feel so emotionally uncomfortable, confused, and out of sorts that you wonder what you're doing with your life and if you're even headed in the right direction.

Instead, courage is about learning to find grace with your process, facing your vulnerabilities, understanding that messy things are simply part of being human, and continuing to show up and try anyway. Courage is creating meaning from darkness and continuing to write our lives with an eye for adventure, resilience, forgiveness, and grace.

Courage is choosing to find the sacred in the everyday and insist on wonder and joy. Courage is knowing that an awe-inspiring life is available for us if we learn to engage with the voice of our hearts. Courage is allowing ourselves to dance with our tenderness and sensitivities, explore our intuition and creativity, and live a radical life of love and individuality.

This kind of courage changes hearts and lives, and I know we each have this courage.

186
What's Grace Got to Do with It?

Grace is a concept that is hard to capture in words because grace is an experience, not a definition. It is always available to us, but sometimes we miss it if we don't pay attention.

Grace is the freshness of bright raindrops and yellow tulips in spring. It is the beauty of fresh snow when it covers all the grey grime of life and makes everything feel magical and new. Grace is the kindness of a stranger, the joy of heartfelt laughter, and the feel of a breeze on a hot summer day.

Grace is the miracle of life, the wisdom of grief's light, and all the tiny moments of love interlaced throughout our days. Grace is the gift of receiving goodness from the universal flow of light; we don't do anything to particularly merit this goodness— grace just is.

Grace is game-changing. It reminds us that life is not a zero-sum game. Our gains and losses are not being checked in an ethereal box, where life only gives us equal gains and losses in like measure.

Grace throws the whole equation out and always tips the odds in our favor. It marches through our lives and helps right what got tipped upside down or pulls us off one path and deposits us on a better one. Grace is accorded to each of us equally, simply for belonging to and participating in this life.

Sometimes grace is easy to spot, and other times, it's disguised, and we miss it. Regardless of appearance, it is always compassionate and wise and operates from a space of helping move us toward our highest good.

Flowing seamlessly through every moment of our days, filling in the cracks of life so we feel uplifted to create a path to a better way. Usually, when we least expect and most need it, grace comes along and holds the power to change everything.

187

GIFTS OF STRENGTH

"Vulnerability is the birthplace of love, belonging, joy, courage, empathy, and creativity. It is the source of hope, empathy, accountability, and authenticity. If we want greater clarity in our purpose or deeper and more meaningful spiritual lives, vulnerability is the path."
—Brené Brown

Don't lose your vulnerability, empathy, or tenderheartedness. We live in a world that likes to tell us it's not okay to be sensitive, cry, or feel something too deeply because we're being "too emotional," but you know what?

The ability to feel deeply, love fiercely, open your heart, and share your vulnerability is a magnificent gift of strength. It is a gift the world needs more of, and we forget that our sensitivities are superpowers in disguise.

It takes more courage to keep our hearts open than to keep them closed.

It takes more strength to cry our way through a season of grief and let our hearts be broken and reformed than it does to make our pain.

It takes more bravery to face our fears with scrutiny and integrity and find the fortitude to still choose the light.

So, don't diminish your big, brave heart just because somebody else doesn't understand it. You were given it for a reason, and you have a light to shine on this world. Keep feeling, loving, laughing, and crying, and allowing your superpowers to help direct your path.

Light your world with your secret strengths and remind those who have forgotten what courage truly looks like.

188

GRACE REBELS

It takes a lot of courage to work on bringing a more radical sense of acceptance towards yourself. It takes a lot of courage to drop into your being and learn to sit within that space. It takes a lot of courage to see the transcendent lovely in the strain of human hard.

In other words, it takes a lot of courage to be a grace rebel. It is a sacred act of rebellion when we choose to bring love into spaces that feel unlovable. It is a sacred act of rebellion to see the holy in the dark.

It is a sacred act of rebellion when we choose to fully acknowledge and make space for our hurt, pain, anger, bitterness, hate, resentment, and sorrow.

Because every shadow aspect is a creature in disguise. Tricksters who teach us about the darkest, hardest stuff inside of ourselves so we can learn about humanity and empathy and actively choose love.

So, we can be grace rebels who answer grace's invitation with a "yes," inviting it into all spaces inside ourselves and realizing they are all worthy of love.

Realizing our process is just that: a process. It's not something right or wrong, good or bad, better or worse— it is simply the evolution of our eco-system of being.

189
Snowflakes

Everybody has their own process, their way of being in the world. Like snowflakes with individual patterns of sacred geometry, each of us forms differently, sterling ice crystals dancing through air, taking a unique path to the ground.

People forget it's not easy being a snowflake.

They forget we are formed through cold, ice, and dust; yet manage to create crystalline beauty on our fall to the earth. Anything sensitive enough to form in these conditions has an underlying strength many may miss if all they see is the seemingly fragile grace.

We often underestimate what looks soft and don't recognize it for what it is— a gift of beauty that only becomes beautiful by allowing life's alchemy to shape it. We miss the lion strength found in vulnerability, emotions, imagination, creativity, divergency, heart knowledge, and love.

It is only by tapping into these sacred veins of receptivity that we can find our unique path. The more we try to quiet our intuitions, diversities, and sensitivities, the more we lose our shape and look like everybody else.

When we look like everybody else, we staunch our call, which is trying to break through and speak truth, helping us return to the home of our soul so we can better see our way and find the beauty of our own divine, crystalline flake.

190
WORDS FOR OPEN-HEARTED LIVING

We care about different things in this world, and the trick is to figure out those who are what you are about and those who aren't. Then, learn to meet people where they are in accordance with your boundaries of self-love.

Not everybody is meant to get the best of our hearts. We can love fiercely while allowing only those willing to love us fiercely into our inner sanctums: we can't carry everybody in that space.

That's the rub of courageous, open-hearted living. At some point, most people trying to live from the heart will try to engage in their relationships from the deepest point of their heart center, believing that others are engaging with the same equity and love.

Yet not everybody is in that space in this life; that is where our wisdom and discernment must come in. Allow people to be where they are, and they will show you exactly where they are.

Don't waste time trying to change or do their hard work for them. Pay attention as you continue affirming and being who you are, so you don't take on their energy or confuse their way of being in the world for your way.

Then, we can make self-loving and self-honoring choices about navigating that relational space. Continuously empowering ourselves to keep walking our path and working on the only heart light we truly can.

191
FREEING OURSELVES OF FAKERY

Younger post-divorce years me— who was smack in the middle of some of my deepest lessons on authenticity— once, rather boldly, wrote:

"I don't know that this world needs any shinier, packaged, polished presentations of self. We've got all sorts of people walking around doing "fine," "good," and "loving life" when they are a compartmentalized, shut-down mess inside.

Vulnerability can feel scary, but I think even scarier is to go through life faking it, faking yourself— for then we become enslaved to everybody's impression of us, and we are not free at all, but chained to an image."

Time has not changed my thinking on this. It is scary to go through life faking it and wasting this beautiful brief miracle on anything that isn't real. Or waste time playing into an image instead of discovering and living our most vital self.

Life is a beautiful gift, and if we want to show up with more authenticity and courage, then we have to give ourselves permission to do it imperfectly. Awkwardly. Beautifully. Bravely. Hesitantly. Elegantly. Messily. Confidently. Curiously. Humbly.

Forever engaged in the art of discovery and knowing all of this is imperfectly, perfectly part of who we are.

The world needs more compassion, softness, honesty, less armor, and more people with the courage to be real. Shallow living and faking good don't heal hearts. Love heals hearts, and to love is to be vulnerable, malleable, broken, beautiful, and utterly whole in our realness.

192
BIGGER AND BRIGHTER

It takes spirit and grit to learn to color outside life's lines and shake off societal conditioning and old ways of being. Old patterns and programming run strong in our family systems, collective systems, and collective histories— learning to be ourselves is a process of gradual unlayering.

As we unlayer, we begin to find that if something doesn't work for us, we can give ourselves permission to rework it, redefine it, and create a new vocabulary. We can rescript success from the heart's point of view and expand into a more beautiful reality. Our world grows more vibrant in this process.

We begin to release rigid categories and learn to see everything as something we can use to further our journey. We start to realize that it's not so much about what happens in our external circumstances but how we choose to take our circumstances and do our inner work.

Life begins to open with new possibilities. We see beautiful horizons where fences once lay and realize the only thing boxing us in was our narrow beliefs about life.

We feel empowered to keep releasing limiting language and thoughts and architect bigger, kinder ways of thinking in our minds informed by the truths in our hearts. Liberating ourselves through our acts of self-compassion and self-acceptance. Finding the creative courage to see that we are so much more than humanity's old programming.

If you don't like the constraints of this world, then free yourself. Unbox the broken boxes. Make up your own rules and keep redefining what success and failure mean to you. Let your heart help you sense, feel, and intuit your way into a bigger version of reality, and then take a step in that direction and begin to see—

Life is so much bigger and brighter than we give it credit for, and it loves nothing more than to generously respond to the energy of a heart setting itself free.

193
Perspective for the Hard Days

"You yourself are the eternal energy which appears as this universe. You didn't come into this world. You came out of it, like a wave from the ocean. You are not a stranger here."
—Alan Watts

On those days when chaos hits, pressures loom, and it feels like tension surrounds from all sides— take a step back.

Stretch. Be. Lift your chin to the sky and ask for support from the light. Look for the grace supporting you. Notice the way the rain falls, the sky's blues, or anything in nature that helps anchor you into the energy of peace, presence, and calm.

You are doing okay. You are here. You will figure it out. You are beautiful. You are spiritual. You are human. You are loved. You belong.

Remember those things and receive from something bigger than yourself.

Remind yourself that this moment, this season, this cycle is but a pinprick in time on this leg of your journey, while you, dear soul— at your core— are an infinite galaxy of light.

194

Diamond Souls

There are times on the journey when our courage falters. Times when we might feel crushed and flattened by our circumstances.

It is hard to feel brave in this space. Our tender hearts feel tired. We think we can't keep going. We feel achingly vulnerable and broken down, but what we cannot see in the breakdown is that there is also a genesis beginning.

Grace, dear one, grace.
Breathe, dear one, breathe.
We are nothing without grace and breath.

Remember that as hard as it feels, there are ingredients in our challenges that the sensitive heart can take to grow a diamond soul. If we can stay with ourselves, witness our struggles, and find a way to bring compassion into this space, we will figure out how to become bigger than our fear and pain.

This is what living with heart courage is all about— learning to dance with the shadows and make something sacred out of our struggles by transforming our pain into light. We can learn to deal with our traumas, griefs, brokenness, and vulnerabilities.

We can use our exquisite sensitivity and creativity to find clever ways to bring healing and love into what feels dark inside. We can enter our cave of self, face what feels dark, and emerge with greater awareness and wisdom.

Through this alchemy of vulnerability and strength, we can withstand life's pressures and still find a way to radiate light.

195
Reservoirs of Love

When I was younger, I used to worry about and feel like I was too much. Being an intuitive, sensitive soul makes you feel the ocean's deep, and sometimes, those feelings and the way you experience the world do not mesh or gel with the general population.

Which doesn't mean those things are wrong. They are just a different level of perception, attention, and sensitivity.

The older I've gotten and the longer I've learned to embrace my own journey, the more I've realized that the question of "Am I too much for others?" isn't very helpful, and a much better question is, "Can I learn to be enough for myself?"

Can I learn to trust and validate my own experience of self? Can I learn to hold my own hand and say, "There, there, my dear one. I know this hurts fierce." Can I learn to honor my heart in whatever way I see fit?

Can I learn to love myself when my emotional experience threatens to unravel me? Can I learn to be big enough to witness my experience with compassion? Can I learn to carry these experiences and own them as part of my whole being, so I don't project and disown them onto others?

It's not always easy. These things are works in progress for anyone, but the answer to these questions is yes— *yes, I can*. And yes, you can.

Yes, we can learn to be enough, present for ourselves, and heal our wounds with self-love, self-trust, and self-compassion. We can learn to forgive ourselves for how we did things in the past and do them differently now.

We can learn to take back our power and see our way of being in the world as valid and needed instead of looking to others to approve of our way of being. We can learn new ways and new things. We can learn to see the journey of the sensitive heart as a sacred journey, for sensitive hearts hold space for more love to take place in this world, which is holy work.

So don't let anybody tell you your heart is "too much." It can't be too much. Love is never too much. And you've already got it inside of you in deep wells and endless reservoirs, which means you are absolutely, positively more than enough for you.

196

MAGICIANS

What people often don't know about the highly sensitive, the intuitive, the empath, the creative, the healer, the psychic, the energy sensor, the heart that feels/sees/hears/perceives to the deep— is that they don't fit the paradigms and boxes most found in this world.

Most of us will learn to make a good show of "fitting in," but it's not the real self. It's simply an adaptive, lesser version of self that was developed as a survival skill because the alternative of feeling isolated, rejected, and alienated is too painful.

So, you learn to tuck away the most beautiful parts of yourself from a young age the moment you hear some version of "You are too sensitive; you need to grow a thicker skin to make it in this world." Growing up becomes a lesson on suffocation and learning to fold yourself into pretzel twists to fit the molds society expects of you; soul growth becomes a lesson on learning to unfold and stretch those limbs and reject old molds that do not fit as you empower yourself to create your own.

You will think these abilities are a curse until you learn to see them for their gifts. After all, not everybody sees and feels in color or can tell who somebody says they are, which may be completely different from the energy emanating from them. Not everybody can hear the trees speak, journey in their dreams, or listen to the wind's voice.

Not everybody can love so hard that you break your own heart and have to keep reforming it anew until your heart gets so big it holds the stars. Then you realize your heart was never truly broken;

it was just being stretched wider and vaster, until it grew so spacious it became capable of grasping love's infinity.

Nobody will tell you these things are gifts as you're growing up. They may not even tell you as an adult. You might be one of the ones out on the cusp, feeling alone as you wander far outside the lines drawn by others, finding your wisest friends are sky and sun and sea.

I will tell you it is a gift. I will tell you your gifts are magic: you are a Magician, with love being the greatest magic of all. I will tell you that your way of being in the world is valid, and it is not you who needs to change to better suit this world. It is your world you need to change to better suit you.

I will tell you that sensitivity, compassion, and love are exactly what we need to bring heart wisdom back into this place. I will tell you never to settle for a box over the freedom of your wings. Most of all, I will tell you— there is nothing wrong with you. You are beautiful. You are perfectly imperfectly you. And you are valued, needed, and seen.

197
THE VOICE OF COMPASSION

The collective voices of this world are not voices of grace but loud, fearful, and conditioned to judgment.

Societal norms, judgmental authority figures, and critical voices from our past and present relationships compound, mingle, and send us the message that we are messing life up, feeling too much, or not doing it "right" according to someone else's standards.

These voices want us to believe we are too much, too little— either way, too something or not enough of something else— because those are their inner fears that they project onto us. These are the judgments we unconsciously marinate in, and it's easy to let them seep into us.

We invert them, internalize them, judge ourselves, and accept those messages as the truth of who we are. Fear will tell us to accept the voices, stay small, and conform to judgment.

It takes a lot of courage not to accept that as our status quo. It takes perseverance to weed out our gardens, rooting out values and ways of thinking that don't support our truth of soul. It takes conviction to say, "I do not comply," and find healthier voices of being. It takes grace to bring a radical sense of acceptance into ourselves.

It takes self-empathy to drop into our being and learn to sit within that space. Yet this is precisely what we are here for. To open the doors we've erected around our hearts. To knock down our walls and lay our best defenses bare. To learn that the keys to freedom are found when we learn to go within.

There, within that heart space, we find the voice of compassion. Compassion's voice can help us see that our inner judgments are rooted in past pain. It gently encourages us to get to work clearing out our inner space. Compassion is always ready to help us accept ourselves and see that despite what we feel are our flaws and inadequacies, we can learn to love ourselves.

And every time we fall into the old stories and feel too much or not enough, and we hustle, scramble, or struggle for our worth, then compassion gently reminds us to relax the reigns. It reminds us to let the light in, and know we're doing beautifully.

198

WEEP

"There is a sacredness in tears. They are not the mark of weakness, but of power. They speak more eloquently than ten thousand tongues. They are the messengers of overwhelming grief, of deep contrition, and of unspeakable love."
—Washington Irving

True courage risks radical exposure. True strength, bold vulnerability. True love, deep intimacy.

Our weaknesses are not found in our tender areas, authentic actions, and honest hearts but in our attempts to elevate superficial successes over soul-directed living. They are found in our refusal to acknowledge and honor what is most real inside of ourselves.

All that is real, tender, and strong will tell us that sometimes the only thing we can do is weep. Be like the rain and allow our sorrows to flow freely and fall gently where they may.

Our tears help cleanse, release, and set us free. So, we don't keep our pain locked up. Sometimes, we just need to let it out in waves of feeling and remember that the heart, who knows how to cry from pain, also knows remarkable ways to love.

199

GUIDANCE FOR TIMES LIFE DOESN'T SEEM TO GET IT RIGHT

What do we do when faith fails? When we fervently hope and pray for a particular outcome, and we are presented with the opposite? How do we cope? What do we find to anchor into during these times?

I return to these questions each time I find myself in undesirable circumstances. I particularly return to these questions when I feel like I've been doing everything 'right.' Be a kind human, check. Stay in my integrity, check. Live with an open heart and try to create love— check and check.

It's hard to find peaceful acceptance when something doesn't seem fair, and we don't get an immediate return on our investment in doing right and being a light. It feels angering when we give life our best and, in turn, something bad happens to us, or someone takes advantage of us or dumps toxic energy on us.

In these moments, we might feel ourselves starting to close up. Shutting down our heart center. Numbing our emotions and feeling something within eroding from emotional burnout after all the hoping, praying, and coming up short.

Sometimes, the path just doesn't look at all what we expected— the winds of fate and luck blow. We find ourselves in circumstances and seasons beyond our control. Hope hurts, and we must become gentle with ourselves during those times.

We must learn how to observe our inner pain with compassion. Draw resources that inspire self-forgiveness and self-grace. Remember that part of how we move through any feeling cycle is through feeling our feelings, acknowledging their presence, and learning to courageously witness our pain.

In these moments, it is enough to pause and breathe, to be still, and to know that the greater cycle of life is carrying all of us along in its tide. We can find solace in nature's life cycles of growth and resilience. We can look for the good still happening in the world and find compassion for our process. We can let our hearts weep and remember that courage is also found in grief.

We can trust that even when it feels like life got it all wrong, that life might still have a few tricks up its sleeve and is still our friend. Helping ease our passage through the troubles and bring us to safer waters of consolation, hope, and a new horizon.

200
THE DIRECTION OF HOPE AND LIGHT

Whatever life brings you and however you react, judging your process rarely does anybody any good.

This is especially true if you are feeling bad about your feelings toward something and telling yourself things like, "I shouldn't feel this way." "I should be handling this better." "I should somehow feel differently, stronger, more mature, happier, less heartfelt, less messy, more organized." "I shouldn't care so much."

Once these kinds of statements start, one is generally shaming themselves about how they are feeling, and in effect, they are now feeling bad about feeling bad when they were feeling bad enough in the first place before they heaped judgment on it!

It's easy to stay stuck in this vicious vat of quicksand for a long, long time. Shoulding on yourself rarely produces the desired results; it usually just leaves things messier.

Be compassionate towards yourself. Have grace for your process. Listen to what your feelings have to say. Be kind to them; they are simply passing along information. Understand that as a human being, you have been gifted with the full range of emotions, and you will experience all of them.

Gently challenge yourself to change if you don't like the direction or emotional pattern you are stuck in. Realize emotions are fluid and no feeling is final. Try doing one small thing differently to bring about change.

Sometimes, all it takes is bringing a little less judgment and more self-compassion into your process to start to feel the tides turn in the direction of hope and light.

201
FIERCE GENTLENESS

You don't have to have the loudest voice in the room to make an impact.

You can be fierce in your gentleness by not capitulating to fear and holding space for a better way.

You can borrow kindness from a flower and weave its essence into the world through each act of being.

You can integrate a bird song into your base chakra, so you always find strength when you remember how divinely supported you are.

You can learn the lessons of a blade of grass and never stop growing or breathing yourself into a greater being.

You can love in spirals, going within to find your light, going without to shine it.

You can make a difference by tending to the sacred face of our earth, by flying an intention of purity through the sky, by diving into hope's seas, and by sharing the gems you retrieve.

You can be like the flower and quietly do your thing, paying no mind to anyone else, and when the time is right, surprise them all with your bloom.

You can walk in outstanding power— just by being you.

202
WHAT IS SACRED EVERY DAY

"To laugh often and much; to win the respect of intelligent people and the affection of children; to earn the appreciation of honest critics and to endure the betrayal of false friends. To appreciate beauty; to find the best in others; to leave the world a bit better whether by a healthy child, a garden patch, or a redeemed social condition; to know that even one life has breathed easier because you have lived. This is to have succeeded."
—Ralph Waldo Emerson

Life is not about perfection and a linear path that takes us to our perception of a relational, material, spiritual, athletic, occupational, or other kind of pinnacle.

There is nothing wrong with striving for excellence. However, when we make striving our singular purpose and tell ourselves that we will be fulfilled when we reach a certain pinnacle, we deceive ourselves and short-change ourselves on the opportunities for excellence life has for us now.

Our "pinnacle" is today, tomorrow, and the day after. It involves keeping our eyes open to what life gives us and responding with curiosity and wonder.

It is courageously greeting a new sunrise with an open heart and closing a day with starry-eyed gratitude. It is experiencing a full spectrum of emotions and finding gratitude for the gift of emotional intelligence.

It is the courage to awaken our hearts and refuse to go back to sleep. It is learning compassion for others through embracing and responding to ourselves with compassion.

Life has something to teach us in our collection of moments through the people we meet, the world outside our door, and our inner world, which is rich with intuition, personal truth, and our sense of purpose.

This is the pinnacle. This place of soulful curiosity and rich experience, and we can keep discovering it when we embrace the art of living well by finding what is sacred every day.

203
GRIT AND GLITTER

When life doesn't go your way, it doesn't mean you've got it wrong. It just means it's time for creative adaptation and courageous transformation.

When the world is spinning, and you're standing still, or you're spinning while life seems on pause— know that life moves counterclockwise at times and is still gently moving you towards exactly where you need to be. Life moves in spirals, and sometimes, when we feel we are going backward, we are just being shown a secret side door to new possibilities.

When your season of grief has gone beyond what seems bearable, know you are seen and held by powers unseen. Your heartaches and life breaks are being poured into by love's strange mysteries. Turn your teary eyes and hopeful palms to the sky and receive the light of grace and ease.

When you feel misunderstood, mistook, and unseen, know that those times can also provide the grist of the sand, which can help us form our heart's greatest pearls. The vulnerability of being human is where we find our real; the grit and glitter of our ups and downs are how we honor the truth in all our feels.

So, may you find peace in the throng of life's upside-down songs and remember that to which you really belong—

Your heart. Your soul. This universe. This life. To the secrets of the moon and the gifts of the night. And most of all, dear one, you belong to the radiance of the light.

204
THE GREAT WEB OF LIGHT

"Humankind has not woven the web of life. We are but one thread within it. Whatever we do to the web, we do to ourselves. All things are bound together. All things connect."
—Chief Seattle, 1854

I know it can be hard to connect and care in this world. There is so much that will break your heart if you take the time to allow it in. We know on a heart level that we are all connected. We know we are part of a greater web of light.

Our hearts break for the individuals, situations, and locations when we see, hear, and read about anything that seems hell-bent on destroying our precious web of interconnection instead of helping fortify and strengthen it.

Compassion fatigue is real. Our hearts can grow weary from the general sense of global grief we often feel. It takes courage to keep our hearts open in the face of this. It takes courage to learn how to grieve. It takes courage to remember our interconnection.

It takes courage to let our hearts break for each other and remember that a broken heart is also an open heart. In that space of openness, more light can come through, and we feel inspired to do what we can to move from broken to focusing our light.

We can do small acts of care and find ways to make a meaningful contribution. In so doing, we cultivate light within and create a dispersion of light.

We can take the time to say a prayer for peace and intervention, light a candle of grace and supplication, visualize clouds of angels descending into situations that require divine assistance, and help strengthen, triage, and support the individuals there. In so doing, we cultivate light within and create a dispersion of light.

We can reach deeper into the collective well of hope composed of the strength of our ancestors, the generosity of the earth, and the human spirits' quest to thrive. In so doing, we cultivate light within and create a dispersion of light.

The things that break us also awaken us. What grieves our heart can also inspire us to do what we can with meaning and intention, even if all we can do is take a quiet pause and offer a prayer of peace. It is enough in that moment.

Trust in the interconnection. Trust in your contribution. Trust that when you cultivate light, it creates a dispersion of light that also touches the threads in our ecosystem. All things are bound together, all things connect, and your contributions of light help strengthen love's web.

205
Expanding Into Courage

Our view of the world is colored by our inner world and relationship to self. Therefore, the world will be as big or as small as we choose to see it, as closed or as open, as stuck and stagnant or as imaginative and dynamic, as fear-based or as love-based, as selfish or kind.

While it's true that we also need to develop discernment and wisdom on the path and learn when to take off our rose-colored glasses and see things for what they are, it's also true that our interpretation of how things are is a choice.

What stories do we attach to things? What do we make something mean? How do we narrate the events in our lives, and how do our narrations serve us?

No matter what ups and downs come, there is still beauty to be found every day. There are still good people of light from all walks of life who continue to invest in creating kindness and peace.

There is still magic and miracles and possibilities. There is still abundance, grace, humility, and creativity. There are still a thousand tiny adventures we can find in the threads of every day if we have the eyes to see.

Cultivate your sense of possibility, and the world will open to possibilities. Cultivate your inner light, and you'll find much outer light waiting to greet you. Cultivate the universe within, and you will begin to see the threads of magic and mystery in the everyday.

As Anais Nin wrote, "Life shrinks or expands in proportion to one's courage." So, find your courage and write yourself into a bigger being of potential, hope, and love.

206

AN EXHORTATION FOR THE TENDER-HEARTED

Don't ever be ashamed of leaving your heart lying on the floor and putting it all out there. Don't ever be ashamed of feeling things down to your bone marrow. Don't ever be ashamed for lacking the compartment for your emotions and taking as much time as you need for your process.

Don't ever be ashamed if you are still weeping tears of sorrow and joy and singing songs of healing— over the pieces of your heart you have gently gathered off the floor— long after everybody else has left the room.

We live in a culture where the way most people live in public does not reflect how they live in private. Many people's experience of themselves is that what they are on the inside does not match how they act externally. People dip their toes in the water of authenticity, fervently wishing they dared to dive in, but hold themselves back because we have learned to fear the emotional depths of the sea.

So many have forgotten how to be real because so little of what they see and hear is, in effect, transparent, authentic, and real.

Love is real. This world needs more love, compassion, care, and integrity. It needs more personal responsibility and action to bring change inside our hearts instead of just talking about change. It needs people who value relationships and wholeness above competition and material success.

It needs tenderness and warmth and people to sing songs over its broken pieces and heal it back to life. It needs people to jump over what divides us and swap seeing sides for seeing people. It needs to know that true success is a whole heart and that if we don't have love, we have virtually nothing.

So, if you count yourself among the tender-hearted. The overly sensitive. The soulful and sincere. The messy, beautiful, awkward, and brave. The "I don't have it all figured out, but I'm still going to show up and try anyway." The heart warriors who know you cannot go to battle if you do not first learn how to weep, for only then are you whole. The people who sometimes think they are just too damn much, and life would be easier if you just had an off switch—

Then congratulations. Your tender heart and sensitive soul are not the problem. They are the solution. So, keep it up.

207

TANGLED

Self-compassion can be a learning curve. It goes against the way society has shaped our grain and the voice of the inner critic, who rings with authority and shame inside. Yet, we have to try our best to learn not to judge our process of life, especially when the hard things begin to hit.

We are our worst enemies, placing expectations upon ourselves regarding where we think we should be in the process, how we should feel, and what it should look like. However, as we travel further, we will find that things will look different than expected.

This is not because we are somehow doing it wrong; this is because life is not a linear process. Growing our hearts is not a linear process. We are not a linear process.

We don't travel on an upward trajectory of healing, growth, and self-development— not if we're dancing with life and living with our hearts wide open. Instead, we will find that our growth process is a tangled mass of yarn that we slowly try to untangle, integrating complex feelings, new experiences, and new self-awareness.

Some processes operate on a timeline of their own accord and will continue long after we wish they were done. As long as you are listening to your heart, giving yourself permission to feel what you feel, and doing your best to keep moving through it, you're doing all right.

And if you're not doing those things and you're fighting your process? Oh well! You're still doing all right! To be human can be terribly difficult and lonely. We are all navigating things as best we know to do without an instruction manual.

The greatest gift you can give yourself in your process is to trade self-judgment for kindness and be merciful to yourself wherever you are. Judgment will only make it worse and make those knots feel even tighter and more resolute, but kindness, with its forgiving touch and gentle ways, has a way of loosening everything and helping it relax and just be where it's at.

Even the most tangled of things.

208

BIG

"I don't want to do this anymore." How many of us have uttered these words during a time of heartache, where our instinct is to emotionally curl up in a foxhole, lick our wounds, and wall ourselves off from the constant stream of pain?

We didn't come here to build up walls; we came here to tear them down. People can try to save themselves from the potential depth of feeling, loving, and losing. We can try to eschew attachment and keep love at a distance. We can try to hold ourselves back from attachments. Still, I suspect that even the best attempts at defending the human heart will backfire, leaving those who avoid meaningful connection feeling more and more like an empty shell of self.

Despite our paltry efforts, our hearts will most likely try to do what they came here to do anyway: love. They have a language of their own and can't help but seek ways to speak it.

If you have loved and life has handed you buckets of heartbreak— find a foxhole if needed. Stop and get off the merry-go-round for a bit if it helps. Cocoon yourself in a blanket fort. Curl up into the cradle of life. Let yourself be scooped by something bigger than just yourself. Take all the time you need with this. Quit as often as you like in this process.

Be compassionate with yourself. Honor what you are feeling until it's worked its way through your system; sometimes, we need to contract before we are ready to expand, and there are gifts to be found in that experience, too.

Just remember, life is big enough for our quits. Big enough for our hate. Big enough for our rage. Big enough for our despair, exhaustion, and bewilderment over how hard it can be to be human.

No matter how often we quit life, life will never quit on us. Life will always respect our need for contraction and support us in unseen ways as we rest, all while waiting at the ready, with arms wide open, for the time we choose to expand once more.

If we came here to be BIG, to shine bright, to reach our full potential, then we must know that it takes more courage to open our hearts back up after hurt than to put up walls. Life always responds to our courage. Our world will only be as big and beautiful as we allow it to be, opening and closing in proportion to the worlds we create in our hearts.

209
STRESS CYCLES AND GREAT SEAS OF LIGHT

We can all get stuck in negative stress cycles and focus on what's not going right in our lives. Over time, when those feelings go unchallenged, it is easy to fall into an apathetic or bleak pattern that goes unquestioned and can quickly become our set point.

This is true for any unhealthy pattern— when it goes unchallenged for too long, it becomes normal. We forget we have a choice to do things differently. If we don't like how we feel, we can learn how to choose differently.

We keep finding the courage to show up in bigger, kinder, more gracious ways for ourselves. Learn how to take deep breaths, breathing in inspiration from life all around us because it is bigger than us. Sometimes, we need to breathe in something bigger than just our own lungs.

We learn greater equanimity and how to take things as they come. We remind ourselves that all we can do is take it moment by moment. We were not meant to carry the whole of it all at once; we are meant to take it bit by bit and allow the whole to take shape.

We learn how to slow down, live with more intention, and be more mindful to create space within the frenzy of the day. Bringing nuance and meaning to our lives and finding the small joys and everyday miracles that help us stay connected to our sense of awe.

We learn how to keep improving ourselves— not because anyone is keeping score or evaluating our efforts, but because the way of the heart is the way of intentionality, peace, presence, and love.

There is so much beautiful life and redemptive change to be found in this space.

Even when things seem bleak, and the best we can do is keep breathing and swimming, all will still be well. Never underestimate the power of grace and love in your life. Or the power of a heart who can keep a small scrap of faith. And let's not underestimate each other, nature, and the hidden realms of the numinous.

We are surrounded by great seas of light; let's keep finding the courage to dip into that ever-giving well and allow ourselves to be filled.

210

MAY GRACE FLOW

The beauty of grace is that it opens us up; like a lotus unfolding, we energetically create more space within us when we offer ourselves grace for our process of being.

When we create space, things can flow: our feelings can move through, our thoughts can shift, and our energy can sigh, release, recycle, and renew— whatever it needs to do.

Grace always creates movement. It feels much better than rigidity, judgment, and beating ourselves up for thinking we should be somewhere other than where we're at.

Judgment constricts while grace opens. Rigidity limits while flow unfolds. Criticism restricts while love allows. Harshness shrinks while kindness grows.

Find grace for your process today. Set an intention to be a practitioner of self-forgiveness and radical self-compassion.

Be in duet with the calm of the trees. Inhale, then exhale, and mindfully send a troubling situation in your life breath; invite in more grace and ease for all involved.

Look up at the sky. Remember, you are so much more than your mental chatter and history. Open to the mysteries and embrace the grace space of your own possibility.

211

SUPERHEROES

The true journey of being human is one that cannot be easily measured. We are all on an invisible path of heart and soul evolution whose progress and steps are not always determined and valued in ways we can see and measure in the external world.

There are superheroes in disguise walking among us, whose depths of strength we'd never know or realize. We can't always see the weight they carry or the endurance it has taken to carry it. There are some braveries that exist, some acts of courage in this world, that simply lie beyond measure.

We find them in the people who got dealt a lousy hand of cards. The ones who had the decks stacked against them from the start. The ones who house losses and traumas and griefs and silent stories of pain, whose words are etched amongst their ravages of heart. The ones who learn to keep going. To keep hoping for better. To keep trying for love and change and healing.

There are lessons of courage we can find and much we can learn from our superheroes if we can begin to see their invisible capes flying about us and value them for what they are:

A testament to the strength it takes to reach up and choose to grow in the direction of healing.

A journey of bringing light into the dark and shining their star into a sea of midnight, so we can better *see* and find ways to bring hope into the light of our collective.

An unseen story of soul who still insists, despite the odds, on leaving this place better—- with a little bit more love— than they originally found it.

212

BLOOM

There are times in this world when all we can see is the gray and the storm and the clouds. We lose our sense of warmth and almost forget that the sunshine still exists. It is during these times that it is hardest to trust, to remember life is still on our side and that we are not alone in this.

Even on the hardest days when it feels like the sky falls, and we are surrounded by broken pieces and a sense of lost hopelessness, a time will come when we eventually come out of the other side of things and see the grace of new light.

When we can't see the sun through the clouds, it is easy to forget that life will not abandon us if we stay the course. Life will not forsake us if we move through it with sincere intent. Life, in its infinite compassion, will support us in becoming our authentic selves.

Sometimes, this means we just keep moving forward, every day a step in a new direction that will eventually reveal a beautiful destination. Sometimes, this means we take deep breaths and keep trying to bring ourselves back to a space of grace, love, and breath whenever we feel lost.

And sometimes, this means we will be asked to find our brave, step blindly into an unknown we do not understand nor can see our way through, and keep trusting that our hearts have the courage to stay the course and new life will be waiting on the other side.

Life doesn't bring us to the edge to abandon us to the darkness. Life brings us here so we can learn to make a way for more light. For without the light, we will never find what we need to bloom.

213
Those That Shine the Brightest

Those who shine the brightest didn't get that way from living life "right" and being "good" or being perfect and having everything add up on paper. Those who shine the brightest have usually walked through fires so strong they burned away all that wasn't real.

They have descended into dark internal hells; they didn't believe they'd find their way out. They have fallen into abysses and grand canyons of soul pain so deep they barely knew how to traverse and ascend the terrain.

They have made hard choices, leaps of faith, and been asked to trust when they couldn't see the way. They have been asked to bring love and healing into spaces that don't look very lovable or healable.

They have been purified, sanctified, and set aside. They have been stretched, broken, grown, shifted, transmuted, transformed, and transfigured throughout their experiences.

They are the ones— from all backgrounds, all creeds, all colors, all beliefs— who have been called to be the healers, light-workers, game-changers, and way-showers of this world. They are the ones— the BIG, brave, vulnerable, courage-filled hearts of the world— who are here to awaken greater consciousness.

They are the ones who have been called to the cause of love. As difficult as it may be, they know they can and must trust their path because they are following something intangible but very real inside of them.

They are following the way of the heart and walking the path of love.

214

Galactic-Hearted Supernova

You cannot be afraid of being "too big, too loud, too different"— too "something"— when you need to be that very something to express, actualize, then integrate an aspect of self.

You are not too much; the critics are too little— remember that.

You cannot shine by hiding your light or fearing what will happen if you shine too bright. Mold-breakers, and game-changers, and love-agitators are usually the ones creating lives wrapped in sparkling holiday lights year-round. They keep their own timetables and push past the lines others have drawn to seek authenticity, truth, and expansion.

Mostly, you cannot NOT be yourself because somebody else, or someone else, or something else doesn't get it and wants you to be different. The world needs you— we need you— to be your truest self.

You can always be sensitive to others' points of view and extend others the same grace and right to be in this world that you would like extended to you. But you cannot, not speak up, lift up, glow up, and love up— or keep yourself suppressed, compressed, and repressed because your growth incites distress.

You have done, and are doing, your work to be BIG. So, don't stay small to try and do the work for others. Let the discomfited do their emotional work to grapple with their own discomfort and wish them peace and wellness on their journey.

But as for you? Embrace your growth, embrace your soul. Shed and reinvent and agitate with grace. Be bold and be lit. Please be all the "toos" you need to be to keep growing into your gorgeous self.

And shine, you Galactic-Hearted Supernova. Shine.

Pearls of Wisdom on Healing, Wholeness, and Finding the Light in Darkness

215
The Importance of Feeling Our Feelings

The tricky thing about emotions is that you can't just experience the good ones if you aren't willing to experience the hard ones. If you don't let yourself feel sorrow, grief, fear, and heartache and let those difficult emotions transform and refine you, then you will never fully experience joy, love, gratitude, and wholeheartedness.

We don't get to control feelings or just pick and choose the good stuff. In a society with an overabundance of pharmaceuticals, alcohol, drugs, the internet, food, material goods, and dozens of other means of distraction and process addictions, there are plenty of means to try.

Those who try to control what they feel can usually find dozens of ways to numb themselves, so they rarely have to feel a thing. But that's the problem: they will seldom feel a thing, and how much are you living if you are not feeling?

An authentic life isn't found in dismissing emotions and attempting control. Authenticity is found in remaining vulnerable to the journey and open to our feelings. Is this hard and uncomfortable? Yes. Will this process break you open and ask you to invest in your emotional health? Yes.

More importantly, might you start seeing how much wonder the world holds? Might you learn to love your life? Might you know you are living a life embodied in essence and spirit? Yes.

Most importantly, is it worth it? Yes. I believe so. It is a necessary shift if we wish to live to a fuller potential and engage in our lives wholeheartedly. It is how we learn to experience our world in technicolor. It is how we expand into a greater possibility and higher expression of self.

216

Unicorns and Mud

There is a huge place for positivity in this world. For rainbows and unicorns, for finding happiness and pursuing joy, for good words of light and loving energy, and for anything that is like an ice cream sandwich for our soul.

But there is also a huge place for the dark.

For the growth disguised as mud, which is really a healing agent here to cleanse and exfoliate us. For the darkness that makes us search that much harder to find our starry diamonds in our heart's sky so we can navigate in the black. For all the hard edges that sharpen what's strongest in us and force us to actively choose the light.

Those dark periods are not the destination; they are just part of the path as we keep moving towards our becoming, spirit expansion, and heart growth.

We are human; our depth of emotional experience makes us whole. And our journeys will keep us traveling, back and forth, from the light to the dark to every shade in between as we grow and become, in our human shells, the souls we are meant to be.

There is a season for everything, a reason for each aspect of ourselves, and there's no right or wrong way to be. Each piece of who we are makes up the greater mosaic of us makes up the greater mosaic of humanity. There is truth in every piece.

Learn to live life in such a way as to embrace and find meaning in all that is shadow and all that is bright, from the gentle happiness of a rainbow to the blackest hole that lines the night. You will find that— from mud to unicorn— there is room for all our experiences, sorrows, joys, dark moons, and radiant lights.

217
Excavating Our Hidden Lights

When I was younger, I had a false belief that being "messy" meant I wasn't doing life right. I had a misconception surrounding the idea that I was supposed to have things together, and if I didn't meet my expectations of myself, it meant I was somehow lost, broken, or doing life wrong.

I had a lot of rooms inside of myself that I'd never turned the lights on in. I wasn't even aware of their existence, and it was only through the process of breaking to awaken, then diving into my breaks, that I began to have a burgeoning sense of their chambers.

I learned in that process that courageous, heart-based, authentic, soulful living is not about having things together. It is about allowing ourselves the permission to break, dissolve, be lost, not know, investigate, grapple, feel, and compassionately keep showing up for whatever is coming up inside of us.

Working through our own "mess" is what inner work and soul work are all about.

That's where we find our hidden lights. That's where we find our buried treasures. That's where we go deep sea diving and return to the surface with our pearls.

There are some things in life that can only be accessed when we are in messy states of grief, or disarray, or great uncertainty, or other states of becoming undone.

If we allow ourselves the courage to sit with our process compassionately, we see that messes can be portals that lead to self-awareness. There are new forms of life to be discovered in the mess that have the potential to be phenomenal teachers. Teachers that help us further unravel our own mysteries and bring new vision and knowing into places within our heart's interior, previously untapped and unknown.

We become soul archaeologists when we do this. Observing what's inside. Excavating our relationship to our existence. Digging for our truth.

Noting our patterns and consistencies. Approaching ourselves with openness, grace, and curiosity. Discovering a wealth of abundance. Bringing illumination and understanding to places inside that once sat unexplored.

218
EMBRACING BROKENNESS AS A NATURAL PROCESS IN LIFE

If you are walking around and breathing, you will be broken by this world.

It is not a matter of whether it will happen. It is a matter of where, when, and how. Then, it becomes a matter of what we choose to do with our broken pieces.

It is a matter of struggling with the whys and finding our sense of resolution, which eventually allows us to evolve beyond a previous space of self and step into our grace and light.

We all have our stories. Many of us are in the process of living those stories as they unfold, not quite knowing how the current chapter will end. We can choose to have faith in the process and hold to the belief that if we brave the dark of not knowing, we will eventually find our way back to the clarity of the sun.

No matter who we are or how black the path may seem, we can hold hope that change is always possible, and we are never alone in the dark.

Life and love can always redeem us if we let them. If we tend to our inner world until it becomes a place where courage, transparency, and bravery dwell.

If we remember that we are here to grow as souls and collect new experiences as we go. If we learn to let our hearts be arranged and offer them up for change.

219
THE CORE OF BEING WHOLE

Somewhere along the way our culture has developed serious misconceptions about how life should be, limiting how we relate to ourselves and our ability to support one another authentically.

Problems, hardships, and tragedies often get minimized and reduced to something that needs to be cheered up, contained, or fixed. Often, these are the very ingredients that provide a gateway for growth of the heart, spirit, and soul.

Life wasn't meant to be a linear ideal, where we live in perpetual states of positivity, good mood, and curative thinking. Life was meant to be lived as a whole. We have emotions so that we can experience the entire spectrum of feelings.

Acknowledging both the dark and light is what it means to be human. Integrating the beautiful and the horrible and finding the lessons from both is at the core of being whole.

We make mistakes so we can learn. Good things can come from what seemed bad, and bad things can come from what seemed good. We learn from both, and through those lessons, experience becomes our teacher of truth. Self-knowledge becomes our teacher of authenticity.

Our job isn't to judge our process but to embody our lives even when we find ourselves in hard places. We can choose to show up for ourselves and be present where we are at. We can choose to draw a map of our emotional experiences and allow their wisdom to support our transformation.

We can practice radical self-compassion, let our souls curl into life, and be supported by something bigger than ourselves. The world can hold us in a stasis of comfort if we let ourselves breathe, receive, and be still.

220

Shadowlands

Our shadows are as important as our light. They are the space where we find our hidden depths and the irritant grains of sand where our pearls form. Anytime I've been through a dark period, a depression, or a grief journey, I always come out the other side and realize I've collected gifts along the way— even if I couldn't see them at the time.

It's hard to permit ourselves to be in a dark space. It's uncomfortable. Often, it's excruciating. Heartache, sorrow, and seemingly intolerable feelings are stormy seas to sail, and we will crave fairer waters and the grace of sunlight.

We crave feeling good. We sometimes judge and blame ourselves for not being able to pull out of it. We wonder what is wrong with us because we think we *should* feel better.

But there is nothing wrong with us. The shadow self is a part of who we are, and learning to work through our darkness is part of being whole and being human. Often, the tools that help lift us up on a "normal bad day" fail us in the shadows. There's just not enough substance, grit, or realness to those tools.

Yet substantive, authentic living is both real and gritty, which means we will get dirty from time to time. Sometimes, we must allow the dirt. We try to navigate dark terrain the best we know how and make peace with the fact that we feel things that aren't often peaceful.

We learn that unpeaceable emotions are part of the full spectrum of being human. Great creativity can come from conflict and chaos. There are gifts in dissolution. Shadows are where we find evolution.

Being in a dark place doesn't mean we're not transforming, shining our soul light, or being of less value or worth. It doesn't mean we've lost our way. It simply means we're busy being human beings who are engaged in the process of allowing for our full scope.

221
Building Bridges

We must keep building bridges to the spaces inside ourselves that are difficult to access.

The spaces where our doubts and fears hide. The spaces where we feel wounded and unhealed. The spaces we often don't like to look at, don't know or perhaps don't like to acknowledge exist— until they are jostled by life and forced to come out into the light.

Fierce examination and compassionate scrutiny are the only ways to explore the parts of us that don't match up or sometimes carry inconvenient truths and stories of old traumas.

This is hard work— necessary, but hard. It's the kind of work that invites us to get a therapist, a journal, or a stack of self-help books. It also invites time in nature, a water ceremony, a healing ritual, or a talking circle.

Maybe a smattering of all the above— there's no right way to go about the healing work of self, just an openness to doing the work.

We build bridges inside ourselves when we learn to build alliances with all our parts, aspects, and feeling states.

We build bridges when we learn to make peace with where we are. We don't have to love it or wish to remain in that space forever. We just have to allow the path of peace within, so we are not at war with ourselves.

Inner divisions are where the roots of strife, fear, and despair begin. So, this is where our inner work begins: we must keep building bridges and reclaiming the parts of ourselves we have outcasted, ignored, or disowned until we start to feel we have a clear space of light inside of ourselves and are in union with our whole.

222

Broken Birds

There are many of us who've been made to feel like broken birds. Somewhere along the way, somebody— maybe a whole lot of somebodies— looked at us askance, judged us, said something cruel, or did something cruel.

They failed to see us for who we are and only saw a break or a bend in what was a perfectly shaped wing. They saw us as broken, not because we are broken, but because the lens with which they view the world is cracked.

Except we usually don't realize they have a cracked lens. So, we internalize their perspective and see ourselves through their lens. From that moment forward, we begin to cringe and shrink. Part of us perpetually bowed in shame. We cradled our wings, trying to heal and mend and make that "break" whole.

Trying to prove we are enough— not realizing that our own lens is slowly cracking the longer we see ourselves through their eyes.

Finding wholeness within ourselves is the realization that while we can't fix somebody else's lens, we can fix our own. We can learn to see ourselves through the eyes of the universe, who supports all life and who says we all have a place here.

We can learn that our innate worth is in our very being, our very breath; not the things we do, who we know, how we look, or who likes us. We wouldn't be HERE, children of this time and space, if we didn't already matter.

We can learn to see the beautiful and imperfect perfection in our wingspan when we find the courage to step into our fullness and embody the only thing we were ever truly called to embody— ourselves.

223

EMBRACE IT ALL

It is those messy human moments— when grief suddenly hits with vast waves of unidentifiable sorrow, and we feel an ache and don't fully understand what or why we are feeling what we are feeling— that we need radical self-acceptance the most.

When we fall between our cracks or discover we've wandered into a gray depth that holds alchemical wisdom, those are the parts of ourselves hungering for embrace.

Sometimes, embracing them is as simple as saying, "Hello. I feel/see/am aware of you. What do you have to teach me?" Then, listen to, learn from, and honor your emotional flows.

Our wholeness of being is all of us. This includes the things we like, the things we're still working on, and the things we've yet to heal. It is our inelegant, gritty humanity and our ethereal, light-bearing divinity. It's the highs, the lows, the in-betweens, and every shade of a rainbow.

The more we see ourselves as an ocean with multiple currents, flows, depths, and beings, the more we can know ourselves whole. All those aspects of ourselves deserve love, which is how we create wholeness in our ecosystems.

All good, all you, all shades, all worthy— always. The more we know ourselves whole— knowing ourselves as our fullest expression by embracing all experiences of self— the more we can love ourselves whole. The more we love ourselves as a whole, the more we light this world up.

Let's light things up.

224
You Are Not Alone

If you feel you've made a mess of life and wandered too long in the darkness, start with gently taking one positive step. This might feel scary, but it might also feel good because it's a step, and steps are important. They help us find the courage to take another step, and over time, even the smallest steps can begin to add up.

When we feel we've landed in a place where we think things are completely botched, remember they didn't get that way overnight. They might not tidy themselves up as quickly as we would like. But remember your courage, dear lion-heart, and know you have what you need to begin the great untangling.

Remember, you are not alone in this process. All significant changes begin with surrender and realizing we can no longer keep trying to contain something that has become uncontainable and has taken on a life of its own. We find healing when we admit our vulnerability.

Begin with surrender. Begin with truth. Begin with an honest assessment of where things are at. Begin with talking to someone trusted. Begin by realizing you don't have the answers and that you're not going to find the solutions you seek by continuing to do what no longer works.

Begin by remembering that one of life's greatest lessons is humility and teachability and allowing ourselves to break open so we can become something more than what we were before. You're going to be okay. You might not feel that right now, but eventually, you will.

Somehow, this world has continued to spin on its axis and find a way to keep weaving out the greater thread of life, no matter how broken things seem. You, too, will find this same grace and realize that life is already busy helping you unthread the seams that leave you tightly bound to circumstances you no longer wish for and find a way to start anew.

Just try to remember, dear heart, that there are people out there who believe in you. Who've sat at the bottom of a rubbish heap— possibly of their own making— and still found a way out, realizing along the way they are turning their trash into treasure. So, too, can you.

Just take that first step. I believe in you.

225
On Healing Wounds

You can't heal the wound by staying in the wound. You just can't. There simply isn't enough space and room to find the healing you need.

If the definition of insanity is doing the same things repeatedly and expecting different results, then sanity demands a compassionate assessment of our truth. It demands an honest evaluation of how we contribute to the perpetuation of the issues in our lives, and a willingness to challenge ourselves to do things differently.

Healing comes in multiple shapes and sizes. Sometimes, it means walking away from a relationship or a situation that no longer serves.

Sometimes, it means examining the core beliefs that keep you stuck in the same old pattern, afraid to make the changes you dream of.

Sometimes, it means finding the strength to simply begin by setting the boundary of "No."

However healing comes, it always means finding the courage to examine whatever has caused the wound by bringing it out into the light. If we don't feel and reveal it to ourselves, we cannot heal it within ourselves.

When we learn to live in alignment with ourselves— to walk a path of integrity and authenticity where we are more vested in learning to be real than maintaining the status quo in our lives— we begin to make the necessary changes that bring wellness to our hearts. And when your heart is well? Everything else begins to fall into place.

If you don't know where to start, an excellent place to begin is to take some space for yourself, try to get out of your mind and drop into your heart, and ask yourself: *How do I best love myself in this?*

Then listen to what you have to say.

226
Listening to the Inner Voice

Sometimes, a good case of "the blues" is just that. The blues. A hard day. A fluid feeling that will pass if you stay with yourself.

Everyone has highs and lows, and if we treat ourselves gently, surround ourselves with friends, do things that feel kind to ourselves, move our bodies, practice self-care, just keep swimming, and get a little momentum during these times, the lows gradually even out. The sunlight creeps back in, and it is once again shining in full force.

When those things are not working, sometimes "the blues" might not really be blues at all, but our inner voice desperately trying to get our attention.

Gently whispering that we have inventory in our internal closets that we are not tending to. Gently challenging us to take stock and make changes where necessary. Gently nudging us inward so we can reflect on whether we are living the authentic life we are meant to lead.

Gently singing us a sad song of love that reminds us we are not loving ourselves and singing the song we were meant to sing.

Many things distract us and keep us from listening to that inner voice. We could spend years dancing the steps of avoidance and denial and continue in the same avoidant, overly busy, fearful cycle in which we have been stuck.

If we do not listen to our voice and learn to honor it, nobody else will do the work for us. Do not be afraid to confront the lows in your life and see if they have valuable information for you.

Be gentle and thoughtful and love yourself in this process. Keep moving, keep reflecting, keep the faith, and let the answers come through by living consciously.

227

MAKING FRIENDS WITH SADNESS

"This being human is a guest house. Every morning a new arrival. A joy, a depression, a meanness, some momentary awareness comes as an unexpected visitor. Welcome and entertain them all! Even if they're a crowd of sorrows, who violently sweep your house empty of its furniture, still, treat each guest honorably. He may be clearing you out for some new delight."

—Rumi

I once spent the better part of a summer in sorrow. My inner sadness belying the bright sunshine and happy summertime activities happening in that chapter of my Alaska life that particular year.

No matter what I did, I couldn't chase my sadness away, press reset, or make myself feel something other than what I was feeling. I chose to stay with my sadness; it felt like a forced choice at first, but over the summer months, I began to see that it had valuable lessons to teach me:

Even the saddest, most pitiful parts of myself held value and deserved my love and validation. My sorrow was a deeper reflection of accumulated griefs, betrayals, and heartaches, all of needing more time to process, integrate, and release.

My grief was just love turned inside out— I realized those who love the hardest feel the deepest, and I grieved because I had loved.

I found a quiet strength in this knowledge that summer. I was a secret bad-ass heart ninja walking around incognito, and my superpower was love. I found something in myself that gave me back a piece of myself I didn't know I was missing, and as I moved through my process and the sadness shifted, I found on the heels of sorrow came a profound rebirth and new vision for my life.

These were the gifts my sorrow offered me in the summer of 2013. I would have missed all of it— all this beautiful wisdom, and radical growth, and soul-deepening maturity— had I not allowed for and invited sadness in.

228

THE POTENTIAL OF NIGHT

Any period of darkness always comes with its gifts. The chance for solitude and stillness, time for hibernation and reflection, opportunities for allowing the seeds and roots resting below the surface to grow strong so they are ready to rise when the light arrives.

Darkness always precedes any creation; the nothing of night is where dreams are born and possibilities conceived. Night has the potential to be a beautiful time of inception— sometimes, there is grace in the in-betweens, and we don't know if we can stay open and curious about life.

In this space, we are invited to look up and find the stars scattered in the velvet, still helping to show and guide us. We might learn to look at something differently and see it from a new perspective than in the light of day. We might see ourselves differently or find the stirrings of creativity and muse being born.

Perhaps in our unknowing, we learn to better belong to ourselves and belong to the strange feelings of uncertainty inside of ourselves, making friends with that which feels clouded and mysterious inside. We might learn to stay with ourselves and realize that periods of darkness help travel us deeper into the cave of our psyche and soul, where the only thing we have to fear is ourselves.

Maybe we realize that if we can hold onto the red strings of our love in this space, we'll eventually find our way through the labyrinth of our uncertainty, so we better learn to trust the process and feel our way through the shadows, allowing our intuition and instincts to guide.

Our eyes begin to adjust to the lack of light, and we learn to better see through the eyes of our heart, which reminds us always to keep faith as we begin to realize the potential of the night.

229

BOXES OF DARKNESS

"Someone I loved once gave me a box full of darkness. It took me years to understand that this too, was a gift."
—Mary Oliver

When somebody gives us a box of darkness, it's easy to get lost in feeling wounded and wronged. We can spend much time directing our energy and anger toward the person or situation we feel wronged by.

These are normal feelings when someone has hurt us and wronged us. But over time, we may feel like a truck stuck in the mud. Tires spinning helplessly, churning up more mud— the more we waste our energy throwing hate darts, obsessing, and checking up on the individual, the more we become deeply stuck.

Ultimately, this hurts our hearts, and it staunches our growth. From one who has been here, no judgment. Sometimes, we need the rawness and realness of letting our process be without immediately trying to better it.

But I have found over time— the longer we insist on holding onto our feelings of righteous anger— that bitterness will creep in and keep us attached to the very thing we wish to shed. So, when we feel ready, instead of staying on a course where we keep furthering our justification of and attachment to our wounding, we are better served by simply tending to the wound.

We do this by tending to our hearts with restoration and care. By releasing thoughts, hurts, systems, individuals, situations, or beliefs— as often as one needs— that do not help serve, grow, or tend our gardens. By doing whatever we need to process, rage, pain, feel, vent, and let it out and then focus on how we would like to feel and who we would like to be.

We must insist on greater freedom in our hearts and refuse to take bitterness as our setpoint. If we stay with it, we will find that over time, we will begin to compassionately detach and learn to move forward with the wisdom we gained, not the pain. We stop overidentifying with our wounds and instead start to embody the wisdom we found through our healing process.

If our hearts and happiness are at stake, it is worth continuing to let go of what we cannot change. Then, lovingly working on what we can change— the box of light inside ourselves.

230

Pain as Teacher

Inner pain is not the problem; it is the symptom. It is there to tell you something is wounded, to inform you of the exact spots where life wants to help you heal, and to teach your heart more about the full scope of being human.

If you refuse to deal with it, it never really goes away and will continue to follow you from one room of your life to another. It seeks your attention and resolution and interferes with your ability to be peaceful in the present.

Your job isn't to judge your pain and build walls around it to protect yourself from feeling it. Your job is— with fierce, blazing self-love— to take a wrecking ball to whatever barriers exist so you can find out what's on the other side.

There is no other way than to explore the space outside of the walls and begin to dismantle them, so you have room to explore what is on the other side. This can feel daunting, but it is necessary to clear out the space inside your heart.

If you want to feel more healed, commit to a life where you do what you can to create opportunities for healing. If you want to feel more spacious, then make space inside of yourself.

If you want to learn to integrate the wisdom of your experiences and release the pain, then you must let pain teach you why it is there so you can be a better student of your experience and begin understanding it with new insight and perspective.

Only then do we find what we need to work mindfully with our pain so we can reveal it, feel it, release it, clear it, and open to receiving greater wholeness in our lives.

231

BECOMING A FRIEND TO OURSELVES

If we can approach the broken parts of our lives with open receptive hearts, we will find grace waiting there.

Our relationship with our wounds, hurts, pains, and triggers is just that— a relationship. It is subject to change and reciprocal. What you put in, you will get out.

When we feed the mouth of bitterness, self-pity, misery, anger, and other internal dialogues that further harden our hearts and diminish ourselves, we create a negative relationship within ourselves and negative relationships outside ourselves.

Instead, we must feed the mouth of extreme compassion and love by creating a relationship of love to the parts that hurt inside.

Let love tear down walls where the world would tell us to build them. Develop a relationship of understanding and compassion for our humanity and the depths of pain we can feel because being fully human is very hard and messy work.

We can accept responsibility for tenderly loving ourselves instead of placing this responsibility into other's hands. We can learn how to become a good friend to ourselves and extend kindness to all parts.

Through that love, we will find more compassion and grace— for our brokenness and others' brokenness. No matter what the question, love is our answer when we learn to see it as a fluid, flowing, creative energy helping us move towards wholeness.

232

TRICKSTERS

Rage. Anger. Hate. Bitterness. Resentment. Desolation. Isolation. Self-pity. Wretched want. There may be some extraordinarily ugly emotions that come when we engage wholeheartedly with life, and we are hit by trauma, crisis, and grief.

While I have learned that everybody handles these experiences differently, I have also learned that we truly do need to feel them to bring healing to ourselves. If we deny the monsters in our rooms, they will only get bigger and louder. They are trying to get our attention as they wait for our acknowledgment.

We all owe it to ourselves and our healing process to acknowledge the full spectrum of our feelings. There are some hard beasts to face inside of ourselves, and they will come out during times of great hardship, but they do not have to be ignored and hidden.

The more we learn to listen to and make peace with our unpeaceable thoughts— by paying attention to what they have to say, honoring those feelings as valid, then choosing to love anyway— the more we realize they are teachers in disguise, here to trick us into learning about humanity, forgiveness, and grace.

That's the bottom line when it comes to monsters. If you sit with them long enough, find a way to look them square in the eye, and face what seems so scary, then you'll begin to find they are not so scary at all. Instead, they are tricksters that help us get in touch with the toughest, darkest, stuff of humanity. We learn to make a conscious choice and choose love, forgiveness, and peace.

Thereby becoming a willing participant in our own growth of the soul.

233
Tuning Into the Frequency of Love

Everybody has broken pieces. It's just a matter of how and where those breaks began. And when we rub against those places, in one another, things can get even further cracked.

We don't often see each other's breaks because that kind of authentic talk and admittance of vulnerability isn't something our culture makes much room for. Sacred stories of hurt and transformation are often misunderstood and turned into fodder for gossip, exploitation, or finding weakness.

This is what makes love, resilience, vulnerability, and courage so powerful. It's not a denial that brokenness exists; it's a choice to choose the good stuff anyway, because it feels so much better.

It's a choice to keep trying to tune into the frequency of love and to find that love within yourself. It's a choice to take responsibility for healing your greatest asset— your heart. And when you are doing your process work on a heart level, the world can come alive to you.

Each time you turn your attention back to yourself and challenge yourself to heal, grow, and expand from life's lessons, you are an active participant in creating your own life. Then, just maybe, you start to see rainbows where you didn't before.

Taking a breath becomes a gift. The trees are a vigilant comfort. The sky is an ever-changing kaleidoscope. Kindness is your sustenance. The full moon is a time of magic. Maybe you even find yourself standing under its light, looking up, feeling much more grateful to be alive.

234

Someday, Someway, Somehow

Our responsibility to ourselves is not to deny the internal damage done to the lands where our scar tissue exists but to embrace the wounds of the land. Then learn to cover them with new life and new love.

Our responsibility is to gently place one foot in front of the other and remember how to breathe, trusting that the air will come just a little bit easier in time.

Our responsibility is to go at our own pace and, over time, see if we can find the beauty in life again, knowing that our sorrow makes life's joys all the sweeter.

Our responsibility is simply not to give up on ourselves and to very gently try to not give up on hope or magic or joy, even if it takes a while to find these things again.

We might sit by a tree for a while, or gaze at a flower, or listen to a cat purr, or do one of hundreds of miniature acts of light to help facilitate our healing process and connect to life's universal flow and endless pools of grace.

It doesn't matter what we do. We just need to keep faith in our hearts, even if they feel tired, disheveled, or worn down. Even the tiniest pebble of faith is enough to start a revolution of love when the time is right.

For now, just keep breathing, going, and resting when you need to. You do have this, and in case nobody has said it, I will—someday, someway, somehow, you're going to be alright.

235

BROKEN AND WHOLE

Maybe we move through life both broken and whole. Where it's not an either-or but a symbiotic relationship; each time we find a break within ourselves, we are afforded the opportunity to heal it a little more, moving us into greater wholeness.

Broken is what it is to be a true human. Whole is what it means to be innately divine. When we realize we are always slightly broken in our humanity, we realize we can never be truly broke. Instead, we learn to see our breaks as the place where we can receive, unveil, and reveal the true light within— the light of our soul.

Being broken is how we also know we are whole. We become chiseled and hollowed out by life's hardships, which carry the potential to move us into a transformative space of mending our wounds with perspective, prayer, self-expression, and love.

Every time we allow another fragment of unhealed self to fall away, we can move from old stories and mistruths— our ego's perception of whom we think we should be— into vital, life-giving truth— our soul's knowledge of who we truly are.

We understand our darkness only sharpens a greater understanding of our light, allowing us to become more whole and alive in love. We become vessels of light when we allow this process to happen. We become columns of peace and grace that continually hold more space for love to come onto the planet.

We've chosen to make space within by holding space for ourselves. Holding space for our humanness. Our brokenness. Our struggles.

Our wholeness is what allows us to courageously attend our breaks; our brokenness is what makes us whole and brings us closer to the truth of our souls.

236

From Grit to Pearl

If you want to embody your fullest potential as a divine being, you must also embody your fullest potential as a true human. As above, so below.

We sometimes seek out the high road and want to find spiritual growth— this is a beautiful space to be. However, if you should find that the high road isn't where life is currently taking you and the demands of being human are requiring your attention, then please remember that attending to our humanity, nourishing our psychological landscape, and embracing our human experiences are what help us open to these experiences and bring them into the palette of our hearts.

Grief can be a rite of passage. A "bad" day is an exercise in being human. A season of darkness is a journey through your inner earth so that you can discover new depths of your soul.

The more we allow the alchemy of being human to transform us, the more our hearts open, and the more we feel guided to set our sights high, look toward the stars, and reach for love. We descend to ascend. We learn the wisdom of grit, so we can find the transformation of the pearl.

We transmute fear to faith with each act of excavating the interior of life's lows and finding growth. That's what it's all about. Whether you're reaching up, down, or out, it's finding all the ways you can to reach for love within this confusing, glorious experience of being an embodied soul.

237
Sunshine in Winter

It is my observation that most people value the beautiful, the light, and the sunshine while missing the value that darkness has in helping us break, grow, and stretch in ways we never did before.

We want the sunshine but not the winter, and yet our winter seasons are just as important as our summers if we want to learn to shine bright in this world.

Winter is our losses, our heartbreaks, and what happens every time we put on our Charlie Brown ghost sheets and optimistically head out the door to go trick-or-treating. Life throws stones into our bag, leaving us shouting, "No fair! I got a rock!"

Winter is what we do with those rocks. The times we cry over them, grieve over them, suffer over them, and then learn all we can from them. Learn to face them, examine them, tend to them, and mine them for all they are worth. Hold them up to the light, then polish them, so they become diamonds of darkness that makes our lights brighter.

Winter is how we learn to carve out a holy space inside ourselves and fill it with the things that nourish our souls. Love, bravery, and finding the courage to do the right thing every time our hearts know the right thing to do. Peace, connection, and kindness.

We fill this space with the sacred and mundane, having learned that magic is found in the simplest of places, starting with our ability to take a breath and experience love. We fill it with the knowledge that life is a gift, and we are here to experience, care for, and tend to this gift in the ways that call to each of us.

We are here to savor life and find our light, even in times of sorrow. Winter is where we find the truth of our soul. Sunshine is simply what comes from that.

238

DARKNESS IS MAGIC, TOO

To be human is to be in both shadow and light. To know ourselves whole is to understand both shadow and light. To free ourselves into greater expressions of love is to work with both shadow and light.

Releasing the past, finding emotional freedom, and moving towards wholeness are not predicated on clearing everything out and turning ourselves and our lives into clean, new spaces. It is a matter of choice to keep turning our attention to the new space we are trying to create and working with the ingredients of the past and the present to heal, inform, and transform our future.

Go gently on yourself if you've been trying to reach for happier hopes and still feel sucked into the sticky quicksand of times gone by.

Find grace for your process if you thought you put it behind you, only to find it sitting in the heart of your psyche's living room, forcing you to examine it and find a way to clear the space.

Be blessed in your spirit, knowing that all of this is part of your spiritual journey and is not a reflection of your worth, value, integrity, or inherent goodness.

How else do we think we will experience maximum soul growth if not for the gifts that eventually come from the depths of our shadows?

Always remember personal transformation is magic, too. Darkness is magic, too. Sorrow is magic, too. Mud is magic, too. Even now, even you, in the entirety of this moment where past and present are interweaving and intervening to manifest the most authentic creation of you—

You are magic, too. You are a soulful, celestial being on a terribly beautiful and difficult terrestrial journey of becoming. And you are doing a damn fine job.

239
Transmuting Pain Into Love

Sometimes, we need to descend before we can ascend. Letting ourselves spiral down into the fiery depths when life calls us there, so we can look through the flames in search of the light. Sometimes, we need to work with our shadows, allow for the full expression of emotions, and grapple with the grit.

Grappling is how we find perspective. It's how we can potentially shift our mindset, gain insight, or find a new way to heal our wounds. Grappling is part of being human. Life's grace is such that we are always spiritually loved, no matter how dark we may feel when going through our psychological depths.

There is potential in a dark space because life holds the grace space for us, which allows us to dive into our depths safely. There is magic in our depths, magic in our shadows, magic in the forgotten pieces of ourselves, who can be powerful teachers on where we most need healing and compassion.

There are also gifts we find in the dark. Our heart's refusal to give up. Our desire to heal. Our vulnerability. Our willingness to break. Our empathy. Our resilience. Our authenticity. Our hidden strengths. Our ability to keep trusting when we cannot see.

Sometimes, making sense of the bigger picture is hard, and we struggle to find perspective. In nonsensical, challenge-filled times when we find ourselves in the depths, it's helpful to still remember—

There is self-compassion. There is self-kindness and grace. There is personal transformation. There is our sacred inner work. There is the wisdom of nature. There is the wisdom of the heart.

The wisdom of the heart is not afraid to grapple or descend into our depths. It helps us remember that we can learn to constructively work with these challenging ingredients of self, mine them until we find our diamonds of light, and use them for personal transformation—

This is how we transmute our pain into love.

240

TO FIND OUR WAY HOME

Do we ever lose what once was home in our hearts, no matter how far we travel in life?

I don't think so, and perhaps this is the part of ourselves that not only yearns for simpler days but feels the need to travel back to the past to re-anchor into the roots of who we once were. In these moments, we can remember— with bittersweet vividness— who we've been, how we've become, and the journey we've taken to travel where we are.

There is a see-saw-like balance of going back and forth from one end to the other when it comes to remembering, learning from, and honoring the past while still allowing ourselves to embrace the gift of presence, reinvent ourselves in the present, and grow in new ways.

Sometimes, our psyche likes to zig-zag back to the past— going through a very soulful, in-depth process of understanding who we were at different points in our lives— just before it's getting ready to quantum leap forward in the immediate future.

This is the invisible process of the soul, which intuitively knows we need to remember, honor, and grieve our former self to embrace and welcome the birth of who we're becoming. This process can also feel psychologically uncomfortable because when our sense of self shifts, our identity feels less certain, and we can struggle to find emotional equilibrium.

We find ourselves searching through the pages of our past to retrieve bits and pieces of our soul, discovering where we might have lost a piece of ourselves so we can heal any lingering grief or trauma that we couldn't fully access at the moment.

As we do this, we can appreciate our journey, witness the growth, and gather our energy back so we can move forward with more freedom, presence, and clarity in our hearts. We can move away from any place in our psyche where we still have an attachment to pain, fear, or shame. We can learn to see ourselves through a greater lens of wholeness and find the grace to look at our journey through a lens of appreciation and love.

We forget ourselves in the fluidity of our humanity only to find ourselves in the divinity of remembering that if we can find love in any lostness, we can always find our way home.

241

SELF-FORGIVENESS

There is going to come a time when you may start to realize that hanging on to the past and your past mistakes is no longer serving you— and I hope we all get to that point sooner rather than later. Life is quite short and precious, and each of us is imperfect. In those imperfections, we don't always get it right from moment to moment.

When we come to those places where we didn't get it right, the best we can do is make amends in the ways available. Maybe we will go to the person and apologize. Perhaps we just send the energy of humble, apologetic intent to the situation or individual and ask the universe to direct that energy to where it needs to go. Trusting that the soft pink light of forgiveness and letting go can happen at any point in time— when we finally feel ready to let go.

More than anything, when we bump into the spots where we feel we failed, we must find a way to make amends with ourselves. We must find a way to forgive the times we may have been foolish, insensitive, hurtful, or wrong. We're only meant to hang onto that stuff long enough to learn our lessons and integrate the heart truths from the situation.

After that, there is nothing new to do or learn in our old territory, so hanging onto it and rehearsing it will only leave us repeating old patterns, acting out, and projecting our stuff onto others instead of simply owning it. This creates a dead-end street that leads to looking backward and getting mired in the past.

We are not meant to be stuck in the past. The past contains old dramas, stories, lessons, and shells of self that keep us from having space to embrace the new. The past was yesterday, and today is NOW. If we want to be joyful and free, we must learn to release our expectation of being "right" and accept that there will be just as many times when we are "wrong."

It comes down to our daily choices and willingness to acknowledge our part in things without attachment to whether we were right or wrong. Be curious. Do the best you can each day. Learn from yourself. Cultivate an ongoing attitude of forgiveness within; be expected to be surprised at how much space this will free up to forgive others.

Become a student of unconditional love; realize this LOVE exists in spades, fistfuls, and never-ending quantities simply because you are a child of the universe. Fight for your right to be happy. Place your hand on your heart and heed its truth: *your soul is so much more than your story.*

Your soul is so much more than your story.

242

A Healer Instead of a Hurter

Hurt people tend to hurt other people. Healed people tend to help others heal. Most of us are works in progress, falling somewhere in between, where our hurts are unintentional.

So, we make amends as best we can, let the situation become a teacher, and try to do better the next time.

This is how we learn, grow, and become bigger. After a while, we realize that somebody else's reaction and behavior towards us is much more reflective of themselves and their relationship with life. Just as our reaction to others is much more reflective of our relationship with ourselves and our relationship with life.

The more we continue to heal that relationship with ourselves— the more we recognize where we have trauma, drama, triggers, and reactions, the more we can work on bringing peace into those places.

Righting our relationship with our inner being.

Bringing love into spaces that are a result of unlove.

Shining light on all our parts of ourselves so we can be seen and whole.

The more we do that, we become a healer instead of a hurter. Our act of well-being creates vibrations of healing and hope in a broken, hungry world.

243

Illumination

We think enlightenment— moving towards a fuller sense of clarity, truth, and illumination in our lives— is a peaceful, Zen-laden path. But I have found that this simply isn't true at all.

Any time we turn the lights on in a previously dark and unexplored place, we will become aware of all the cobwebs, clutter, and dust that have collected and will need to spend some time cleaning before that space feels clear. This is hard work, unglamorous, and sometimes miserable.

We cannot step into a fuller awareness of ourselves without the painful process of examining and sorting through our emotional, spiritual, and relational spaces. In this process, we might feel squeezed and stretched or emptied out, like life is tugging at both ends of something invisible but tangible inside— pulling and siphoning, clearing and cleaning— trying to make space for something new.

There is nothing Zen about it. But there is something honest: our unvarnished truth. This can lead us to a greater sense of purpose, insight, and awareness of our place in the pattern and the direction we want to continue to shape our lives. Crisis, challenge, and hardship can shine a light into every corner of us if we let it, and there is much we stand to gain when we allow the light to stay on.

A deepening relationship with life and ourselves, helps us live with greater intent, meaning, and authenticity. A deepening relationship with our spirituality holds the potential to help us step more fully into the truth of who we are. A deepening relationship with love holds the key to changing the shape and scope of our hearts.

Humanity is messy, Spirit divine, and we are lucky enough to be graced with both. It will take both— plumbing the depths of our recesses and bringing whatever we find out into the light so we can live an examined life AND finding perspective and relationship with life that extends and embraces something beyond just ourselves— if we want to find the courage to live a life of illumination.

244

Purpose It to Love

I believe in transmutation. When we take something we are experiencing individually and use it to increase consciousness, compassion, and interconnection, it transforms our experience into something more.

It allows us to transcend. Even if just for a brief moment. We rise above the pettiness and grit of the pain we are feeling, and we say a prayer, create an intention, and offer our hurting hearts on behalf of other hurting hearts.

We send the energy of love out to someone. Or imagine our pain is being crystallized through the fires and turned into a diamond of light— we watch it drift among the energetic realms and ask that someone else in pain receive the love we've poured into it.

We write a poem, make art, or choose to do something kind for another. We fold our sorrows into origami cranes of peace and then send them into the sky like lanterns of light to make the journey easier for another.

Sometimes, we don't understand why something has happened in our lives, so we have to create our own meaning. Through the act of creating meaning, we create light in a situation where it didn't previously exist through our willingness to reach for and purpose it to love.

This is a mindful act of alchemy when we choose to do this transformation work. It's one of the ways we can find the hidden lights in our pain, learn to work constructively with our darkness, and make a choice to transfigure something terrible into something edifying and bright.

When we know how to do this, we don't have to beat ourselves up when we're in the thick of chaos and overwhelm, and we aren't our best selves. We just need to retain a tiny seed of belief that this, too, shall pass. When it does, we'll begin to discover all these juicy gems of growth and insight that came from that time, which help us to continue to become a fuller expression of self and to use our light to uplift others.

Bright lighthouses of relentless hope, we cast out more kindness and light into the world and remind ourselves and one another that beautiful things can come from seemingly difficult times.

Pearls of Wisdom on Grief and Finding the Light in Darkness

245

HEART

Sometimes, you just have to feel it.

Let the natural expression of pain flow, which honors the strength it takes to try for love. The absolute courage it requires to tangle your heart with another and risk the words "I love you." Risk vulnerability, risk hurt, risk all the unknowns that may come your way. Risk the potential loss that may someday hit with unexpected suffering.

There is no shame to be found in having a hurting heart when your hopes haven't gone as planned and life has brought you to a point of break. No shame at all. Your heart is doing what it is built to do: love, feel, break, heal.

The human heart is one of the most achingly fragile and sturdily resilient forces on the planet. Don't be afraid of what it has to say. Don't be afraid of its depths. And don't be afraid to let it do what it needs to do to release, remember, repair, and renew.

We contract so we can expand. It is the only way a heart knows to grow.

246

HOW TO GRIEVE

People will be willing to tell you how to feel, how to grieve, and that you need to let go, but I have found that at some point, you are simply going to have to realize that people are not you, and you are going to have to give yourself permission to make up your own rules.

You are going to have to come up with your own vocabulary for what you are feeling, figure out what you need to grieve, and define what letting go means to you. Maybe you want to redefine the entire concept of letting go so that it means you work on releasing yourself from everybody else's expectations, attitudes, and values toward your grief, leaving you with the freedom to love, lose, grieve, rage, and heal as you see fit.

Your grief then becomes an opportunity to test the boundaries and wander outside the lines to feel beyond the grief models, books on loss, and what worked for somebody else. Your grief then becomes an opportunity for you to make a break from anything that doesn't support your process and anyone who doesn't allow you space to determine your own needs.

Your grief becomes a doorway to greater authenticity, giving you the courage to own your experience and know it is valid. Your grief then becomes the ultimate lesson on self-care, self-love, self-healing, and listening to yourself. The best thing you can do for yourself is to create space to nurture the needs of your soul. This is a job that nobody can do for you but you.

247

Blank Spaces

We don't always realize the spaces somebody fills in our lives. Physically, emotionally, mentally, and energetically, we get used to arranging our gravitational orbit to accommodate their presence and learn to revolve in accord.

We develop a unique emotional set point toward them and an imprint of feelings we only hold for that relationship. We form an introject in our mind that represents our thoughts, templates, and perspectives of them.

We create memories, stories, and narratives about who they are and what they mean to us. We get used to them occupying all those spaces. Then, one day they are gone, and there is nothing left but the void of empty space they once filled and a lingering sense of feeling lost at sea.

Loss will give you blank spaces, and you will feel lost for quite a while. You will struggle with how to fill that empty space and how to feel that empty space. It will become very important to give yourself both space and time to let life slowly help you find your footing again.

Be kind and gentle to yourself as you do this. Something that was sacred feels ripped from you, and it's going to be a while before life forms itself around that void. In the meantime, give it space to heal. And give yourself space to just be with it. Sometimes, that is the best we can do; just allow the space for it to be.

248
GRIEF, THE GREAT EQUALIZER

Water is an element that cleanses everybody. It strips away dirt and grit, purifies, and renews.

Grief has the power to do that, too. It's supposed to unravel, it's supposed to undo— that's the chaos of it— like a storm hitting our lands.

Grief is designed to deconstruct our finite ego and take us into our infinite soul. It can potentially purify through its wisdom because grief's wisdom is the wisdom of love.

Love, even disguised as grief, is always the great equalizer. It cuts through all layers, barriers, and boundaries, asking us to peel away our ideals so we can travel closer to the soul of what is most real.

249
SMALL WAYS TO HELP CARE FOR ONESELF IN GRIEF

Honor your emotions. Everything you feel is real and valid, no matter what you are feeling.

This is about you and your grieving process— there is no right or wrong.

Recognize that grief is a process, and it's not linear; it's multi-dimensional. At times, it can feel messy, chaotic, and nonsensical; just let it be what it is; not everything will add up.

Remember that other people may not know what to say, and that's okay. This is a beautiful time to practice self-love by telling yourself what you need to hear: "We are going to make it through this. I am here for you. I love you."

Remember that grief is disorienting, and it takes time to feel reoriented again. Practice being kind to yourself if you feel sideways, upside down, and topsy turvy, and find small ways to center and ground.

Release expectations for how things should look. Especially for how YOU should look— your process may be different than expected, and that's perfectly alright.

Know that time may not heal all wounds, but time does help us travel away from the deepest point of the pain, and that is its own form of comfort. One breath at a time, one day at a time, one step at a time— you are moving through. I promise you.

250

Sideways

Sometimes, grief hits you sideways. You're looking ahead, not expecting it to come along, and then it runs right into you, making you lose your balance. At times, it's those moments that will knock you over hardest, as you weren't prepared to be swept into grief land and tumble into the missing ache.

But there are things you can learn in the tilted slant of this space, which forces you to shift perspective.

We learn how grief is almost always inconvenient, and yet it doesn't have to be unwelcome— it exists to help us process our pain and to help bring us back to a space of loving memory, so we remember what's most important in this life.

We learn how we think we know our emotional terrain yet can be completely surprised by what's sometimes buried in our seas until we lose ourselves in our mysteries and must swim to greater depths of being.

We learn how massively strong and courageous the griever is, for the griever is on a grief odyssey not of their own volition. They aren't allowed to get off the boat, and they must find a way to keep going and pressing forward into uncharted terrain with only the stars and love to guide them.

The sideways space is where you begin to learn your composition. The sideways space is where you face your most brutal pain and find your way over, up, around, and through. Most of all, the sideways space is a potential invitation to opportunity.

Opportunity to honor your love for those you've lost, kept in the most sacred place— inside your heart. Opportunity to honor and respect your grief process, growth, and self. Opportunity to honor and deeply cherish the precious gift that is this life.

251

BOUNCE

There are many times we have a say about what happens in our lives, but sometimes we have no say. You can be walking along, focusing on the path in front of you, when you are completely blindsided by something you never predicted or saw coming. A tragedy, a trauma, a cataclysmic change that knocks you off that path, landing you in lonely, unexplored terrain where you are forced to become an inadvertent participant in a journey not of your making.

It is a journey of life's making, and regardless of purpose or reason, you find yourself staring at that mountain, wondering how you can possibly climb it, then somehow finding the courage to take that first step.

There are days when you want to turn away and crawl back into the cocoon of normal that encapsulated life before all this happened. Days when you trick yourself into thinking you are further along than you really are. Days when you search for shortcuts, bailouts, and time warps and learn the painful truth that the only way out is through.

Some people will understand the passage you take, for they, too, have walked these lands, but many will not. It is not their load to carry or their journey to make, and they will sit expectantly, waiting for you to bounce back, waiting for you to reach that distant horizon so life can resume as it once was. What they do not understand is that this is an unseen process of heart and spirit and soul, and you will not look the same upon its passage— there is no bouncing back.

We can't undo the strings of irrevocable loss that are pulled loose when grief enters our world and life turns upside down on us. We can't tie them back the way they were and return to the skin of self we previously wore. For better or for worse, we have been asked to step into a new version of ourselves.

However, if we allow for life's breaking and find the courage to embrace change, grief holds the potential to shine a light on our souls. Stripping us of all the facades and pretenses that hide our authentic selves. Revealing an untapped well of love, courage, and strength that awaits us in the darkest need.

Helping us realize the intangible things that are most real while introducing us to our deeper, spiritual selves. Teaching us a new, resilient language of the heart that helps us become deeper, wider, and more than we were before. After its initial contraction, grief offers expansion— if we learn to let its light in.

Once the face of grief has shone its spotlight on us, things may never return to how they were, but most often, they aren't meant to. We didn't come here to stay the same; we came here so our hearts could be rearranged. The best any of us can do is learn how to courageously take the journey life hands us. Believe we will find our bounce again. And learn to land wherever we may.

252

WATCHTOWERS OF LOVE

Perhaps one of the cruelest truths that comes with loss is that you can't return to who you were before. You can't crawl back into your old shell of self. You can't rewind to a reality where your loved one is still here because you are constantly reminded that your life has definitively changed. And with that change, you will be forced to change as well.

There is no road map for who you become after grief. Those of us who've passed through grief's wasteland and found ourselves on a new shore know that each step forward will be a step into something new and different than who we were before. It's the kind of change that can be incredibly lonely; nobody but you can bear the burden of this change.

Yet, change also holds the potential for new possibilities and the spark of new life if we can learn to fan the flame.

It may not be the life we would have chosen, but we can try to accept that this is the life we've been given. Since we've also learned from our loss that life is an infinitely precious gift not to be taken for granted, we try not to take our own lives for granted. It is in this space of gratitude that we can transform that spark into a blaze and become a brighter light than who we were before.

The kind of light who learns to see the sacred every day. Who decides to use their light to try and warm the world. Who takes the pieces from the wreckage of their grief, builds a watchtower of love out of them, and then shines the fires of their love light so bright and high it is visible for miles and miles.

We reach out to others who feel lost and alone in the dark and help them begin to see the path to find their way home.

253
Get Over It

You don't have to get over it. You don't have to get over it six months from now. You don't have to get over it six years from now. You don't have to get over it sixty years from now.

In fact, there may always be a small part of you frozen in the thick of grief. Curled up by the tomb of the loss where you laid a piece of you to rest the day you lost them. Kneeling in honor for that which fell too soon.

You do not have to get over it. But you do have to keep getting on. Trying to put one foot in front of the other. Trying to do life. Trying to move through and see if you can find new life on the other side.

You owe it to yourself; you owe it to your grief, which reminds you how fiercely you loved; you owe it to your massive heart, who is busy crawling forward, struggling to try. To move. To search for all that is good and true and bright.

To find the light amidst the pain.

In the hopes that someday, whenever that day may be, you find that while you were busy watering the land with grief, life grew roses around the place where your loss resides. Giving you hope and a reminder that despite the pain that marks that place, life will find a way to keep growing. Easing the pain. Reminding you profound good happens, too.

Covering what aches with the only balm that will soothe the pain: love.

254

How to Swim

There is a reason grief is often compared to the ocean. As you churn about in its watery grips, you can't help but know the strength of the sea.

One moment, you will be standing on the shore, and the ground feels solid— you are making it through this, you are going to be okay. Then a rogue wave unexpectedly pulls you in, and you are floundering in the middle of the water, drowning for all you're worth, until you realize the ocean has spit you back out, and you are once again on the shore. Though you don't know how you got there, there is solid ground beneath your feet.

While you can't stop the cataclysm that is grief when it comes, or keep yourself from being pulled into that tumult of an ocean, or ignore the difficult and necessary tasks that go along with caring for your heart after loss, you can choose how you go through it. You can choose to fill in the gaps and cracks and in between moments with as much self-compassion and kindness as you can.

You can learn to let your giant heart and your fervent faith in the process of life be a lighthouse in your storm. You can teach yourself how to swim in the watery depths by surrendering to the waves and letting them float and carry you for a while when you feel you can no longer carry yourself.

Even in the middle of the ocean, you can learn to take in life, look to the hope of the stars when you lose your way, and choose to let the one thing trying to pour from the seas of your heart flow: a song of grief rising from the void in your deep.

255

THE THICK

If you are in the thick of it, please tread kindly with yourself. Grief is a confusing and jagged process; loss creates a sense of internal lawlessness that knows no rules or bounds.

You might find that your psyche devolves into disarray as the constructs and schemas on which you have built your sense of reality tumble down, obliterated. What you believe to be true turns on its head, and it's so mentally disorienting that it is difficult to know which way is up. Gravity doesn't exist in the thick of grief.

The way you once saw the world becomes an ideological pile of debris you are forced to sort, as your neural networks turn into traffic jams and dead-end roads and abrupt cliffs of irresolution. You search for the answer of what it means for someone to cease, and you find that the model of grief you are living is one where every stage is mixed, an emotive mass of finger paints with a tiny dot in the middle that says: "You are *here*."

You are here. This is good news because it means you are still going. You are still finding a way to swim through molasses, walk through quicksand, and put one foot in front of the other, even though you're floating untethered in space. While it is a sticky and messy process, one without a time limit or rulebook, you are still going, still breathing, and still trying to show up.

I'd reach through these pages and give you a hug and a gold star for doing that much if I could. This may be the hardest thing you will ever endure and have to drag yourself through. Your gravitational orbit will never look the way it did before, and it's going to take your brain, your body, and your heart some time to undergo reconstruction, rebuild, and repair.

In the meantime, go gently on yourself, for you are in the thick of it, and you are still moving. Which means you are doing beautifully, you wonderful, brave human.

256

LABYRINTH

Grief is an amorphous language I'll be learning to speak for the rest of my life. New words and phraseology are forever being introduced; old words that I thought I had memorized suddenly shift and change in composition or accentuation.

I think this is part of what makes grief so complex— there are all these tiers and layers and dimensions to it, and you can warp throughout these dimensions multiple times in a day. That's why it's so nuanced: it's a labyrinth with many levels, twists, and turns— that keep changing— and at times, it can feel impossible to find your way out or make sense of the passages.

Some days, that labyrinth feels less complex, but there are other days where I still find myself wandering in it. One moment, I'll travel to the deep, desolate mud of earth's crust, then I'm on to the sorrow of sad, lonely ocean waves only to find myself transported up into the dissolution of the clouds, drifting and lost.

Then I'll time warp back to 1980 when we were little kids, and life was simple: cartoons, the sandbox, Mom's meatloaf, trips to our Methodist church, Dad driving us in the car while the soundtrack to "Sound of Music" plays on.

Because those who traverse grief's labyrinth are also time travelers, able to cross great spaces and spans in mere seconds and breaths and heartbeats, you don't know when you might be called to travel or where or when you'll return from the journey.

And the only thing that I have found that helps you make your way through that labyrinth is love. Because love isn't linear, there is no start and finish to it. Love exists always. Circular, infinite, limitless, enduring, eternal. Transcendent. This means no matter what layer or tier or time you find yourself at, love is there.

Enfolding us, helping us, guiding us, holding our hand, and lighting our path. Reminding us that the only reason we find ourselves in the labyrinth in the first place is because we loved. And when we tap into love, we automatically create a doorway we can step through, so no matter how lost you feel— love will always help you find a way to return to your home.

257

THE WASTELAND

People say that grief is like the ocean, and it is in many ways. It can come and go like the tide, washing you into its powerful waves, churning you upside down until you don't know which way is up, each shifting moment a different shade of sea.

Yes, grief can be like the ocean, but I have found the heart of grief to be more like the dry, barren wasteland. Endless in view. Oases few. The blast of the relentless sun is unforgiving in nature.

Grief eviscerates. It makes you feel like you are crawling, trying to scratch your way through the haze of parched pain. Grabbing for anything that might quench your unquenchable thirst.

The wasteland is where you come face to face with the heart of your pain. The wasteland is where you will feel destroyed and erased. The wasteland is where you fall off the edges of yourself and the edges of reality as you knew it. The wasteland is where you find out what you're made of when life knocks you to the ground, and you are forced to go on all fours.

I know it may seem like you will never emerge, find your feet again, and be forever crawling. But *my dear friend*, I can tell you from one who has had many a crawl herself, there are gifts on the ground that we do not always see from the height of the sky.

Gifts of sand, stone, and roots remind us that we are being held up by the power of the earth and are supported by more than just ourselves. Gifts of cooling, underground water reserves when we learn how to dig deep.

Gifts of a humble heart, tired spirit, and hurting mind that leave us desperately seeking— and therefore more likely to *see*— grace also exists in this space. Gifts of strength that come when we look back, see the ground we've passed, and realize:

This is horrible and brutal and hard, but I made it this far and see how strong I've become. Because. I. Am. Still. Going.

258

BECOMING

Loss can take you to some dark places. Places you don't want, but can't help, to go. Places marked by despair and great pain, anger, and a sense of senseless want. Places where it is hard to hang onto silver linings or fragile hope or any sense that the sun will shine again.

These are the places where you may encounter what feels like the very worst of yourself. A time may come when you begin to miss the old you: the you, you were before this awful loss.

You might want to squeeze back into that old shell of self— take your old problems back, take your old sense of normal back. Take back the luxury of not having to live with the heavy press of grief.

A time may come when you look in the mirror and don't like what you are becoming. But that's just it, isn't it? You ARE becoming.

All this awful, nasty, sticky mess is part of the passage of grief and holds the potential to help shine a light into our darkest spaces, where we will be forced to face our debris. Forced to find ways to dig deep and bring a blaze of bright into our darkness. Forced to find the stars that help us navigate this night.

This is the place where we learn to expand. This is where we learn love is big enough to love over our most miserable parts of self. This is the place that holds the potential for incredible heart growth.

This is the place where we come face to face with ourselves and find we are always stronger than we think we are, always have a little bit more to give than we think, and are filled with an infinite supply of grace to see us through the journey.

259

BREAK

What does it mean to live a life where we let ourselves break in the direction life is breaking us? To be certain, this is easier said than done. There is a reason the word "heart" usually prefaces the word "break." Our heart wisdom is stronger and bigger than our mind wisdom, which is why most of the time, when we are broken in life, it is the heart that takes it the hardest.

Heartbreak is the hardest break to heal. Unlike a broken bone, which can be reset and realigned, the heart doesn't heal back into the same shape it did before it was broken. The grief-changing work of self becomes an invisible process that those who've been broken go through. They journey onwards from the bitterest point of their loss as they process their pain and go in search of healing and perspective.

Breaking is painful, yet it is part of life. The bottom line to learning to break is that while we want to think we are the ones in control— in the past, I have clung to situations until my nails bled and my knuckles turned white, trying to keep change from running its course— the reality is that life is bigger than us. There are times when we will be asked to yield to it.

We can't control our breaks, but we can choose what to do with our pieces. When life swings its wrecking ball into our walls, we can rage, cry, and grieve. We can learn to break. Learn to crumble. Let ourselves take space to be a mess, and then let life fill us up with new pieces so we can be rearranged.

Let ourselves disintegrate and reintegrate and integrate, and learn to trust the process, even when we don't know where the process is taking us.

It's the best any of us can do. Follow our process in the bigger process called life. Allow our shells to be shattered when something shattering comes along. Trust life to help us put our pieces back together. Look for the hidden lights in the darkness that will help guide us along the path. Learn to release instead of cling. Find the courage to just keep showing up and trying to find the love.

Fight relentlessly for a free heart that learns to transcend the break.

260

Shine

There will be days when the sun shines a little bit brighter. If you're not there yet, I promise you they will come. There will be days where the grief isn't as potent, and the light slips its way through the clouds and brings you warm grace.

When those days come, let them. You have nothing to feel guilty about for feeling good. The grief is there; it isn't going anywhere.

Feeling good doesn't mean you're not grieving. It just means you are beginning to open to life again, starting to take in the joys and the goods that will slowly begin to impress upon your psyche, reminding you there is still life out there waiting to be lived.

Everything has a season— even grief— and makes itself known in its own time. So, on those days when the clouds part, the winds stir, and the light comes in, let it shine. Bask in it. Take it into you like a medicinal balm.

Let it warm your spirits and help restore you to life, and know you've been given the medicine of grace.

261
BRAMBLES AND ROSES

There is always joy among the sorrow and roses among the brambles. Our emotional experience isn't relegated to just one thing when it comes to loss. It is relegated to all emotions joined together by the word "and," helping us hold both love and grief side by side in our hearts.

Part of grieving is the work of clearing the brambles, pulling them out in thorny lots, and dealing with the pricks and wounds where they've made us bleed as we allow ourselves the time and space to mend and heal. Our roses are never any lesser for the brambles, but we will find that when we clear them out, the roses become even more pristine, pure, and distilled.

Our enjoyment of the rose is that much more intense because we know the stinging rub of the brambles. When you know the sting of the thorn, you learn to value those roses with a ferocity of gratitude that can only come from learning about pain from the inside out.

Life's gifts become a testament to grace when we have experienced the knowledge of the wound. Grief then becomes the catalyst for distilled joy. Sorrow is a doorway to goodness. The work of the heart— in this space of loss— is to acknowledge all the beauty and all the ugliness in this world, then join them together with the AND.

262

Essence of Grief

This is the essence of grief:

It is the loving and the missing and the reminders that hit suddenly of all the ways your life has changed and all the opportunities you will not have with your loved one. It is the deepening, widening, and stretching grief brings to your heart and the soul wisdom that comes from loss.

It is the ache and hole you carry inside that is uniquely shaped to who you've lost— nobody else can or ever will fill it. After a while, you learn to till the soil of that hole and plant roses of love in that space, so you always have a sacred place inside where you can kneel, talk to your loved one, and honor them.

Honor them, and in so doing, honor you. Those who carry grief know things others do not.

What you feel is real. It is valid. It is complex. It is dynamic. It is achingly, shatteringly human, and it all exists because you have loved and lost. We grieve because we love, and we find healing and strength in that very same love. Love is our question and our answer and everything that lies in between.

263

HOME

We cannot return to innocence once we've passed the threshold of loss, but we can return to ourselves. We can reach up, stretch out, dig deep, and do whatever we need to do to excavate our own sense of self and find a home there, within our hearts.

There is one task on this earth each of us is better able to do than anybody else, and that is to try and be our most unequivocal, authentic, true-blue self. Even in grief, we can do this by finding ways to honor our losses that feel authentic, real, and loving to the whole of who we are.

There is much in this world that will break us. Shatter us into shards, make us aware of parts of ourselves we never knew existed, turn a light on in our darkened rooms so we can see the full scope of who we are. Even in this darkness, we can learn to embody what it is to be real.

Loss can break. Life can break. Our hearts can break. Our tears can fall. We can re-mend, repair, rewire, and reinvent, only to find life comes along and breaks us all over again. But there is a fundamental wellness in our souls that goes unharmed. It is called love, and no matter how often our pieces break, they will reform themselves around that core again and again.

Some things cannot be broken, and so long as you hold love in your heart— no matter how far you wander off the path— you will always find your way home.

264

WILDFLOWERS

There will always be a hole in the shape of the loss inside your heart that cannot be filled by anyone or anything.

Each life is a unique imprint upon this planet; of course, we cannot fill or replace or just get over one another when someone has exited our lives, nor should we heap expectation upon ourselves to try. People who do not understand the nature of loss may not understand how it can hurt so much after all this time, but I say a hole in the heart will always hurt and to treat our losses with casual expendability— to deny their ever-changing impact— is to deny what it means to be most human.

However, time is a mysterious elixir. It doesn't always heal things, but it does change things, and if things change long enough, we might begin to find that new life has found the courage to grow around the area where the barren hole once lay.

Wildflowers begin to pop up with stubborn hope. A few birds fly by, reminding us that the world is bigger than this space, and life continues. The soil digs in with resilience and chooses to support fresh seeds.

A tree that looked chopped down begins to regrow. It has unshakable roots, for it has withstood some of the worst life has to offer and still found a way to believe in the sky and rise towards the sun's strength.

No. It is not that any of us will ever, ever forget whosoever touched our lives and left them too soon. It is more that time offers the necessary seeds of nourishment for us to remember our roots. Slowly grow out of the desperate dark of devastation and find the heart-growing grit to look up and receive the light.

265

NOODLES

Grief is a strange beast. It's twisty, not linear. Like a bowl of noodles where everything gets whirled and twirled together, chasing each other, weaving in and out in a cluster of slippery swirls. So it is with grief, our experience of it swerving and curving, twisting and taking us on emotional detours whose destination we didn't anticipate.

Grief taps into us on multidimensional layers, intersecting in multiple places across our timeline. It can make you feel very young and childlike, like a little kid who just wants to cry and scream, "Not fair, not fair, not fair!"

It can ask you to time travel. Journey back into the kitchen of old memories where life seemed simpler, and a bowl of spaghetti with tangy marina sauce and watching Donald Duck was a stellar Friday night when life felt filled with imagination, innocence and bright possibilities.

It can also make you feel ancient as if your heart holds the heavy stories of a thousand-year-old grove. The concentric circles around your soul, each telling an epoch of your journey through grief.

There's not a single emotion grief doesn't tap; you never know what you are going to get in that bowl, each noodle being a part of the whole, each noodle equally valid, and simply one more expression of the love that underlies the loss.

We are reminded that our grief comes from a place of love, so we allow it to wash through and remember the love. But we also remember that we can't build a home out of grief and our memories. There is no presence or joy there.

We can only examine the tangles of grief as they come our way. Do our best to be open and honest with each strand. Acknowledge it as valid. Release it when ready. Then keep pressing forward, doing our best to be here now and find the joy.

266
WE WILL HAVE JOY

There are going to be days when, despite our best efforts, we just can't connect to that which is good. And that's okay. Especially when suffering and processing loss, it is important to know the scope of the darkness so we can learn to find the stars that guide our way.

But when it is time and those stars have led us through the worst of it, we have to make a choice on how to see this life and what we choose to nurture inside of us. If we want to find what is beautiful in this world, then one has to be rather persistent when it comes to joy and gratitude.

These gifts can quietly start to dissolve when we are not actively tending to them. Over time, we'll notice a slow continental drift, where gratitude diminishes, and that leaves us with only tiny shards of good.

Every day, we are given a choice. Life asks us the question: Who do you want to be in this world? The way we choose to live is our response. Our perspectives, attitudes, thoughts, heart energy— that's all on us. Nothing external can change that. Change is an inside job.

We are the ones who must insist on finding joy. Even when life has handed us a heap of gritty muck, at some point, we have to choose to find the gifts anyway. To see there is always space for new ideas, new moments, new intentions, new loves, new letting goes, new skies, new experiences, new interactions, new beginnings, new moons, new creations, new imaginings, new places, and new heart spaces.

All are just waiting for us to recognize them, grab onto them, and shape them according to our energy, efforts, and intents so we can choose to find the gifts of each day. The gifts that increase joy, love, happiness, and gratitude.

Some days, we just need to work a little harder for it, but we all have the capacity inside of ourselves to do the work. To change our set points. To challenge ourselves to be more than our circumstances.

To insist that in this moment, on this day, no matter where we find ourselves— we will have joy.

267

ECLIPSE

Grief will bring you to an eclipse of the soul. It is where you will find your darkest hours and know your darkest nights. *But my friend, please know that any good dark night of the soul is a possible gateway to light.*

This is the space where you will begin to discover your truth. Where everything else is burned away except that which is meant to matter. Where clarity becomes a companion and these bones of humanity the place where you learn just how deep and far and wide love can stretch.

We have this illusion in this life that we are somehow separated from love. That it is outside of us and something we need to seek out, grasp for, and cling to. But the truth is, *that* is only an illusion: love has been within us all along. We just had to make space to find it.

And if you have dared to stare grief in the face and make the passage of dark back to the hope of light, discovered new strength to carry on, scratched your way out of the shadows, found the sacred rhythm beating through the veins of these times which allows this world to keep on spinning, then you know grief for precisely what it is.

The hardest, most powerful teacher of love we have ever had.

268

Everywhere

They never really leave us. Those who've left too soon. We find them in each breath, each heartbeat, each laughter, each joy. They reside there, smiling with us, resting between grace and gratitude.

Certain songs may come on that tug at the heartstrings. Happy memories may fly, seemingly out of nowhere, into our memory stream. Birds and butterflies and bunnies act as messengers of spirit speak. Nature is often a medium to send messages in between.

We find those we've loved and lost in the creases and folds of life's fabric, where the veil is thin and permeable. We find them when we notice ourselves extra thinking of them, almost hearing a whisper, catching their scent on the wisps of the wind, seeing them clearly in our mind's eye.

They reach down and tuck us in as we sleep, hovering close by and singing the songs of angels. See our tears and gently blow them from our eyes. "I know you will be okay," they say, "I believe in you. I BELIEVE in YOU."

Unbound by time, unboxed by gravity, freed from the limitations of this realm, connected to a source where love is eternal, all things are possible, and light is the gracious law guiding the way.

They can be there while still touching here. Forever carried in our hearts, forever a soul returned to love, reaching out through infinity to remind us they're still with us— they are always, forever, everywhere.

269

IF YOU STRIKE ME DOWN

What if love just grows more powerful when someone leaves us? If that love is good and pure and true, what if removing the shells of a body and the physical act of being in each other's presence, well, what if it removes that which is material in love and simply leaves us with that which is divine?

What if love somehow grows stronger after? What if there is more to come? What if there are lessons for our hearts that we haven't yet imagined because that spiritual and emotional shell had yet to be broken prior to our loss? What if those we love are still out there teaching us, guiding us, helping us, and the act of learning to let go holds more significance than we grasp?

What if Obi-Wan had it right all along when he said, "If you strike me down, I shall become more powerful than you can possibly imagine." What if the power of love just gets stronger after, and the act of release and surrender become the ingredients we need to grow and ascend and make space in our hearts for more love?

What if you remove all the physical manifestations, and the love still lives on, and we still hang onto the essence of love for who and what we've lost? What if it is we who become more powerful than we possibly imagined?

Then, we are not just those who have loved and lost. We become beautiful, powerful beings who find a way to transform and transcend the dark of pain by finding the courage to see our love for what it is: an expression of divinity shining out in the darkness, reminding us that no matter how much pain it holds, there are still forces in this world capable of magic, mystery, and light.

270

All That Is Shabby and Bright

Loss will take you to the core of what it means to be human. Like the cycle of the seasons, which teach us how to release, return, rebirth, and reclaim, it is okay to be full and complete in this task.

Remembering that is so hard for us at times. We expect ourselves to entertain life with our best foot forward and a sense that we have it together. We place expectations and judgments on how we think we should be handling things. We feel to be messy and vulnerable and chaotic is to fail at this misdirected, self-appointed task.

But loss is completely chaotic. Undeniably vulnerable. Sloppy and disheveled. Achingly untidy.

Our emotions do not turn off when something is over as if relationships are a linear process. We cannot expect something to end and expect our hearts to accordingly end all emotional attachment as well, like we can simply dispose of those emotions and move forward to what's next. And if something ends because of death, which is the most final ending of all, then we can expect to take all the emotions that come from heartbreak and times that by the thousands.

Whoever they have been to us— those who've touched us in a profound way, those we intertwined ourselves with on a deeper level, those who left our lives leaving scrapes and holes and pangs in our hearts— they will never be disposable. There will always be traces of someone who left a footprint in our internal gardens.

Our responsibility to ourselves isn't to deny that these imprints exist, but to make space for those who've impacted our lives, to make space for those we've loved and lost. Our responsibility is to honor the mess of our response and know there is room for all our feelings. Our responsibility is to remember our relationship with grief isn't linear: it is fluid.

Circular, cyclical, seasonal, full. Subject to movement and change, as it continues to seek healing that waters and weeds and grows and warms our gardens to wellness. Our responsibility to ourselves is to learn to love ourselves wherever we are and simply accept that this, too— all that is shabby and all that is bright— is what it means to be human.

271

HONOR THEM

There is no right or wrong way to grieve, process our losses, or remember those who've passed in this place. Some signatures are written so strongly inside us that they will forever remain engraved. Years may go by, and you may still feel the ache and the love in the place they hold inside your being.

This is the cost of loving and losing. To feel that love and ache and realize nobody else will carry that experience, carry their remembrance, carry that love inside of you in the unique way you do. Since you are the keeper of this precious task, you should not be afraid to remember and honor them in any way you see fit, whenever you see fit.

Make up your own rituals of remembrance. Throw flowers in the river in release. Write letters and burn them in a fire; let the smoke and ash curl up towards the sky and reach the ears of those you love.

Light candles of intention and memory. Surround yourself with pictures or prized possessions. Name a star after them. Talk to them daily. Talk to them in the moon, your mind, and your memories. Believe they hear you.

Keep moving forward, yet never get over it. Let your heart break, even as you let your heart mend. Find something that speaks to your soul. Go to nature. Go to where it's quiet. Go to holy places. Seek out the divine and seek out the human. Seek out whatever calls to your heart and fills you with meaning and purpose. Realize the more purpose you have, the more you honor those who've passed through your life.

Do your best to be kind to yourself, whatever your process may be. This isn't about judging whether your process is right, wrong, or normal— this is about doing the best you can. You are a human being who has taken a rite of passage you never wanted to take. You are brave, courageous, and full of heart and spirit for everything you feel.

Honor you and honor them. Piece all the ways you care, grieve, cry, mourn, and joy around you like a patchwork quilt, which you have stitched together with your love, depth, and humanity. Wrap it around you: your superhero's cape of love comprised of all you were and all you will be.

Know each time you don that cloak, look to the star, feel the ache in your chest, and each time you notice the missing and yearning and happiness and lack: That yes, this life— their bright light— did indeed matter.

272

Grief's Doorway

Honoring our grief is not about focusing on what we've lost— not at all.

It's about our relationship with ourselves and our relationship with life. It's about making space to remember what matters most: the love we give and the love we are in this place. It's about creating opportunities to grow in relationships and connection with the world around us.

Our losses are doorways to a greater space of remembering, appreciating, releasing, loving, grieving, and growing. When we honor, we are reminded of our true nature: we are not separate; we are connected to everything, our past and present continually weaving together to unfold the mystery of our future.

Honoring is about giving ourselves permission to be our full selves. To feel our full selves. To feel the full scope of our lives, which includes our losses. To honor our process of being, our unique relationship to grief and loss and love, our trail of being a true human.

We honor so we keep resolving, dissolving, and evolving our relationship with life. We honor because we have loved, and in so doing, we discover that love is grief's antidote.

273
WHAT LOSS HAS TO TEACH US

"In this moment, there is plenty of time. In this moment, you are precisely as you should be. In this moment, there is infinite possibility."
—Victoria Moran

We don't always recognize the sacredness of our lives. We have to learn to tap into the precious quality of our breaths, the potential we each hold as individuals, and the nature of our own light. We don't come here knowing it.

That is the heart wisdom we gain along the journey, something we must first experience to embrace truly. Experience is the difference between knowing about something and living and embodying something. And we can't fully embody life if we haven't been through heart-wrenching loss.

Loss is our teacher who heightens our life experience and creates a greater awareness of how beautiful and finite it is. Loss is the catalyst that can catapult us into a new consciousness. Loss holds the potential for tremendous transformation when we can grasp its full lessons.

There is no greater teacher on life's brief, glorious wisp than the death of something— a relationship, a dream, an ideal, a season, and sometimes that death manifests in physical form, and we lose someone we love. It is only through knowing finality that we can see how sacred our wisp of self is, how sacred the journey is, and how sacred the ALL of life is.

Because we are here— here in this place's beautiful, difficult, finite, possible space. It means we have chances, choices, and possibilities. What a gift is the light of our possibilities. It is inherently holy and hallowed, precious and cherished, prayerful and revered, sublime and divine. What a privilege to be present and embrace the opportunities that are our lives.

Our deepest darks are often found in the loss of something or someone that was sacred, precious, and dear to us. Our brightest light can be found when we grapple with the terms of life— that all things must end so they can come around in new form.

We hold the potential to find new openings when life hands us a close. An opening, which can help us realize how sacred everything is. From the most heightened to the most mundane, from the beautiful to the awful, from the sorrow to the joy. It can all become a chance to embody each moment we are given as best we can.

To be full in our grief. To be full in our love. To own and stretch and delve into whatever emotional experience we have on each given day. To embrace the presence of a moment, whether we like the moment or not. To live more courageously, honestly, boldly. To simply sit still and belong to this world. To see the sacred in the whole of our lives.

As long as we are here, we have the gift of possibility. The gift of growth. The gift of hope. The gift of falling deeper into love. The gift of reaching and lengthening and evolving into bigger, more nuanced beings. The gift of hurting when we are in pain.

Celebrating when we joy. The gift of carrying our losses in our hearts and letting those losses strengthen us in love and affirmation of our humanity. The gift of continuing to strive to embody the peace, change, and grace we so wish to see in the hallowed halls of these precious, sacred days.

274

Non-Sequitur

The longer I deepen my relationship with grief, the more I realize that grief truly is a non-sequitur. We live out its irresolution the rest of our lives and our being, breathing, and loving becomes the resolution, even as the missing and nonsensical never fit.

We might still miss our loved ones every single day. Perhaps not a day goes by when we don't think about them or have an ancient awareness of how losing them has altered us. We may know exactly how we got from point A to point Z, even as some days we still wonder how we got from point A to point Z.

Some things in life are like that. Irresolute. They don't fit neatly into a bundle. They don't logically add up with a conclusion that makes sense. Their emotional experience cannot be contained, quantified, or reduced to a model. They are what they are: tangents and detours and traumas and unfinished stories with ongoing questions whose answers we seek through our living.

We might move forward in our lives all while wondering who we would have become if we hadn't had this loss? How might our life have been different? What unfinished business of self did we leave behind to show up for our grief?

There may still be a sense of abrupt departure. A ripping. A quantum leap. A life ended too soon, which forced the life as we knew it to end too, morphing us into someone else.

We may never know those answers. Time may bring more peace to our questions, but perhaps it won't, and we'll continue to smack into those questions, which sometimes still startle and jar us. They may leave us saying, "Is this really my life?" Perhaps those questions will always be a part of us, and we just have to keep making peace that some questions are unanswerable.

The grief process teaches you that you can't find a resolution in the middle of irresolution. Sometimes, all you can do is press pause, recognize the disjointed Salvador Dali-esque surrealism of this life, and just make space for it to be what it is.

I have found that grief can develop a softer tone the further we step from the deepest point of the pain. Once a flashing neon sign, placed directly by our heart's window, glaring and jolting and relentlessly reminding us of our loss— our attention is initially fully centered on that intrusive, blinking light.

Over time, it might no longer feel so glaring. Grief's colors and presence become quieter. More subdued, settling into our joints and cells. It becomes part of our story and part of who we are, giving us an underlying sense of sorrow even as it can heighten, sweeten, and help us find gratitude, possibility, and an expanded love for the gift of life.

Maybe our losses will always feel like a non-sequitur, like the story doesn't add up— the conclusion an irresolution. But the love we find as we carry our loved ones inside of us becomes our solution and my salvation. It makes us so much more than who we were before.

And for that, I am grateful.

275

Forever

There were times when part of me felt like all I wanted to do was stay in a state of depression and grief after my brother died. But all along, the wiser part of me knew there was a lesson in love to be learned from all of it. My job was to decide whether I wished to receive it.

My job was to decide whether I would close myself off to the hurt of this world or find the absolute courage to open my heart just a little bit farther and receive. Receiving meant turning my attention from what I had lost to becoming cognizant of what I had gained. Receiving meant letting go of *what was* to accept something greater in *what is*.

"What is" turns out to be a massive recognition that you can remove the material and earthly realm of a relationship, but you cannot touch what we hold in our hearts.

I believe this to be love in its purest, most divine form. Just because you can no longer see its physical manifestation when something has passed doesn't mean it's not there. As long as you hold love in your heart, those who've passed are only a heartbeat away.

If you can grasp that concept, truly grab onto it, letting it envelop you with an unalloyed truth that burns through all but that which is most genuine and true, then you realize even though everything has changed, absolutely nothing has changed. They will always be with us. Forever. The energy of love cannot be reduced; it only continues to multiply every time we realize and express it.

I cloak myself in this knowledge: You can lose a life, but you can't lose love. This newfound awareness makes me stand strong and straight and realize that I am not a broken being after all. I am a walking container of all the love I've collected— big and strong and full of life.

The love that ripped me apart is the same love reknitting my seams. Love has become my revolution and my absolution.

Pearls of Wisdom on Letting Go and Embracing Change

276
Change Cycles

Whether or not we realize it, we are in a constant cycle of change. If we are here and have air to breathe, we will be forever changing and developing.

Sometimes, change comes in giant waves and big flows. Sometimes, it's an ebb, and we feel like we're going backward and retrograding in our lives when really things just appear to slow down so we can be ushered into greater alignment when they speed back up.

Change can be hard for us to embrace, but the sooner we can embrace change, the more we shift into a fluid paradigm of evolution and growth with lots of room for creativity, reinvention, and rearrangement. We release more rigid ways of being, and instead, open to a more gracious relationship with our lives.

We stop imposing ridiculous expectations on ourselves about how life "should" look, wasting precious time lamenting what isn't. Instead, we embrace how life does look. Viewing whatever comes across our path as a potential teacher to help us grow, so we can open our arms to the gifts of what is.

Our minds like to resist change, so it can be hard to take the mental leap from resistance to acceptance. This is why our heart and intuition processes become the tools we need to navigate change. Sometimes, the best and easiest thing we can do is give ourselves permission not to know, have faith in the change process, be in the nebulous feelings of the moment, then put our hand on our hearts, drop into that energy, and ask:

"What do I need to know right now?" And then heed the wisdom that comes through.

277
GO, BE YOUR CHANGE

If nothing ever changes, it means that nothing new is growing. If nothing new is growing, then the space in which we are comfortably resting quickly becomes a comfortable resting place for stagnation and a means of a slow cessation that leaves its bearer with a gnawing unease and the persistent question: Is this all there is?

Life is here to interrupt that stagnation. To make you think, to make you expand, to make you become, to make you grow. Allowing life to have its way with you to bring about this process can be one of the scariest things you'll ever do because it is not comfortable, certain, fixed, or controlled.

It is creation through chaos. It is also needed for true growth because nothing new ever happens from sitting around and doing the same thing over and over. You will never find what you require for your soulful growth if you keep repeating patterns.

If life is calling you to change, if YOU are calling You to change, then listen. Take notes. Heed the warning. Nourish that intuition. Do something different. Step new. Give yourself permission not to see the big picture and not to know. Trust your process. Trust your heart. Stretch your wings.

Leap into the chaos. Give yourself space to make a mistake. Or lots of mistakes. Keep moving forward anyway. Whatever you do, just don't shut that voice of change down because you already know that road leads to a dead end whose questions you've lived the same answer to a thousand times.

Life cannot sustain itself without new growth. And you deserve to grow. You deserve to give that side of yourself the space it needs to breathe new air. You deserve a life defined by its abundant meaning and not its abundant lack. You deserve LIFE. Go, be your change.

278

Who We'll Be

"Who in the world am I? Ah, that's the great puzzle."
—Lewis Caroll, Alice in Wonderland

We can spend our entire lifetime finding and losing and rediscovering ourselves. We're meant to spend our entire lifetime finding, losing, and rediscovering ourselves in a constant dance of creative, dynamic expansion.

The challenge is that it doesn't feel very dynamic or expansive when we are in a change space. Change creates a nebulous void where we lose track of ourselves as we stand on the brink of uncertainty— no longer the person we left behind, not quite certain who we'll turn out to be.

I always feel intense, immense, sincere swells of discomfort in this space. *Who am I, where am I going, and who will I become?* But I have learned and keep learning that in all my losses, and findings, and rearranging, there is a part of ourselves— some still, invisible wisdom of soul— who knows exactly where we are going and who we will be.

This part makes itself known at its own pace and process. A new thought here, a different action there, an old belief shed, a new belief slowly embraced. It reveals itself in its own time. You slowly unpeel sticky layers of a cocoon until one day, you realize all those layers have dissolved into cups of compost for old ground. You find yourself cleared for new space, blinking in the face of fresh light.

Our deeper selves have a process and rhythm all their own. They change as change is needed, growing in their unique shape and way. We unpeel when it is time, leave our layers behind, and begin to learn to use new eyes.

It feels dark when we're in the void of change, but we can learn to sink into the pregnant space of the nebula. Somewhere inside, an emerging self will slowly begin to form. It asks us to protect and nurture our incubation, so it has the space to become.

We cannot rush this process, but we can send our unmet selves love and cradle the seeds of who we'll be.

279
The Nature of You

We can be very impatient during our change process. We judge a bad day, a bad month, a bad season as evidence we are not changing quickly enough, or we have wasted time and gone backward. Then, in our self-judgment, we feel even further away from where we are trying to get to.

Isn't it fortunate, then, when we get into the shameful spaces inside of ourselves, where the mind says, "You're not doing it quickly enough, and you will never get there," we have magnificent teachers in nature who teach us the exact opposite.

Nature teaches us we can't stop change from happening. We can't stop a season or force a season. Nature teaches us change often happens on its own accord. Just like the trees, flowers, moon and sun, and natural rhythms of life, we are in a constant state of transformation within our cycle and rhythm of self.

If you are seeking change and trying to get somewhere but don't feel like you are doing it fast enough— rest easy. All things truly do happen in their own time, including you.

If you are seeking change, yet feel stuck and like you're not taking the right steps to make things different— rest easy. Just because you can't see the seeds being planted doesn't mean they won't bloom and bud in time, helping you find your momentum.

If you don't know where you're at with any of it— rest easy. A tree cannot help but be a tree, and a flower cannot help but be a flower. A cloud will naturally embody the nature of a cloud, and a stone cannot help but embody the energy of being a stone.

If you just relax around all of it and allow yourself patience with your growth and truth, you will find that so as with nature, you cannot help but embody the nature of you.

280
The Importance of Tiny Anchors

We need the small things in life that help anchor us to ourselves. Particularly during transition, challenge, and change when life feels uncertain— and we feel like we are losing the usual tethers we've come to depend upon.

The small acts of constancy can help us stay centered during times of life change, transition, or any situation where our world is in flux and we're feeling scared, unsure, and bowled over by uncertainty.

During such times, it can be extraordinarily helpful to develop comfort rituals to help anchor you. Comfort rituals can be very grounding and soul-nourishing, and they are especially needed during stress and upheaval when some TLC becomes a necessity and priority.

The solidity of a familiar mug of coffee or cup of tea and time in nature helps contain us and dust off a layer of stress and fatigue. Soothing words and inspiring quotes or listening to a playlist can feel healing and supportive.

Find the people, places, and animal companions that warm you. Tap into the small things that feel comforting and help give you a sense of continuity in a shifting landscape.

A person can find their way through many a winter of the soul by depending on such tiny anchors. Little acts of faith, comfort, and grounding help us self-soothe and stay connected to something familiar as we learn how to weather life's storms and trust that eventually, things will calm again, and everything will be right as rain.

281
LEARNING TO LEAN

Life is a series of letting goes. A constant cycle of birth, death, and rebirth that evolves our relationship with ourselves and the world around us. A teacher who tells us to stop grasping so hard, open our palms, and let what we cling to fall through our fingers so life can place something new in our hands.

When we learn to do this, we learn to lean into the rhythm of life and follow its flow instead of constantly fighting the current and trying to turn back the tides of change. Most people resist their seasons of change. They don't want things to be different; they want them to stay as they were. They desire what is already secure and known and fear the ambiguous future space of what they cannot see.

Sometimes, we cling to ideas, people, jobs, material things, our notions of how things should be, and our ideals of who we should be in an effort to fight the current and try to keep the order of life to our liking.

Life is continually whispering, trying to tell us something so we can better embrace change. Yet, we often don't know how to listen and are scared to lean in. We resist, bargain, and compromise, trying to contain the change and keep the order of life as we know it, which is a bit silly if you think about how we are single-handedly trying to stop the greater process of life from happening.

This is why we must learn how to lean in. There is beauty in the lean— a sense of rightness when we yield to life and don't try to avoid, distract, or dance away from the truths it is trying to impress upon our hearts. The lean is where we can begin to trust its process, even if we don't understand our direction and can't see where our steps will take us.

The lean teaches us to let go, even if we are scared, and to tolerate our feelings of discomfort, dissonance, and fear. It also teaches us to trust that no feeling will last forever and that there is new life on the other side of release.

We can't always see the shape our days will take or know how life will work things out. But we can learn to keep learning to let go and lean— to let our loves, losses, griefs, and leans shape us. We can always remember, no matter how unforeseeable the future may seem, that life will not let us fall if we have the courage to trust it.

282
MAKING SPACE FOR UNCERTAINTY

"Life is a series of natural and spontaneous changes. Don't resist them — that only creates sorrow. Let reality be reality. Let things flow naturally forward in whatever way they like."
—Lao Tzu

There is a tendency for us to want to go back to the way things were when we've been through big changes. We feel vulnerable and uncomfortable when unsure, and we might yearn for simpler times and easier days.

Except life isn't hardwired to return to the way things were. It is hardwired for change and never returns us to the way things were but asks us to evolve ourselves in the greater process.

So, it is helpful to find ways to create a certain level of comfort with uncertainty and make space for this feeling state. We can learn to engage uncertainty with curiosity, humor, and radical acceptance. Making peace with the idea that we don't know what we don't know, and it's okay not to know.

We can embrace the principle of not knowing as a lifelong journey. We can see ourselves as travelers and adventurers who are continually discovering how to become increasingly adaptable and resilient in change. Who keep learning how to detach from the way we thought things should be and open to the way things are.

Uncertainty can feel like a tilt-o-whirl, where we don't know what twists and turns are coming next. We are invited to lean right when we think things are going left and learn to go left just when we think things are going right. We learn to better be in the experience, not take it too seriously, and try to find a sense of paradox and play.

When in doubt, keep it simple. Remember how resilient, capable, clever, and resourceful you are. Return to your heart. Do the things you can. Trust in a bigger picture. Remember that even though the world is constantly changing, some things will always hold true— nature heals, kindness rocks, grace exists, and love will always win.

283
Authenticity, Grit, and Light

Changes that keep you moving in the direction you feel you need to go often require hard choices and a bit of sacrifice. It may not be comfortable, but it does make you stand behind your choice and keep your feet solidly on your path.

There is something transformative about owning your choice. If the change were easy, if it didn't require letting go of something, if it didn't require acknowledging loss so you can move forward—it wouldn't be much of a change. You wouldn't find something new and better within yourself that will help you courageously stay your course.

This requires a lot of digging deep, finding untapped courage within, and learning that even if someone isn't holding our hand and guiding us through the change, life is holding our hand. Life is cheering us on and helping line up our next steps. And really, what better partner to have than the ever-resilient, creative, resourceful force of life itself?

Each time we let go, each time we bravely forge forward on a new path, life supports us. We find unexpected allies and respite. We are gifted with synchronicities and signs that help us keep going. Blazing our trail becomes a little less daunting, for we see there is unexpected sanctuary and support along the way.

We notice a more solid sense of belonging and strength within ourselves. We realize we are truly being our change, owning our choices, and putting action to belief. The path forward may not be the easiest, but it is wrapped in untouched beauty, wild adventure, and unparalleled authenticity, grit, and light.

284

JUMP

Change requires courage. Great, great gobs of it.

The challenge is that we want to know what known truth will come in the unknown. We want the answer before we've barely begun to explore the question. We want to know how it will work out before we've even committed to the change.

We want to guarantee that if we leap off the cliff, life will be waiting there with the safety net to lessen the fall and a guide to lead the way to uncharted territory.

We want to know that if we leave the relationship, the job, the situation, the old way of doing things, the old way of thinking, the old shell of being, the lesser skin of self— something better is waiting for us on the other side.

The strange thing about life is that the only real way to find out what's waiting is to leap without guarantee. You can't keep one foot securely on the ground and still jump. It doesn't work like that; you have to go for it.

Write your signature on the stars with your fearless fidelity of intent. Jump off the end of the precipice— crash or fly or fall or sore— trust that whatever happens next is just as important as where you'll end up.

Maybe whatever happens next, however it looks, is exactly what you need to experience for you to end up exactly where you were meant to be. There is another word for that kind of jump.

It's called faith. You can trust it. In the end, it will never let you fall.

285

Each Brave Step

There are many reasons we stay stuck. Maybe we take the keys to our personal freedom, responsibility, and freedom and hand them to someone else, making our ability to change contingent on them.

Or perhaps we find it easier to stay within the familiar lines of a comfort zone, no matter how much we dislike that space, than to wander outside the lines and find the courage to navigate a new land.

We might lack the faith to believe there is something better on the other side if we just walk across the invisible boundaries of limitation we have set in our minds.

Maybe we suddenly think we can see into the future and talk ourselves out of change, making excuses and convincing ourselves, "It won't work." We close our hearts and minds to unseen possibilities, so life is robbed of opportunities to explore these new possibilities.

Mostly, we want to bargain with life, keeping one foot safely in the land of the secure and familiar while our other foot slowly and halfheartedly dips its toe into the waters of change.

We expect things to be different without fully committing to diving in. Instead of finding change, we split ourselves between the world of the familiar and our yearning for something more. Neither get our full selves nor our best efforts, and we continue to feel tired, stuck, and convinced things can't be different.

Life doesn't work like that. Life responds to the amount of energy we put in. We wait for life to show us the way and carve out our path, while life is waiting for us to choose the direction we wish to go so it can help us create the path.

Take a step in the direction of change, and you will begin to see a path where none seemed to exist before. The ground will rise to meet you, and you will find that what once looked like a dark void of nothing is turning into a trail, bridging you into a new beginning— created through each brave step.

286
LITTLE ACTS OF CHANGE

Any day can bring a new start. A change in perspective. A change in behavior. A release of something that's not yours to carry. A step towards reclaiming something critical to your well-being.

Try on a new thought, have a new experience, learn a new word. Put on a pair of sassy yellow shoes you've been saving for a special occasion just to put a new spring in your step— any day can be the beginning of beautiful change if you choose to purpose it so.

Set an intention for things to be different. Grab onto a seed of hope. Practice radical gratitude. Smile more. Take one step in the direction of a goal or dream you've been contemplating. Envision a fresh start with a sprig of reinvigoration. Ask the universe to grant you new eyes to see your life through a wider scope.

Celebrate whatever sliver of moon is hanging in the sky. Take a walk in the woods. Spend time with an animal friend. Cook something zesty, craft something fun, or go to a space you've never been.

Make a tiny list of your favorite things. Pray in a new way. Write a poem. Discover a new song. Try something novel that feels right to your heart.

No matter how grand or small, all it takes is one little act of change to create momentum for a positive shift, and any day can bring a new start and be the beginning of beautiful change if you just choose to set an intention for growth and make it happen.

287

Chop Wood, Carry Water

When transitions and big changes happen, it can be hard to stay grounded. Unknowing terrain always comes with uncertainty, disorientation, and not knowing exactly what or how to feel.

We might find we keep shifting in feeling states: one moment, we feel positive and can-do, the next, we grapple with anxiety, unease, and long-term questions. Sometimes, we make things worse for ourselves by getting so caught up in our anxiety over what will be that we miss the opportunity to work on just being there for ourselves in the moment.

When life shifts underneath us, we are also invited into greater presence and self-love. Instead of thinking we are our feelings or mental chatter, we can witness what we're feeling and thinking, notice where we are, acknowledge our vulnerability, and practice extreme self-empathy with our experience to bring compassion into our space of self.

It is also very good to keep it simple during this process. Stop trying to figure everything out and focus on what's immediately in front of us. We need small tasks and little to-do's that help us feel more organized. To focus on nature's constancy, daily gratitudes, and putting one foot in front of the other.

There are times in life when we cannot see the bigger picture, and we're not meant to. The more we overfocus on our anxiety about the future, the more untethered we feel. In these moments, it helps to show up for ourselves with self-compassion. Focus on being in the change process instead of trying to interpret the change process and finding the acts of grounding and goodness we can do.

As the old Zen proverb goes— "Before enlightenment, chop wood, carry water. After enlightenment, chop wood, carry water." Remembering it is always enough, no matter where we find ourselves on the journey, to just show up, take class, and be a diligent student of life.

288

UNSTICKING

"In the process of letting go you will lose many things from the past, but you will find yourself."
—Deepak Chopra

Letting go isn't easy. Sometimes, we hang on knowingly, but most often, I think we don't even know we're hanging on to something until our grip is nudged and we're forced to begin to release.

This is a highly uncomfortable process. Our attachment to our attachments often acts as a psychological glue that holds together our mental constructs, beliefs, and templates for how we understand ourselves and our relationship to the world around us.

Unsticking ourselves from that is hard. Sometimes, it hurts and feels disorienting— we've untethered ourselves from older ways of being, which leaves us floating around in a void as we seek something new to ground into.

This void space is necessary for a time because it's only through the void space of release that a hollow is formed where something new can originate. New ideas, new ways of being, new attitudes, and beliefs can begin to take place. New grace can come in and fill us.

One of life's most poignant ironies is that we must let go of what has passed to free our hands and receive what life has for us now. But here, in the now, is where we are. Today is where we are. This moment is where we are. In each breath, we find the now is where our joy is found.

289
Questions for Letting Go

How do we help ourselves when we realize we are clinging to something, and we need to let go? How do we begin to create space and loosen our attachment? A good place to start is by staying curious and investigating our experience to find insight into why we feel stuck.

If we start to understand our hesitations, motivations, fears, and other unconscious patterns, we can find new awareness. We begin to see what's blocking us and how we might be holding ourselves back from experiencing greater freedom and peace of heart. This supports us in making more conscious choices to help us find a way to begin to let go.

For times of stuckness, here are a few questions that might feel helpful to use as contemplation tools and journaling prompts to better understand your dynamics and find new insight:

- What am I gaining by holding on to this?
- What is stopping me from letting go?
- Who would I be without this?
- What am I afraid will happen if I let this go?
- How would it change me if I didn't have this in my life?
- How might it feel if I were to let this go?
- How might I start releasing my attachment to this person, pattern, belief, etc.?

Stay curious. Start digging deep. Start finding your truth by figuring out what is driving you to hold on so hard. Begin figuring out where you feel stuck and take small steps towards softening your grip, doing release work, and surrendering your attachment.

As we work on loosening just one knot of our attachments, we find that other things that have been feeling knotted shift as well. We begin to feel more open. We start to see our way through what has held us back from release and feel more empowered to keep choosing new space.

290

Choosing Growth and Change

A time might come when we look back on our choices and say something like, "Wow, I've really blown it." We smack into regrets and self-blame. We obsess about where we went wrong; self-recriminations become quicksand, and we feel more stuck the more we ruminate and dwell.

We can't get over ourselves or what we think we did wrong. We know we should have chosen better, and yet we didn't. We blame and fixate without realizing the more we do this, the more we just keep hanging on and staying stuck.

It's okay. You're okay. We've all been there. Take a deep breath. Your inner light is still intact. If the only way out is through, you can find what you need to make it through and move in a new direction.

Nothing in life is ever beyond change or without redemption. If we can remember that we are souls on a human journey, here to learn as we go and grow, then we can begin to find a little more grace and courage to face ourselves with compassion and care. We can find what we need to let go of where we've been, confront our vulnerability and fallibility, and choose a better way.

Things are never hopeless, and we are never helpless. But we do need patience in the process of embracing change. We can't unknot a tangled ball of yarn with one pull; sometimes, things take a little while to untangle. As we work on addressing the snares and snags in our thread, we'll find that life's grace meets us in this space and assists us in gently easing the knots.

Begin where you can. Start with something small. Start with honesty and self-scrutiny about your desire to act on your behalf and change. Identify a proactive step you can take and then take that step. Ask for support. Learn to be vulnerable. Stay humble.

Commit to a path of growth and change. Look to others who have also chosen growth and change, then surround yourself with their stories, inspirations, and encouragements. Know that change is possible. Know that you are worth change.

Know that nothing is irredeemable or irreparable under the light of love's gaze— including you, dear one, including you.

291
THE FACE OF CHANGE

"The only way to make sense out of change is to plunge into it, move with it, and join the dance."
—Alan Wilson Watts

Yes. Surrendering into your heart and the heart of the universe will take you in directions others haven't trod.

Perhaps your choices won't add up on paper. Perhaps your successes won't look like others. Perhaps you won't know where you'll be called from one month to the next or how your life will look. But it will be beautiful. It will be magical.

You will learn things you couldn't learn any other way, and you will grow in ways you couldn't grow any other way.

Sometimes, growth happens in mysterious ways. We spiral and corkscrew upside down. The notes in our song get all mixed up until we realize we've been writing a symphony out of order, and we begin to see our bigger composition.

We can go from feeling lost to found overnight. Realize we grew wings from hardship and strife. We can feel directionless and like we can't see our way through, yet still be moving towards our light.

Trusting there is wild joy when we release the reigns and move more deeply into a relationship of trust, surrender, and faith. Sometimes equilibrium is found by learning to fly sideways, softly, swiftly— straight into the face of change.

292
A Clear Heart Ready to Receive

It's never easy to let go of the people and things that may have hurt us or the pieces in our life that didn't entirely turn out as expected— but those energetic, emotional, and situational endings are often the catalyst required for a new beginning.

Living with the clutter from the past is the equivalent of emotional hoarding and will only prevent us from having clean and open spaces to receive the gifts of the present.

We have to learn to clear out the space in our hearts, so we have a new room to shift our focus to the things meant for us. We clear that space by feeling it to reveal, heal, and release it, which, admittedly, is never easy; some emotions and feeling states are difficult to process and grapple with.

Yet part of being human is feeling it all— the grime, the gloss, and all the hidden gold in between— and remembering that our emotions are just information flowing through. What matters most is how we choose to work with that information and embrace the opportunity to practice radical forgiveness and grace in our relationships with ourselves.

Allowing for all our feeling states and aspects of being. Learning to see them as part of a greater ecosystem of soul. Choosing to work on releasing whatever doesn't serve us— even if it's hard to let go.

Everybody deserves clean, open, honest spaces. Let go. Clear space. Cut a cord. Do a ritual. Listen to a sound bath. Donate a box of stuff. Release it to the full moon. Press your palms against the earth and shed your psychic debris, trusting it will be composted into new life.

Find both practical and symbolic ways to let go as many times as you need. Stay with this for as long as you need. Sometimes, letting go isn't a one-time process but an ongoing commitment to release, so we can keep moving forward with a free and clear heart ready to receive.

293
BREATHING OUR WAY THROUGH ANYTHING

A good bit of chaos and discontent is often needed to help clear space and help us reflect on how we're doing in life. Change is disruptive but also creates space. Space to sift. Space to evaluate. Space to be in the mess. Space to trust. Space to receive.

Space to breathe. Because if we're still breathing, it means we are here. Here, in this love. Here, in this universe. Here in this space. Here, at this moment.

Here is a miracle in its own right: here is a possibility. Here is a chance for better. Here is what it is to be human. Here is life.

Even on the darker days, it is a gift to be here rather than not here. Each time we take the simplest of breaths, we can be reminded of our "here-ness" and the possibilities of our lives. Un-Zen stuff can happen. We can still have an irate chat with life about why.

We can also learn to keep an open heart and listen. We can learn to respond. We can learn to breathe, receive, and be. We can learn to tolerate ambiguity, restlessness, and angst through curiosity, space, and breath.

We can learn to breathe our way through anything, and, in the words of my younger, poetic-mermaid-soul self, we can remember—

"It will be okay: life. What life knows we need and what we think we need are often not the same.
But there are endless opportunities to find your way along the path, a million possibilities alight in the sky of who you can be, and if you learn to turn your heart inside out, you'll see love has been there all along.
Laugh and do not fret— a heart can change in the span of a blink. You're doing better than you think. And the truth of the universe can be held in a single breath."

—Cranberry Dusk

294

The Wild Unknown

It takes courage to be vulnerable and sink into your own space of change. To let the silk cocoon of the unknown wrap around you for as long as you need until it falls away and you see your path with clarity.

Most people fear this space and do what they can to avoid it. They try to hit rewind, reboot, reset, and make things return to how they used to be. Even the body responds differently in this space, as the nervous system searches for certainty and something to anchor itself to; anxiety and fear are easy companions to find here.

I think of this space as the wild unknown and liken it to being dropped off in a spiritual wilderness and forced to find your path. Trusting your soul to help you navigate in the dark. Trusting that the right support will come along at the right time. Trusting that you have been called here for a reason and that you will be given invisible guides who help you along the way.

Some days, you're in awe of the vast beauty surrounding you—there is so much space for growth and room to stretch out and explore, and you realize that learning to navigate by starlight is a gift.

Other days, you realize how scary it is to feel so alone in uncharted territory, and you work to calm the mental chatter that tells you to turn back, realizing there is no going back; there is only moving forward.

Most days, though, you aren't quite sure how to feel, caught somewhere between who you once were and who you are becoming. So, you try to let your body and heart feel whatever they need to feel and reassure yourself that although the soul process may feel invisible, it is very real, and you can trust it. It is your soul, after all.

You have not been called to the wild unknown in vain, and you have universes within you that will help you find your way through. So, you trek across new terrain, finding new ground and gifts on the journey you didn't realize existed until you arrived in that space.

Trusting the divinity in your soul knows exactly what it is doing, even if your human mind can't always see the full picture. Trusting your internal compass to lead you where you need to go. Trusting you are never alone, even when it feels like it.

Trusting, trusting, trusting.

295

TIDES

Life has a way of moving us along. Crisscrossing and interweaving us in endless spirals of overlap and letting go. Sometimes towards one another and sometimes apart; the siphoning of being moved apart from one another is usually more painful and stretching than the connectivity and receptivity of moving towards.

We are not meant to stay the same throughout our timelines, nor are our relationships meant to stay the same. Relationships are fluid, dynamic, and subject to growth. Change happens to us individually and happens to us with each other.

It can be difficult to experience changes in a relationship, sometimes downright heart-ripping and mind-splitting. I have found the more abrupt the change is, the more we are left with feelings of disturbance and irresolution and the more we may struggle to accept the change.

But I have also found that it is possible to make peace and accept something that feels unacceptable if you just make a little space to accept that part of it may never feel okay. In this paradox, we find the crux of letting go— we must learn to make space for our whole experience of self in the matter.

Sadness. Regret. Reminiscence. Good Memories. Wishes that it was different. Anger. Confusion. Grudging acceptance. Forgiveness. The pain of separation and the echo of something we once belonged to and no longer do. The light and the dark. The love and the hate.

The only way I know to embrace change is by learning to embrace the whole of who we are. We can't learn to let go if we are turning a blind eye to or willfully engaging in denial of part of ourselves. And we can't let go of somebody we have loved— whatever the nature of that love— if we don't acknowledge the part of ourselves that wants to hang on.

Sometimes, the best we can do is take the hand of the part who wants to stay and stick and gently say with the utmost care, "There, there, my dear one, I know this space was beautiful in its time, but there is no life for you here anymore." Then, help that part of ourselves continue to learn how to turn their face towards the light of what is ahead.

Such is the paradoxical nature of change. We can't fight the tide of life. Nor were we meant to, for no matter how resistant our minds may feel, it is in the nature of our soul to reach for change. We have a way of seeking expansion, even when we don't always know what we are seeking. And life has a way of moving us along.

296

STRINGS

How human it is to want to hold onto something. Yet how transcendent it is to let go in love, an act that speaks to the core of unconditional love.

Because unconditional love releases strings and expectations, it just is. Pure and undiluted in any situation. We learn to love simply for the act of loving, without an expectation attached to what and who we love.

We learn to love without promises or guarantees. And so, if the time comes when what we love needs to change or grow, we can choose to unstring, release, and let go. Because, ultimately, that's what love does. It lets go.

We can learn that when we release and let go, there is always new life and new gifts on the other side. That doesn't mean there won't be bumps, grief, hurt, and heartaches throughout the process.

It doesn't mean life won't tip sideways during the change and throw curveballs at us. It just means, on a fundamental level, when we yield to life, release the strings, and try and lean into the change— there will always be new life and love waiting.

297

BALLOONS

As much as I'd like to be like the proverbial girl in the picture about to release the last of her balloons, I have never found release this easy.

Letting go of something doesn't occur in one fell swoop or a single instance.

It happens in small bits and pieces: the time you cry it out over there, the time you sit with your sadness over here. It happens in the quiet of your waking hours, and it happens deep in your subconscious as you sleep.

It happens as you bravely step forward and create new memories to add to your timeline that help soften the distance between the immediacy of the things you're trying to release. It happens in giant bursts, small drops, and all the in-between moments where you find yourself just trying to do the work of living life.

Letting go is a process and not an immediate one. We are best served by releasing all expectations of time constraints on when we should let go. Twenty-five years might pass, and your heart will still ache in that same spot, reminding you of the magnitude of the consequences that occupied that place.

Hold those balloons for as long as you need, and only release them when you know it is time. We'll let go when we let go, in our heart's way, in our heart's time, trusting that whatever is released will always return in new form and new light.

298

MOVING FORWARD

You don't have to move forward. Moving forward is a choice, not a requirement. Sometimes, staying in the same place can be a good thing. Staying in the same space isn't always stuck.

Staying in the same space is sometimes a break, pause, or rest. It's getting a quarter of the way along the trail, knowing you have a way to go, and judiciously taking a respite, allowing yourself time to breathe and reflect before you get up and begin taking those next few steps.

Grief. Trauma. Heartache. The hard stuff. We don't like to see people uncomfortable; it's hard for us. So, these are all areas in our lives where it will be more comfortable for other people to see you move forward than stay where you are, and they may not get why you appear to be in the same place.

But they are not you. They may not know that your lungs are almost empty, and it will take you a while to fill them back up. Or that something is cracked or broken, and so, you're going to have to find healing where you are before you find what you need to move forward. Or that you're plain old, not ready. And that is okay.

Moving forward is a choice, and you should make it when your heart feels ready, and you realize that staying in the same spot is not serving you.

You might find you've filled your lungs up and healed your cracks as much as you can from your current vantage point, but you can't find deeper breaths until you've cleared the muggy thick of the trees. You can't find deeper healing in your current space of self because you will only transcend that space if you stretch beyond and venture forth.

When you realize those things, you know you're being called to move. You'll know the sunlight is beckoning you, asking you to receive its medicine of hope. You'll know that life has new gifts if you dare to release and step into new terrain. You'll know that though you'll never forget where you have been, it now feels okay to think about where you'd like to go.

Most of all, you'll know that your own pace of self and process of movement is humanly, divinely, imperfectly perfect for you.

299

THE LOVE INSIDE

Sometimes, we want to hang onto what we've left behind. We tunnel back into old memories, cling to nostalgia, and yearn for a time that has passed. It's as if we are keeping something we've lost alive inside of ourselves. We resist moving forward, clinging to every little memory like precious jewels.

We don't want life to move on; we want things the way they were. Every step away from how things were is a step towards something new, foreign, and highly uncomfortable. Embracing the present moment means that life is moving on when we are afraid to let go.

It is profoundly beautiful how deeply humans hold onto what they have loved. It is difficult for us to release the reigns back to life, acknowledge that life is moving on, and admit that we don't know what the future holds. The future is always an unwritten possibility. It is new, foreign, and highly uncomfortable. It is okay to feel lost until we find our way again.

It is so achingly human to fear letting go, yet here is the vital thing we must remember to free ourselves for the present: the love inside, we take it with us.

It will always live on— beyond the physical, circumstances, timelines, and change. Love is greater than death, and so it can never be taken from us, even when those we've loved have gone on.

The new experiences, beauty, and love in our lives do not diminish what was there before. They only strengthen and enhance it. Memories may fade, and, indeed, every step towards what will be is a step away from what was, but we are not here to stay in the same place.

We are here to venture into the new, foreign, and uncomfortable. We are here to learn about love. Learning about love requires great courage to face the come what mays. It requires loss. It requires the admission things have changed. It requires letting go of what was, so we can make room for who and what we'll be.

That's okay, though, because, in the end, we will never lose what matters most. It will always live on through new loves, new experiences, and new characters in our scripts. Wherever we go, we take it with us— the love inside.

300

On Leave-takings, Becoming, and New Springs

"I said to the sun, 'Tell me about the big bang.' The sun said, 'it hurts to become.'"

—Andrea Gibson

Usually, the harder we try to hang onto something and resist change, the more likely it is that we should release and let go. We love the idea of rebirths and new springs: the transformations that come after intense conflicts in our lives, which encourage us to make positive changes that take us to the next step in our journey. A chrysalis followed by the butterflied flap of new wings. The life getting ready to spring up after incubating in the decay of fall all winter long.

But it is harder and sadder to contemplate the loss, the release, the cessation, the death, the leave-takings that precede new beginnings. Endings come in many forms, from a quiet acknowledgment that gently nudges us into accepting a chapter is closing to the rupturing heartbreak that leaves a path of wreckage. We wonder if anything will ever be okay again and what possible metamorphosis can come from such devastation.

Though it has the potential for exquisite transformation, letting go often comes with the price of pain. And how we like to avoid pain by constructing illusions of security. We bargain with the universe to avoid change, reassuring ourselves that this moment will last forever, though we know it won't.

We cannot bear to contemplate the loss of something, so instead of embracing change, we throw up walls against it to convince ourselves that life will stay the same when the truth is that the only thing permanent is impermanence.

Some people spend their lives in denial and avoidance of the pain of the road not taken and miss living the road they are currently on. Living often requires us to walk straight through the pain to break our hearts so wide open we emerge into a deeper and more brilliant love for ourselves, the world, and our lives when we reach the other side.

We find new gifts, though, when we choose a new beginning. A deeper sense of gratitude for the sacred wonder in our world. A heightened appreciation for the gift of the present moment. A greater acceptance of the life, death, and rebirth cycle, which teaches us that all endings lead to new beginnings— we are asked to stay open to both.

For myself, my prayer has always been that I try and accept my leave-takings as they come with grace, dignity, and an open heart; allow myself to continue becoming; and embrace the rebirth that comes after loss, for there will always be new springs.

One could spend a lifetime answering this prayer. It would be a life of becoming. It would be a life very, very well spent.

301

THE SACRED TOTALITY

I've never quite grown used to the psychological discomfort of change. When I'm going through big changes in my life, it can often still leave me feeling vaguely uncertain, unanchored, and strange. As if I'm grieving something or losing something I can't entirely understand, even as I feel an ambiguous premonition that something new is seeding itself within this space.

Despite the discomfort, I have learned the lesson many times by now that we are here for change. Life will keep changing. Things will die off. Something will be born. We attach and detach over and over. We love and grieve. Joy and sorrow. And the world carries on.

I have also learned that if we can transcend the density of our pain and try to find the light in loss, tragedy, and uncertainty, it can all become a chance to embody each moment we are given as best we can. We don't disown or reject anything but learn to embrace, own it all, and find the wisdom.

I call this carrying our full. We can carry the full in our grief and love, own and stretch and delve into whatever emotional experience we have on each given day, embrace the presence of a moment— whether we like it or not— and live more courageously, honestly, and boldly. We can simply sit still and belong to this world.

We can see the sacred totality of our lives.

We were never promised that life would look a certain way. We were only promised a chance to make the most of what comes our way. We were given our spark of self, soul growth, a chance at humanity, and a chance to evolve our hearts. We were given opportunities to learn about love in all its diverse forms.

We were given the gifts of possibility, growth, hope, falling deeper into love, reaching and lengthening, and evolving into bigger, more nuanced beings. We can hurt when we hurt, celebrate when we joy, carry our losses in our hearts, and let those losses strengthen us in love and affirm our humanity.

This is how we embrace it all: stay open to life. Let your heart break when it needs. Contract and then expand. Try to focus on the wisdom gained and not the pain. Take all experiences into you and let them nurture this process. Grow in love and keep growing in this fullness. Give gratitude as often as you can for the sacred totality that is our lives.

302
WE OPEN AT THE CLOSE

We hold the potential to find new openings when life hands us a close— openings that can help us realize the alchemical mystery of life. After we've done the release work of change and grief, after we braved the nebula of not knowing and traveled the black box of nothingness in our lives, life begins to bravely grow once more.

The clouds in our minds begin to open— we notice a few sunlit rays of hope. A rainbow arcs in the sky— we feel a flicker of inspiration. We meet a new kindness— we notice our heart is warmed by it, and something that felt inwardly frozen has begun to thaw.

We bravely trudge forward, taking steps to move on, and despite our reservations and lingering feelings of uncertainty, yearning, and grief— we see the potential for new life to form. We realize our heart hasn't died with the loss of what was, just a piece of it, which has been busy mourning and taking respite.

But the whole of our heart has always remained intact, and in this new opening, new light gently surrounds the space that feels closed off and dead inside of us— a daffodil pops up; the first sign of spring. We notice our inner soil has fresh nutrients of strength and resilience to help us grow towards the sunlight. We know that we cannot replace what we've lost, but we can embrace the hope of new beginnings.

This is a gift. This magic alchemy and ongoing dance of the life, death, and rebirth cycle teaches us that nothing is ever final but always returns to us in new shape and form. Perhaps not as we'd known it before, but if we can keep courage about ourselves and continue to do our work of making friends with uncertainty and change, we will find bright beauty in this new space.

Maybe at some point, we'll even find a few shreds of teary-eyed gratitude where we thank our closings for bringing us our openings, bowing our heads in reverence at life's strange beauty, and great mysteries, and the undefinable, astounding ways love continues to reveal itself in our lives.

303

Dancing Leaves

Any undoing, shedding, or losing creates a space where life has room to pour new things into us. Endings are a genesis for potential. Metamorphosis happens in the void when we must find a way through the darkness.

It is the metaphorical space where the caterpillar reaches the end of his world and becomes a butterfly: desperation provides the ingredients for inspiration, chaos the material for creation. The space where the leaf learns to free itself by falling from the tree, returning to the ground so it can become the soil and seed for new life.

It can feel terrible when life brings us to the end of the world as we know it, to the end of something inside ourselves. When we can't see anything but black space beyond our current space, we are left to trust that if we go forward, relinquish control, and have faith in the process, we will discover our chrysalis.

We all have our paths to this precipice of change. We arrive through the loss of a relationship, through hardship and difficulty, through illness and injury. Through the end of a chapter, we sometimes realize we were done writing long before we set down the pen. Sometimes, we are deposited here unceremoniously when we suddenly lose something we never believed we would lose, and we find ourselves at the mercy of life's forces.

We are brought here so we can choose whether to contract in fear, trying to squeeze ourselves back into an old shell of self that no longer fits, or to expand in faith, venturing into the black space of the unknown, believing we will find new ground if we are brave enough to see the journey through.

The journey requires a great deal of surrender, for it is only in letting go of how we think things should be that we can develop into who we are meant to be: a never-ending cycle of dancing leaves who learn to grow when it is time to grow and when to drop when life calls us to release. We are undone so that we can become.

304

LET THE SHADOWS FALL BEHIND YOU

"Keep your face always toward the sunshine—and shadows will fall behind you."
—Walt Whitman

Letting go is not for the faint of heart. After all, not everyone can defy sorrow by turning their face to the sunlight and still choose joy despite their knowledge of the night.

Not everyone can release broken dreams on the golden wings of days gone by, fixing their gaze toward the ocean's soft, forgiving lines. The sea reminds us to be in the flow of right now, for only love endures, and all else will pass in time.

Not everyone can take a broken heart, smashed against life's shores of hard-chipped pain. And rebuild it into something bigger than before, staying open to their change.

So, if you happen to find yourself in such a space where life is asking you to relinquish, release, and trust in its unknown grace—

Then, remember the scope of your brave. Know that all we release will come 'round in new ways.

Each fleeting beat of life's sweetness is worth the bitter tang, and in the place where grief and love meet, your heart will mend again.

305

The Ongoing Unknowing

It happens in layers and waves, over many moon cycles, sea tides, and the turns of the season's trees. We peel back old pieces, release mistruths, and shed pale imitations as we move closer to our authentic selves.

It's not a one-time process but an ongoing unknowing of self so we can know ourselves in more soulful ways: we unbecome to become. We unknit old threads to knit the new; we wander outside old lines to discover new terrain.

We heal in small intentional increments, big messy squiggles, and little grace notes that help us patch together a bigger, wiser mosaic of self.

We lose ourselves to find ourselves and then find ourselves again. All of it working together in a gorgeous alchemical process of soul as we keep moving closer to love, our purpose, and our truth.

If we can find joy in the unknown, embrace our void, trust things to unfold, and remember that love knows us and we know love, then love becomes the thread that keeps leading us through the labyrinth of change and bringing us to a new beginning.

This is one of life's greatest mysteries and endless treasures—the ongoing unknowing.

I will never be able to put language to the infinite mysteries of the heart's ability to be perennial; something dies, and something new is reborn; we grieve, and our grief waters the grounds for a new life, and somehow grace wraps around it all.

But I will gratefully put my trust in this bigger process, stay my course, and put my faith in the path of love.

Pearls of Wisdom on Happiness, Creativity, and Meaning

306
ON THE EXPLORATION OF HAPPINESS

Happiness is many things: a choice, a gift, a state of mind, and a state of heart. Some find it fleeting and hard to grasp, while others find ways to create a more sustainable relationship with it.

I love the exploration of happiness. It is a lifelong journey, and my relationship with it changes as I change and discover different facets of what it means to be happy.

Sometimes, these facets complement each other, and sometimes, they are more disparate. But I keep finding that no matter what facet I'm exploring, these things about happiness are overarching principles that hold true:

Our relationship to happiness is closely tied to our relationship with intention, creativity, meaning, peace, and gratitude. When we cultivate any of these qualities, they enhance, heighten, and amplify each other.

Feeling happy is not necessarily the same thing as being happy; nuance matters when it comes to the question of happiness.

We each deserve to define happiness for ourselves. We can share each other's ideas and wisdom on this subject to grow our own understanding. However, ultimately, happiness is an experience we are invited to partake in and map out for ourselves.

We can still work on creating and choosing happiness— or at least aim for the general vicinity of appreciation, warmth, and goodness— despite life's pain.

The choice to move towards happiness can become a loving act of rebellion against the collective weight of stress, struggle, and chaos that often drags us down and threatens to steal our joy.

Never underestimate the power of your imagination to turn a mundane day into a grand adventure and insist on finding color, happiness, and joy.

307

MEANING, WHIMSY, AND LAUGHTER

It is not so much about what happens as about the meaning we attach to it. The stories we tell ourselves about what happens to us determine our perspective, viewpoint, and story arc.

We can write ourselves out of dark situations. We can look for the untold story of the superhero in disguise. We can tell a story of becoming, courage, resilience, hope, and perseverance.

Our interpretation of life makes the difference between having a bad day and having a good day. We can choose to be a victim or empowered, feel in lack or have abundance, be resentful or peaceful, feel entitled or grateful, feel unloved or loved, or see life as an enemy or friend.

Narratives create the lens through which we see the world; the longer we tell ourselves something, the more we believe it.

People with peaceful, happy hearts don't arrive at that space inside because everything goes right in their lives. They have a happy heart because they've learned to take their lemons and write a story about learning to make lemonade through perspective, meaning, and intention.

Even when our stories feel dark, we can find ways to bring in authenticity, grace, and compassion. We can still notice the strengths, look for the gems and pearls buried beneath the sediment, and write about the courage it takes to be human.

Our self-talk and thought constructs matter greatly, and our words hold great power to shape our world. So, choose them judiciously. Kindly. Generously. Graciously.

Ascribe the meaning of your life you wish to make, and please throw in a great deal of humor for good measure. Goodness knows that life just goes down a little easier when one keeps meaning-making, whimsy, and laughter close to one's heart.

308

HERE AT THE INTERSECTION OF LIFE AND GRACE

Life is not here at our issuance; we are here by life's invitation. We are not owed or entitled to its gifts and, as such, can choose to respond accordingly as gracious guests who show up in appreciation or not.

Life is not happening to us. We are happening. And life is happening. Where the two intersect, we have our personal experiences and timelines. Every day, we are called to be active participants in that timeline, choosing how best to utilize the considerable resources we've been given, like our minds, time, thoughts, intents, wills, and hearts.

Life and you. You and life. It's a symbiotic relationship. It can take a while to figure all this out and shift from a self-centric point of view to a heart-centric perspective.

The heart knows that we are continually invited to step into a softer gaze that includes the qualities of intention, compassionate detachment, forgiveness, and warmth. When we engage from the heart space and decide to take life up on its offer to participate with it mindfully, a profound sense of gratitude opens for every little thing.

Gratitude is no longer limited to externals that have to do with status, accomplishments, achievements, or prestige. Instead, gratitude becomes an internal state of appreciation—

The loveliness of a blue sky, the awareness of breath, and the love of a faithful animal companion. The colors of nature, the kindness of strangers, the minuscule simple things that compound into greater moments of peace and contentment.

You realize that the possibility for goodness and joy is unfolding before you with each passing moment— here, in the heart space, at the intersection of life and grace.

309
Every Day, a New Creation

Every day, we create something new. A kindness. A gratitude. A discontent. A fear. A love. An imagining. A joy. A presence. A dream. A hope. A grief. A peace.

All of it is a creation— each moment we are here— even if we don't realize we are creating. The more mindful we are about our relationship to creativity, the more we can bring intention to the process and reflect on what we want to make of our days.

The point isn't to judge our creations as better than or worse than, but to embrace our creations and appreciate the sum of art. Even on our difficult days, we can create a moment for self-love and discover a new insight into what it means to be human.

All colors have value if we choose to see the value. And if we don't like the colors we are using on the canvas of our lives? We can always make changes and focus our creative efforts on generating more of the things we'd like to focus on.

Whether we see ourselves as artists or not, we are still artists who hold the tools to sculpt, carve, and paint our lives through utilizing the treasures in our experience, finding meaning so we give our lives shape, and cultivating curiosity and discovery so we can keep living with intention and openness.

Each day, an opportunity to say— "I wonder what I shall create?"

310
Meeting Happiness Halfway

"There are always flowers for those who want to see them."
—Henri Matisse

As with any other relationship, our relationship with happiness is reciprocal and does not happen passively; it requires us to actively participate in the relationship.

We can become active participants by creating opportunities for happiness, developing a perspective rooted in gratitude, and taking the time to notice and reflect on the good when good things come our way.

We can choose to be fiercely protective about our right to feel happy. We become vigilant gardeners who diligently tend to the weeds in our lives that block the growth of more vitalizing, beautiful things.

As with all the best things in life, happiness is an inside job. It has less to do with our external circumstances and more with our perspectives, beliefs, and the degree to which we choose to open our hearts and how we choose to see the world.

The potential for peace, contentment, and happiness is happening right now. It is reaching for us and moving in our direction. It is up to us to take a few steps toward it, so we put ourselves in its path and meet happiness halfway.

311

Finding Sunshine on a Drizzly Day

"Happiness is a choice that requires effort at times."
— Aeschylus

Some days feel dreary and drizzly, and it's easy to get into a dreary and drizzly mindset. Like an automatic default setting that leaves us feeling kind of sad, tired, and gray. Which just won't do for any length of time if we wish to live with greater well-being, vitality, and peace.

When we feel ourselves falling into the drizzle of default, it is also an invitation to find a wider lens and see the day as we want to see it. This has less to do with our circumstances and more to do with what we want to experience—

Self-love. Kindness. Wonder. Breath. Grace. Ease. Appreciation. Imagination. Connection. Warmth. Forgiveness. Creativity. Rainbows. Poetry. Peace.

These are all ways we find sunlight in the drizzle. While creating our own sunshine can take a little effort and make us exercise our minds and challenge our perspectives— our minds, our lives, our thoughts, our smiles, our laughter, our joys, our passions, and our experiences are at stake.

Maybe that's worth a little bit of effort on our behalf. Maybe remembering what's at stake can help us remember that there is always some form of sunshine to be found in any season in life.

Even if it means we work for it, stretch ourselves, and remember how to reach toward the light on life's gray days.

312

THE ART THAT IS YOU

You are one of a kind. Your authenticity, your unique way of being in the world, your alchemy, which brews and potions an elixir of real and goodness as only you can. It is invaluable, the essence you bring.

So, don't distrust yourself. Or discredit your dreams and the visions in your heart. Please don't dismiss the new pieces of you that you are slowly gathering, even if you don't entirely understand them. Good things take time to come together— including the good things within you.

You are allowed to collect, sort, figure yourself out as you go, and keep reinventing yourself. This world needs the art that is you and the beauty you bring that is unique to your being. This is your essence and your soul.

Keep asking the questions: What meaning can I create with my life? What meaning does life have to teach me? The meaning we make gives our lives subtext and context and directs our path, helping us stay connected to our true north.

So, adventure on. Don't overthink it. Be imperfect. Be messy and glorious. Allow for new ways of doing things and new truths. Be original. Stay curious. Try out new colors. Try new ways of being.

See yourself as an evolving art; let the process of creativity both inform and form you. Paint your life and your world into being with each unique experience, and pay attention to the colors that life brings to the equation as well.

Remember, it's about reciprocity. We are in a creative relationship with the sentient universe around us. Our thoughts, wishes, hopes, dreams, actions, intents, goals, and the unique art we each have to offer the world mean something and shape our path.

When those desires intersect with what the world offers to shape us and teach us what we are here to learn on our journey, we find life's sweet spot where creativity, destiny, and discovery meet.

313
Progressions on the Path of Happiness Circa 2013

I used to think of happiness as those blithe, carefree periods when you felt on top of the world. While I still consider those wonderful, magic times a part of being happy, they weren't always sustainable.

Some days, life is really hard. It doesn't mean it isn't still beautiful or I can't find happiness.

These days, my relationship with happiness is deeper, quieter, and more peaceful. It is rooted in something with greater gravity inside of myself. It is being able to look with courage at what is sorrowful, ugly, and painful in the world and in myself, and still find peace, beauty, and wonder.

For me, that is happiness: the fullness of our experience. Embracing the All. It's a more generous description than I ever allowed it to be, but I have found it real and sustainable, filled with self-compassion and a gentle embrace of the fullness of my life.

On those days when the stars line up and I am floating on cloud nine for no particular reason, that gets to be extra good icing on the cake— with buttercream roses.

314
RESISTANCE AND INSISTENCE

There is value in fully acknowledging and expressing our emotions. Feelings are just part of being human, and our frustration, anger, confusion, disappointment— basically all the hard stuff— always have lessons to teach us. Always, always.

I don't believe in skipping over them if you feel them. They absolutely deserve exploration and expression. Sometimes, you must hang out with them for quite a while and get to know them; you must meet and greet your difficult feelings before releasing them.

However, I have also come to value my right to be happy and learned that a happy heart is a peaceful heart. A peaceful heart chooses to move through hard feelings and not let them fester. It requires finding forgiveness, letting go, and accepting the past to move life forward.

When our hearts are in a space of peace, we realize that authentic, sustainable happiness isn't about self-gratification. It is about self-actualization and taking the harder road of integrity and compassion to keep pushing through negativity and expanding our access to love.

As such, I have found that I'm motivated to insist on finding ways to get back to my center when I'm knocked sideways. To fight for perspective and wisdom, which sees life as a friendly ally instead of "Why is life doing this to me?" To take a stand for my right to experience joy and not let that be taken away based on something else, somebody else, or circumstances.

It's easy to stay in that sideways space when life isn't going our way. It's easy to develop stories that will subtly and blatantly give away our power. It's easy to allow circumstances to be our set point instead of being the creators of our set point.

All those things are easy, but they don't help us create fuller, more satisfying lives and limit our sense of possibility, magic, and wonder. And we deserve to live our best lives filled with astonishment and awe.

Even if we have to insist, resist, and persist in embodying a heart where possibility, magic, and wonder exist.

315
THE CULTIVATION OF GRATITUDE

Gratitude can be an elusive thing if it's not carefully cultivated. I've often said we have to be relentless in our relationship with gratitude. We can't wait for it to come to us; we must go to it, invite it in, and look for ways to bring it into our moments and days.

Sometimes, it's easy to tap into, but sometimes, it's harder to find. Yet just because you can't see the sun on a cloudy day doesn't mean it isn't still up there, shining above it all and beaming in the sky.

There are days when we must look for the sun. Notice the places its light is peeping through. Swing higher than the clouds to catch a glimpse of glow. Reflect on the gifts it's already illuminated and grown in our lives.

Like the ability to breathe. Laugh. Live and love. The ability to feel and learn from your feelings. The ability to not know and think about it and the chance to figure it out.

The possibility that comes with each new day. The opportunity to notice the beauty and to find meaning and purpose as you go. The liberty to make mistakes, learn, change, and become. The reassuring rhythm of nature, whose rhythms and seasons remind us that life is not a controlled environment, but life will always go on and find a way to grow.

Even on our hard days, we can try to grab onto something good. Pull it into our hearts and find the gifts. Insist upon appreciation, revelation, and the solace that comes from learning how to bring oneself back to a space of acknowledgment and reverence for life.

Transcend old setpoints, neural patterns, and messages from a lost culture that say, "I need X to be content, peaceful, and free." Instead, we can demand and claim our right to find contentment, peace, and freedom on our own terms.

Terms whose only guideline says: tapping into gratitude and the sacred is a heart state available to us right now— it's just up to us to learn to choose it.

316

THE PLACES JOY LIVES

Joy will spontaneously find us at times, but I often think we must find it by developing an eye for it, where we take the time to see the spaces that joy is already living.

The love of an old dog. The beauty of fresh flowers. The cheerful color of golden sunflower. Fluffy things. New sky and moonlight. Taking time to count our blessings. Soft sheets and naps. Fresh breezes and warm mugs of comfort drink. Monster cookies. Rainbows. Finding any cause to celebrate. The mood boost you get when you smile.

Somewhere along the way, we lose our childlike sense of wonder and delight. Adulthood can be heavy, and joy seems a silly luxury, yet the energy of joy is holy energy. It makes us feel lighter, brighter, more at peace, and at ease.

We laugh more, and wherever there is laughter, there is always love. In those moments, we feel more connected and can transcend the drama of this world and our own mental chatter. The energy of joy invites us to appreciate and be.

Be in the moment. Focus on the good. Notice what matters. Notice the good things surrounding you and cultivate the energy of the feelings evoked by those good things.

In those moments of being, we are invited to remember that joy is our birthright and our natural state of soul. And so, every time we tap into its radiant energy of light, we are, in essence, returning home.

317

THE PALETTE OF YOU

Sometimes, the harder you look for something and try to force it, the more elusive it becomes.

Sit back. Be calm. Love yourself. Live well. Smile a lot. Create a life that you love. Nurture and tend to your inner garden and let it bloom. Learn to be the art of you.

Find joy in all the ways you can. Never underestimate the impact of small acts of kindness or the difference grace can make. Find the laughter. Find the good. Be wise.

Take good care of yourself. Tune out when you need to ground. Listen to your intuition. Allow your heart to lead. Transmute darkness into color. Keep space for whimsy, hope, and compassion.

Be happy with yourself, and if you're not happy with yourself, commit to discovering how to cultivate inner happiness.

Life will not withhold the good things meant for you. After all, they are meant for you, not somebody else, and so while you are busy tending to the happiness in your heart, you can trust that life is busy tending to bring you more happy things.

The right people, the right opportunities, the right situations, and the good things your heart desires will come along at the right time, increasing the joy and value in your life.

Adding, enhancing, and giving a new dimension to the giant stock of love you have already created within the palette of you.

318

CELEBRATING WEE VICTORIES

Remember how far you've come and a time when you might have wanted what you have now.

It's a strange paradox in life that we work so very hard to reach a goal or life stage, and then once we do, we become used to it and turn our sights to the next thing we wish to dream, achieve, or create.

This is why it can be so helpful to take stock and reflect on our journey from time to time. Make little lists of all that is going right and celebrate all the wee victories and micro wins, even if some days those wins are completing simple tasks and checking off the mundane to-dos of life.

It's important to remember how far we've come, the challenges we've already overcome, the growth we've experienced, and the wisdom we've gained through the lessons we've experienced. For many of us, there was once a time when we wanted what we have now.

Now we are here. Are we happier? Do we feel satisfied? Do we feel content, or have we already become used to this space and are restless for something else?

Reflecting on our lives with a thankful heart helps us develop appreciation and respect for our journey. It helps us shift our minds from a negative space of regret and lack to a gentler space of wholeness and self-acceptance.

Acceptance is always a more peaceful, soulful place. Acceptance creates space and self-grace. Accept reminds us that all is still well. Acceptance is good medicine for our hearts and opens us up to receive and be at ease in life's flow.

319
Happiness is the Act of Being Whole

Happiness can be a mercurial concept, but I find it helpful to approach happiness with a more gracious, forgiving, holistic perspective.

Not as an elusive singular force whose ultimate destination signifies an arrival or achievement. But as a living, breathing entity that emboldens and empowers our hearts every time we dare to strive for joy, beauty, truth, and light— especially in the face of difficulty.

While we may not always feel happy, happiness can still be a core principle that guides our path. We can make choices in alignment with our truth. We can stay open during dark times to search for hidden light and find new pearls of wisdom that transcend emotional pain.

In the process, we can continue to become a deeper, more nuanced, more healed, and whole being. Perhaps the living, breathing essence of happiness can plant new seeds in us during such periods. Perhaps those seeds will flourish in time with water, joy, and sunlight, and our emotional body will catch up to what our hearts have known all along—

True happiness isn't something you feel; it is the act of being whole. It is the continued work of freeing yourself from all the things you are not so you can become who you really are.

The path to true happiness will not always make you feel happy, but it will free your heart to become your highest expression, and there is immense joy to be found there.

320
YOU ARE THE ART

We collect pieces of ourselves as we go— clues, cues, tiny gems, and treasures— which we tuck away until it's time to unfold a fuller story of self. The soul leaves cake crumbs to help us follow the path.

The poem you wrote years back may become part of a book. The strange sense of restlessness you felt months ago may have been the first stirrings and dawning of a new invitation for growth.

The vision you once had of yourself doing something different than what you do now may someday come to fruition. If you just stay with it and let that part of yourself emerge, you'll eventually find your own brand of artistry.

Each scrap and pearl and shell and tiny pebble, each little bit you discover each day, is a piece of the greater mosaic of you. Wings don't unfurl overnight. They start to develop in the cocoon, and sometimes, you may not even realize you've been in a cocoon until you're ready to break through its silken strands of incubation.

A heart can change in a beat, and you never know what might change your heart. You may feel directionless in one lunar cycle, unable to see your bigger picture, then find your deeper clarity somewhere between the moon's next wax and wane.

The feelings, insights, dreams, and heart states we sometimes dismiss, disregard, and discount because we don't understand them are often inklings of the soul helping us paint our fuller picture. They don't always have to make sense; they are here to help us delve deeper into our own mysteries so we can better know their depths.

There can be a lot of layers to dig through to get to your depths. Tiers and stripes and stratums of sediment built up through the years of who, how, and what this world told you to be. But underneath all that is your authenticity, essence, and diamonds of truth, which can only be found in your depth.

So, don't distrust yourself. Or discredit your dreams. Or dismiss the pieces of you that you are slowly gathering, even if you don't entirely understand them. You are drawn to them because they resonate in your heart. Because each color, line, shade, and tone creates a fuller picture of you: your soul is your canvas, and you are the art.

321
WHAT IS UNWRITTEN

"Write your own story, be your own hero. Speak your own truth, live your own dream."
— Raphaella Vaisseau

Try not to get stuck in a place of dejection when things don't work out how you hoped. It's hard, it stings. I know. Failed expectations always do, and they can be a hefty weight to carry when we allow them to weigh us down and harden.

Nobody likes being disappointed, dealing with a change they never asked for, getting hurt, feeling chronically discouraged, or sorting through the complicated feelings of loss that can come when we realize we are living a story very different from the one we originally wrote for ourselves.

But the beautiful thing about life and our stories is that there are literally millions of possibilities waiting for us, and all of that is still unwritten.

So, do not limit yourself to an idea of how life is supposed to be. Your story will be defined by those self-imposed limitations and become chapter after chapter of hurt, anger, fear, bitterness, and despondency.

It is your story to write, so when the time is right, punctuate the end of the old chapter and begin a new one.

Write yourself out of a situation where you previously felt stuck.

Invent a side door or a twist in the plotline that you never saw coming.

Outline a new dream and pen a vision of reinvention and growth.

Broaden your expanse and allow for a new opportunity that moves your story in a supportive direction.

Open yourself up to the infinite possibilities for life, love, beauty, self-compassion, beginnings, relationships, new ways to find yourself, and new ways to write the book of self that only you have been given to create, breathe, and write into being.

322
Aim for Peace

We might not always be able to grab onto happiness during times of struggle in our lives. If you're living authentically, happiness is not an end state but a fluid energy that weaves in and out of our path.

When we open ourselves up to not only the things that bring us great joy, we also open to that which brings great sorrow. One cannot exist without the other. And so, if happiness feels unrealistic during certain times in our lives, maybe we can still aim for peace.

Peace is not the same as happiness, but it does help open a door for happiness to enter our lives. Peace is gracious and welcoming. It builds bridges between the disparate parts of us and helps harmonize our experiences of joy and sorrow, love and loss, beauty and pain. Peace offers us the gentle light of hope, allows us to be in the flow of and trust that it is all moving toward wellness.

In 2013, I set the intention that it was the "Year of the Peaceful Heart." At the time, I was learning difficult and beautiful lessons on maturation and what it means to be whole. These are the words I wrote on a day when I wanted to feel happy and instead felt colored by the blues:

"I reflect on a favorite quote by Rumi and try to take his advice and welcome my sadness into my guesthouse. I ask it to have a seat, tell me of its sorrows, and help me learn what it has to show me. It has a lot to say. I serve it tea, cake, and sympathy. I thank it for the wisdom it has to share.

I find that instead of rejecting it and telling it to go away so I can fake happiness, I have cleared space for it. As it turns out, the offer of space was all my sadness really wanted in the first place, and after finishing the last drop of tea, it thanked me for being a gracious host and quietly took its leave.

I am left with a few specks of cake crumbs and a sense of solidarity with myself. A wholeness that comes from embracing all of me— not just the sunny side but the side that can rain on a parade, while violins sadly play in the background, and a tiny kitten pitifully mews.

Solidarity.... wholeness... embracing all...I think these might just be the stuff of which a peaceful heart is made."

—Sunshine in Winter

Those **are** the things of which a peaceful heart is made. When we embrace all our experiences, we bring harmony into our ecosystem of self, which generates self-acceptance and a peaceful heart.

Something I have learned on my wanderings through the adventures in happiness is that a peaceful heart attracts happiness. So, on those days when happiness eludes you? Aim for peace. You'll be moving in the right direction.

323

THE DANCE

"Dance when you're broken open. Dance, if you've torn the bandage off. Dance in the middle of the fighting. Dance in your blood. Dance when you're perfectly free."
—Rumi

When you approach it with discovery and curiosity, life holds the potential to become a dance. A weaving-in and weaving-out of experience and interconnection that continue to weave together the bigger picture of you and the bigger truth of your journey.

Dancing with life and the universe is not about perfection—it's about holding the mutual rhythms of being both human and divine. It's about learning to engage with life from a paradigm of fluidity, faith, and humor, where we recognize our need to be both agents of movement and change in our lives. We allow ourselves to be led and respond to life's changing flows.

Since life loves a good surprise and can sometimes be a friendly but unpredictable partner, there might be many seeming missteps or feelings like you're going in the wrong direction, but there will also be so many times that you leap and soar and step in time to a bigger rhythm.

Don't worry about how others are dancing. This is your creation, your interweaving, your experience, your invention. This is how you understand the voice of the numinous inside yourself and create meaning, purpose, and a relationship with the world around you.

So, let it be what it needs to be, and remember that you can't miss a step. As Rumi also wrote, "Both light and shadows are the dance of love." And you, dear one, are heart in motion, adding more love into the world with each step.

324
CREATIVE ADAPTATION

Patience is often difficult. There are many things we wish we already knew, which we may not be any closer to knowing. There are things we want to happen now, when the timing isn't there.

What a strange contradiction being human is: we often seek the stability that comes from knowing. We think that knowing will give us a sense of control and constancy— even though we all know that change IS the only constant.

So, we must find perspectives to help stabilize us. We must find something substantial within ourselves to ground into to help create a sense of cohesion and solidity in the fluidity. We must find ways to stay connected to the compass in our hearts, while surrendering to the greater flow of life, if we want soul growth.

We must find a way to make peace within the contradicting energies of movement and pause. Balance is often overrated and unobtainable, but creative adaption is a beautiful waltz.

Creative adaption allows us to stay open to possibilities and make art out of unexpected circumstances. We can lean one way one day and then another the next, and eventually learn that WE are the constant in the aventurine streams of life's flow.

We can become co-participants in our creative process as we accept life's grander invitation to create with it and make rainbows where darkness once lay. We enter the mystic field and work with life, love, and the numinous. We triage action, surrender, and faith in an evolving dance of conscious creativity.

We come to realize that perhaps the things we wish we already knew— the questions of our life whose answer we still seek— will be unimaginably better than anything we could have foreseen when we take the steps we can and then let go, trust, and allow life space to happen.

Patience can be difficult, but it's also necessary if we wish to receive the life of creative existence our hearts seek and are designed to be.

325
Snow Falling on Happy

Sometimes, happiness falls softly, like a gentle, unexpected layer of snow that falls in the night; we wake up surprised and delighted to find it there.

Happiness didn't arrive the way we expected. We thought happiness would come in with a bang. A giant marching band of cheerful noise and cacophony announcing its triumphant entry, while majorettes twirl batons, and a kick line keeps time.

Instead, happiness comes modestly. Like Carl Sandberg's fog creeping in on little cat feet, it slides in unannounced. Perhaps it's quieter than the happiness of days past. It is more deeply rooted in peace and satisfaction from the lovely garden we are busy tending to in our inner worlds and noble, quiet lives. It is not contingent on any one person, idea, or plan for our life. It is gracious and accommodating to whatever the Now holds.

When we are younger, happiness often feels breezy and reckless. A young puppy tearing through the house in abject glee, unaware of any havoc he may cause. You can't help but smile at his hasty joy even while you yell at him to get off the couch and notice the yellow puddle he left on the floor.

Sometimes, we get so used to equating happiness with that wild, carefree state that we are unprepared for the unceremonious arrival in the middle of the night. Happiness simply entered in on her own accord, helped herself to a cup of warm-hearted tea, and settled into our guestroom.

This version of happiness is gentle and wise; she grasps the bigger picture in life. She understands that life's grit might make joy weightier, but it also makes it substantive and real. She doesn't turn a blind eye to the grit— the feelings of loneliness, the ghosts of heartache, her greater awareness of the sorrows in this world.

She calmly accepts these things instead of avoiding them and simply allows herself to experience happiness anyway. She is peaceful like snow gently falling outside. She accepts the cadence of life and has a depth of experience that allows her to know on a heartfelt, cellular level that seasons do turn.

This isn't a flashy sort of in-the-moment happiness. There's no artifice, no falsity, no shallow foundation. It's richly nuanced. Judicious. Circumspect. Deeply rooted.

Quiet and unexpected, like the arrival of the snow's magic in the night. Amicably glowing and warming our hearts, she gently makes space for herself in our lives. One day, we realize that out of nowhere, we notice a deep-rooted sense of quiet happiness. It is a very good day.

326

YOU ARE THE JOURNEY

"It is easier to go where there already is a path forged. But the most rewarding trails are the ones we make for ourselves. Those are ones we can leave behind for others to follow. It also means we find new places few others haven't gone before. Though going where there is no path can be more difficult, it will be worth it when you get to your destination."
—Ralph Waldo Emerson

Life can be a journey, but so are you: You are the journey.

A holder of the potential for unending discovery. A keeper of the keys that only you can turn to unlock the wealth within. A maker of magic when you learn to believe.

A collage of emotions, which hold wisdom when you follow their intelligent flows. A collection of experiences that compose the ongoing symphony of your notes.

You are the journey. If you keep saying "yes" to whatever is inside yourself, you will explore and expand in ways you may never have imagined.

You will take unknown paths and look for new delights with adventure and curiosity. You will realize that every time you choose the unknown over the familiar, you are entering into a deeper relationship of trust with the universe's intelligence and life's creative mysteries.

The answers you seek, the questions you don't even know you need to ask, the endless spirals of galactic grace that will travel you closer to the truth of your soul.

It is you. Within you. Inside you. You are the journey when you make the space for discovery, evolution, and growth.

327
GRATITUDE IS A GATEWAY

If we don't put energy into gratitude, it's easy for our sense of gratitude to slip from our grasp. Daily stressors add up, and our attention is often pulled in multiple directions at once.

The struggle is real— this human thing can be hard. It's easy to fall out of rhythm with appreciation, and we must tune our hearts back to a more grateful space. We do this by learning to radically notice the good in our lives. We do this each time we realize we are focusing on stress, worry, and lack and, instead, shift our focus so we are open to receiving the medicine of gratitude.

That's the thing about all this gratitude stuff— it IS medicinal. Gratitude is healing. It opens our hearts, helps us feel interconnected, and supports our minds in paying attention to what is good and hopeful. Gratitude is the key ingredient in the elixir of happiness; we cannot find nourishing happiness without gratitude's supportive alchemy.

Gratitude is a balm of goodness in a world filled with stress and strife. It teaches us to anchor into the frequencies of contentment, inner peace, and lovingkindness. When we are anchored into these energies, we feel brighter and lighter and can give to ourselves and those around us.

Gratitude becomes a gateway to beautiful things. Each time we appreciate, we let the universe know— "Yes, this, this, this. Please bring me more of this." We unlock the treasures of our hearts a little more, and we contribute our unique alchemy of gratitude to the energy of our world.

There is no big secret to gratitude, but there are practices that we can use to cultivate its seeds with grace and temerity. Where our focus goes, energy flows and becomes the foundation upon which we create a life of abundance, purpose, and sincerity.

328

Personal Artistry

"I took a deep breath and listened to the old brag of my heart. I am, I am, I am."

—Sylvia Plath

Sometimes, we must get busy with the art of living and creating by simply digging deep inside ourselves. Nourishing a relationship with our spirit, nurturing a connection with our soul, and finding the courage to excavate our hearts so we become well acquainted with their contents.

Our experience of the external world reflects our experience of our internal world, and we will find that life will only be as expansive, open, loving, beautiful, compassionate, and filled with possibilities as our relationship with ourselves.

Our inner world becomes the lens through which we view the physical world.

If we want art, we must learn to be the art. If we want nuance, we must not fear our shades of self. If we want fluidity and expansion and to learn to push the boundaries, we must be fearless in discovering and cultivating those qualities inside ourselves.

So, we will find it is with life and our world: if we want change, we must learn to be the change. If we want acceptance, we must welcome acceptance within ourselves. If we want more, we must challenge ourselves to grow and learn to become more.

If we want kindness, compassion, love, joy, mercy, and grace— if we desire greater for our lives, for each other, and for humanity— then we must keep learning to drop out of our heads and into our hearts.

Then listen to the words written upon each beat— I AM, I Breathe, I Love, I Live— reminding us of who we are. So, we can keep learning to become the genesis of our creation. Because our globe, our planet, and our actions will only be as beautiful as our art.

329

JOY IS VITAL TO OUR SOULS

Times of challenge and trouble will always offer us opportunities to return to ourselves.

The nature of uncertainty is disquietude and unease. Finding ways to anchor into our deeper selves is necessary in our modern-day world.

Anchoring in is how we listen to our intuition, heed our inner voice, return to the wisdom in our hearts, and make choices aligned with our truth.

We return and anchor in many ways: Calm. Rest. Creativity. Appreciation. Joy. Nature. Loved Ones. Solitude. Small comforts. Simple pleasures. Through contemplation practices. Through meditation and quiet. Through time in nature.

Through acts of self-expression that circle us into our truth. Through tiny comfort rituals that give us a sense of continuity, pleasure, and peace. This is how we return to our soul, find the light within, and move forward feeling energetically nourished, intentional, and aligned.

In these spaces, we feel brighter and centered. We shed the energetic debris we accumulate from life's stress. We find a newfound lightness of heart.

We remember that joy is vital to our souls. Joy anchors us into our soul's natural condition. It cuts through the uncertain dark and returns us to a pure space of light.

Joy is the currency of vitality. Focusing on joy is not trivial or frivolous— it is sustenance and a natural antidote to antipathy, fear, and compassion fatigue. Joy helps us feel more energized to engage in the world with compassion, warmth, and hope.

Sometimes, we must stretch a little higher to touch the good. Every time we reach up and grab onto peace, truth, beauty, curiosity, and wonder, we tap into joy's golden veins. What a healing balm joy becomes in difficult times.

Be a channel for joy today. Pour that frequency into the world through your words, energy, and essence. Like daffodil yellow sunshine, let it seep into the places where fear and anxiety have crept, helping warm and soften them.

We sometimes forget that simple acts can have a big impact. We don't have to hustle to keep up and prove our relevance. We can stand still and embody fierce change. In a wanting world, we can allow joy to flow from our hearts and trust it to do the work of love.

330

Manifesto of Hope

I believe in people and their ability to change themselves. I truly do.

I see our minds and hearts and bodies and ability to reason, feel, love, breathe, and engage with the world around us as the biggest game changers there will ever be.

I believe when we need support and community it's important to seek out the spaces we feel supported and connected to. But I also believe people are their own experts and wisdom keepers and harbingers of love. The right supports can help hold up a mirror to reflect those gifts back to us, but they can't do the work for us.

After all, you are what YOU have. This means your own experience of self is going to be the most valid. If thought patterns, and belief systems, and ways of being are not resonating with you, then I believe in changing them.

As Walt Whitman said: "Dismiss anything that insults your soul."

We learn so much through trial and error. What worked for us at one point in time may not work at another. We are continually breathing, evolving, and being. That's why life can often be so messy. There's a lot of experimentation going on throughout the whole thing. Most "experts" may have a lot of wisdom, but they don't have your answers— only you do.

So, keep being present with yourself. Keep listening to you. Reevaluate thoughts and internal constructs— especially when they aren't working for you. Be an architect of thought who roots your ideology in radical self-love.

Draw close to people and ideas and perspectives, which support you and encourage your process. Release all else that wasn't meant for you. Drop into your heart, body, and intuitive wisdom. Allow yourself to be moved by the winds of your own change.

Keep going about the work of constructing a life in this world— from the inside out— which supports the whole of you.

331

DREAM YOUR WORLD, CREATE A BEAUTIFUL REALITY

Surround yourself with whatever brings out the "real" in you. Fostering love and truth in your life will help you foster love and truth in yourself.

Be a student and allow nature to be your teacher. Talk to the stars and listen for their answer echoing in your soul. See shapes in the clouds and dragons in crowds of swaying trees. Believe in magic and mystery.

Remember the ancestors who walked here first. Know that we step where they once trod and now rest. Know that all land and ground are sacred. Reestablish a connection with it. Learn to set your heartbeat to the beat of the bones of the earth. Learn to beat as one. Learn what true connection means.

Stay away from people and places that tear you down. Don't change your shape to fit any boxes that don't suit your glorious bursts of sunlight, sky, and sea. Realize your experience of self is right, real, and worthy. Realize your experience of life is the only experience that is going to be most helpful to you.

Don't wait if it's in your heart to do it and you have the means to do it now. Become a waking dream and dream your world. See the world through a rose-colored lens. Create a beautiful reality.

Grieve as often as your spirit requires over the cracks and ruptures in this place. Let your heart break daily, if need be, and make up your own sacred ceremonies to honor the pains that you feel and see. But don't let this hurting world make you forget that the healing and binding balm of LOVE unleashed far surpasses everything.

Pull anything into you that encourages, supports, and nourishes you into blooming like the gorgeous, mad wildflower that you are. Grow and keep growing and grow some more. Until your roots are bound in the ruby ground of the earth and your platinum petals reach up, up, up to the Pleiades, forming their own Milky Way galaxies.

Become so BIG you can't ever go back to small.

332
WRITE ABOUT THE WORLD WE WISH TO SEE

"Write about the world you wish to see. Hold space for truth. Hold space for peace. Hold space for learning to dance with the shadows and find the light.
Hold space for courage. Hold space for reinvention. Hold space for evolution. Hold space for change.
Hold space for love and keep following the way of the heart, for that is the path forward, which will help us create a better way."
—Akashic Magic

I once wrote these words like I was spellcasting. Creating a verbal vision board of a better world. A world where we grow love forward and find the creative courage to let go of what's no longer working and create something better in its place.

I learned long ago that we can write our lives into being through intention, faith, and words. Maybe we can't change everything, but we can change ourselves, and I think that is more than enough.

I wrote my way through a difficult divorce, a shedding of an old self, and a recreation of a new me. Each time I wrote, I found myself ending my words with hope and vision of who I'd like to be and what I'd like to dream into being.

It might be too much of a stretch to say I authored myself into being, since I think there are much bigger forces— like life, love, spirit, and the intangible threads of fate and destiny— that also had a lot to do with it. But I noticed, over time, that I was becoming my vision of self.

We can create millions of things in our lives, from the tiniest drop of gratitude to the biggest wave of grace and change. So why not save a little space to create a more beautiful world inside ourselves and envision a more beautiful collective world?

Through tiny scraps of art, little love notes of kindness, and vision boards built of positive quotes, grand ideas, and dreams, we can add more beauty to this vast universe. Inspiring the greatness in each other, inspiring humble acts of change, and inspiring ourselves to write about the world we wish to see.

Those inspirations and words of love might feel nothing more than a dream today, yet they hold the potential to create the energy that builds the steppingstones to a better tomorrow.

333
LIGHTHOUSES OF HOPE

When I get discouraged about the world—

When I notice that hopelessness and helplessness are setting in. Or empathy and compassion fatigue begin to creep in. Or a news feed brings more angry faces, words, and events that make my heart want to give up and split.

When I get like this, I am reminded it is time to lay it down, turn it off, let it go.

Breathe. Look up. Shift.

Shift my focus to all that is right, all that is joy, and all that is the distance I've come. My repository of recollections and collections of good become my lighthouses of hope in the huge sweep of life's storm.

They light my way with words of grace:

"Keep walking. You haven't quit yet. Don't start now."

"Keep on with joy. There is always joy to be found."

"Cry when you need and laugh like you must, for laughter will always be the true magnetic compass that leads you out of the lost forest of despair."

"Breathe, my dear one, breathe. We are nothing without breath."

"Stop looking to the world to set your tone— you were never meant to be well-adjusted to a maladjusted system. Instead, bring it back to the only world you can control— the space inside your heart."

"Be still, be you, be peace, be real."

And let the energy of love flow from there.

334

Joy is Happening Right Now

When we develop a heart-based eye, we begin to learn to see that moments of gratitude, joy, and appreciation happen all the time.

We find them in the beat of our hearts and the gentle sense of purpose and intentions that order our day. We find them in nature's abundant gifts. We find them in the things that make us pause, smile, and feel lighter.

We can find them in life's challenges, too— the situations that shape us and grow us, the challenges that leave us feeling bedraggled but wiser and stronger in our sense of who we are. They can be a little more hidden in these spaces, but our hearts will teach us how to notice hidden lights.

We find them in breath and time, moon cycles and tree cycles, and the steady passage of day to night, demarcations that mark the cyclical movement of life.

We find them in the good, the bad, the beautiful, the cracks and the fissures, the flowers that bloom, the questions and the answers. We find them in the lows of the valleys and the highs of the mountains, each breath, each season, each new moon, and the words of truth written on our hearts.

We find them in the magical gifts of life and all its euphonious fist-pumping highs, the in-between moments when life feels grayer and amorphous, and even the difficulties and lows that force us to feel, grow, be challenged, and become.

We find them through all these experiences when we learn that all these things mean we are here. We are breathing. We are co-participants in this wonderful, messy thing called life. We find them in our totality of all that seems dark and all that seems bright.

There are days when I lose my sense of appreciation. I stop and pause at the ordinary ingredients of my life and try to see the totality of the whole. I remember that I will never recreate this unique moment again; this moment is its own sacred gift.

I'll look at the sky and say to myself— "BethAnne, pay attention. Joy is happening right now. And you don't want to miss it."

335
A Life of Appreciation Is a Life Well Lived

It's easy to get lost in the constant stream of movement in our world and the ceaseless anxieties so many of us seem to face. Whenever we get caught up in the bigger picture, I find it very helpful to return to our core through gratitude.

In gratitude, we remember that no matter what else happens in this spiraling world, a life of appreciation is a life well lived.

Quiet evenings. The way the clouds illuminate just before sunset. Love in any form. Noticing kindness. Moonlight. Developing a keen eye for things that feel meaningful.

We can collect appreciations like pennies and dimes and tuck them into the bank of our hearts, so we keep a cache of spare goodness on hand.

Instead of getting ahead of ourselves and wondering what the future holds, we can stay in the moment by trying to appreciate exactly where and who we are right now:

How life's strange ups and downs have transformed us and shaped our path. The courage it takes to stay with ourselves and the ways we've shown up for our journey. Any small wins or victories that feel important to us individually. Nature's constancy and clarity help ground us in the cyclical nature of change.

These are small ways to stay in harmony with our hearts and find our way to a space of inner integrity.

Life's bigger picture will eventually emerge if we just stay with the process. Solutions to ongoing challenges will present themselves, and new creative visions will come to life in time. Things will even out and feel calmer.

But perhaps you don't find yourself in that space today, which is okay. This is what it means to trust the seasons in your life and remember that when all else fails and you don't know where you're going, or what you're doing, or when the answers will come—

Find thankfulness for the smallest things and know that a day spent with a grateful heart is never wasted. A life of appreciation is a life well lived.

336

On the Heart of Being Human

It is a contradictory process, the art of being human. We are asked to transform and release while we also step into and create. We balance the tensions of self-improvement with self-acceptance with self-forgiveness and somehow cobblestone all shades of self into our being.

Phew, it's a lot, right? So please be self-kind, and here are a few things that may help along the way:

Don't be ashamed of who you are now, even as you always allow yourself space to grow and the grace to be wrong and change.

Take up, fill, and embody your beautiful space, even as you maintain awareness and respect for others' spaces. Be kind, and when you see unkindness and you can do something about it— do something.

Learn to sit with your anger, your pain, and your darkness and find ways to transmute it to love. Start by bringing love into those spaces of self. Fierce, gritty, dark, deep love that buckles down and knows how to withstand.

Strive for more in your life if it's in your heart to do, yet also remember that you are already enough and need not change to earn more merit in the eyes of love. Change because it calls to you, not because you have to, and know that freedom of choice makes all the difference between sky and cage.

Last, laugh more. A lot more. Laughter has a way of changing the energy in anything and helps us move towards a kinder space inside of ourselves where we remember joy is a revolutionary space.

Remember that the art of being human is closely connected to the heart of being human— complicated, gorgeous, raw, real, ever-changing, marked with imperfection and riotous color. It is something meant to be understood through experience, embodiment, and a great deal of patience, compassion, and grace.

Pearls of Wisdom on Purpose, Presence, Impact, and Wild-Hearted Living

337

How to Live Wild-Hearted

To offer oneself without apology, choose a path of authenticity, and continue to show up from the most honest space you can.

To keep shedding, releasing, reinventing, transforming, and freeing oneself to become a more vibrant expression.

To use life's challenges as ingredients for personal transformation, seeking to understand the darkness and discover the light in disguise.

To find joy in the brambles and dignity among life's thorns and embrace the value of both shadow and light.

To find the buried treasures in life's mess and imperfection and notice the strange beauty of the whole.

To learn to be at ease, belong to oneself, and become a relentless practitioner of self-love, self-compassion, and self-grace.

To empower oneself to create a life of one's choosing and refuse to give up on crafting a beautiful reality and envisioning this world a better place.

To know when to yield and when to be an unyielding force, dancing with life's ebbs and flows, and finding the love in all experiences.

To claim joy as a core value and insist on finding the beauty and magic in this world.

To keep choosing faith over fear, explore the vast wilderness of the soul, and learn to embody the wisdom gained—

This is how to keep our hearts open in a world that will make them want to close.

This is how to let the energy of love become what both shields us and reveals us.

This is how to live wild-hearted and walk the way of the heart.

338

A Life of Untamed Love

As bad as it feels to disappoint another, I think the real disappointment lies in not being our true selves. At this point in my journey, I'd rather disappoint someone else and handle those sticky feelings than shape myself to fit what doesn't fit my heart or light.

I've learned that true disappointment lies in not living out the unique blueprint written inside each of us.

In not acting on the gifts and talents that only we can offer through being our fullest, brightest selves.

In abdicating responsibility for our life to anything or anybody our heart doesn't recognize as truth.

This is a brave path we've been called to— a path of surrender to our heart's truths that paradoxically leads us away from being self-centric and toward being heart-centric. We'll find that the more we move closer to our hearts, the more we grow in empathy, compassion, and love.

We'll still feel highly called to share ourselves and show up for others, except the difference is that it will not come from a space of expectation or obligation; it will come from a space of our responsibility toward love. It might not look like what others expect, but it will resonate because you will feel a sense of rightness.

A life realized, a life of authenticity, a heart that strives to live in alignment so our outside life matches our inside life as best we can, is a life of untamed love. It is a life spent honoring the gift of your life by loving yourself fully and wildly.

Your very existence becomes a radical act of love. That love will spill over onto everything and everyone around you as it becomes a natural extension of yourself.

Become the light you wish to see in this world. It begins with you, in your heart, and your personal artistry. The act of being you is carefully cultivated by showing up in the world with truth, beauty, and love.

339
LITTLE DEEDS OF INTENTION COMPOUND

Speak good words and do kind things. Offer this as medicine for a world that needs healing balm.

We have the gift of choosing our thoughts and words, so why not make them good ones that encourage, love, and show compassion for ourselves and others?

Our small steps of courage and little deeds of intention compound. They offer the medicine of joy, transmutation, and grace in a world that can feel heavy and lost. Every kindhearted thought and endeavor contributes to the whole. What might seem paltry to you might mean the world to someone else.

Share a smile. Pick up a tiny piece of litter and do something good for the earth. Be mindful of an animal. Thank a tree for standing tall. Do something warm-hearted for a fellow human. Walk on the earth with reverence, acknowledging all who came before you.

Say a simple prayer. Look up at the heart of the sky. Breathe in peace and imagine your energy leaving a trail of grace wherever you step today. A life of devotion and beauty is created when we take the ordinary and make it sacred through our intentions of goodness and care.

Insist on magic and see the world open in possibilities and color. Whatever you do, do what you can. Set an intention for light and make it count. Live your life in such a way as to leave no stone unturned for love.

340

The Vibrancy is Here

Ever get ahead of yourself? Wanting to be something or somewhere or somewhat other than what you are? Somebody else or someplace else. The future you instead of this version of you.

It can be difficult to learn to occupy our present space, especially if we have dreams, hopes, and goals we want to fulfill. Sometimes, we tend to focus on where we are going instead of where we are at, and yet our present space is where the gifts are found. Not the future— we're not there yet, and it may look entirely different anyway. Nothing is promised or certain.

While the past holds gifts in the form of memories, they are fading gifts. It's like looking at a pressed prom corsage with tender nostalgia compared to smelling a vibrant rose bursting with life and bloom.

The vibrancy is here and now. Even on days that don't feel particularly vibrant, there is almost always beauty to discover, joy to be noticed, love to cherish, and small moments of gratitude. There are acts of compassion, prayers to offer, intentions to set, and drops of goodness to add to the greater ocean.

There are reflections and insights on growth to discover. Daydreams and imaginings that make you smile. Comfort rituals to be savored. The truth of a breath to be realized. A new sky to fold into a poem.

Sometimes, you just have to be still, claim the current space you are standing in, and know it is perfectly, wonderfully, divinely, magically enough in this given moment. The vibrancy is here. In this breath. In your heart.

In the power of being present, accounted for, and engaged in your life.

341

CHANGE YOUR HEART, CHANGE YOUR WORLD

"A change of heart leads to a change in behavior, and a change in behavior leads to changing the world."
—Marianne Williamson

When we tap into a deeper sense of self-love, forgiveness, and compassion, we heal ourselves and are better equipped to live bigger and braver lives.

We change the world by changing our hearts, and when we are engaged in our change, we can trust that the ripple effects of that change will make an impact.

Change your heart, change your world. Change your world, change the world. If you want to be a mover, shaker, and change maker— even if just by making small and meaningful contributions of compassion, kindness, and love— then the epicenter for that change is in your heart.

As such, we need to tend to our hearts often and work with our heart intelligence. Here are some questions I like to ask when I start to feel like I'm wandering off-center and need to come back to a heart-directed space, do some good old feng shui, and change things up in my heart:

- How can I bring more healing into myself through this?
- What lesson can I learn about love right now?

- How can I move through my day with more peace, authenticity, and kindness?
- How can I bring grace into this situation?
- How can I stay present and witness my experience?
- Where is joy waiting today, and what do I need to receive it?
- What does my heart want me to know right now?

Work regularly with any of these or your own heart-inspired variations through contemplation and journaling. Keep learning how to bring life back to a heart-centered space.

This is how we grow our hearts and claim the vast wilderness within: we take whatever life brings us and use it to cultivate sacred meadows of self-awareness, vibrancy, treasure, and grace.

342

LET YOUR PURPOSE BE A POEM

Find the spaces where love is growing and plant your seeds there. Learn how to embody a bigger self by refusing to capitulate to judgment or fear.

Make quantum leaps in your heart that take you from a space of shame to grace. Follow your soul rhythms and let them play you a different kind of music; teach yourself to flow to them and become like the sea.

Be a sacred rebel who listens to your drumbeat and follows your heart to your musicality. Give your imagination and logic the same respect and accord— both are designed for interpretive dance, weaving back and forth between experience and knowing.

Go to secret places, especially inside of yourself. Create as often as you can. Remember, an act of creation can simply be a mindful exhale intended to send more kindness into the world.

Stay close to nature and learn her secrets by following the wisdom of the trees and seeing where that knowledge leads. Become an ambassador for radical self-belief.

Search for quiet gratitude and develop an eye for the hidden gems. Be present for the sun's riotous rise and the moon's starlit shifts. Make an impact by practicing grace and choosing to uplift.

Let your purpose be a poem. Write an ongoing love letter to the universe with your acts of sincerity and truth. Create a gentle uproar with your gracious refusal to be anybody but you.

343

REAL

"Real isn't how you are made,' said the Skin Horse. 'It's a thing that happens to you... It doesn't happen all at once... You become. It takes a long time."
—Margery Williams Bianco, The Velveteen Rabbit

What does it mean to be real?

Being real and walking the trail of a true human is a process. One in which you keep peeling back the layers of the self and fearlessly examining what is there. One in which you seek self-honesty and welcome compassionate scrutiny.

One in which you allow uncomfortable feelings, thoughts, and experiences to bubble up to the surface— instead of avoiding or denying them. You learn to invite them into your awareness and see what they are there to teach you.

This process requires you to take full accountability for yourself, your energy, your heart, and what you bring into the spaces you occupy. And that's hard work. It can feel scary, unrewarding, and unglamorous. It will probably require dark nights of the soul, unintentional public gaffs, lots of mistakes, and falling down often.

It will call you to make changes in your life every time you find pieces that are out of alignment with your truth. But doing the work will also ground you and invite you into a deeper, fuller, richer relationship with yourself. It will expand your heart's wisdom and give you inner peace.

It will make you unafraid to turn the lights on in the dark spaces within and clear and organize those spaces. You'll realize that's all enlightenment really is— turning the lights on in previously dark spaces. The more you do this, the more you radiate your truth and begin to shine brighter and brighter with sincerity and genuine, nourishing light.

This work will deepen your compassion for others. It will increase discernment and decrease judgment. Real is kind and curious, not arrogant and closed. Real is humble and equal to, not expert and better than. Real is slow to judge and quick to try and understand.

Real can't be faked. Real always brings you back to the heart and a place of love because love is the building block, molecule, and essence of real. And what becomes real cannot go back and be unreal; the real we choose to become cannot be undone.

344

LET YOUR HEART BREAK

There are seasons in life that break your heart. Sometimes, it's the capital H kind of Heartbreak that cracks you wide open, but I also think there is lowercase "h" heartbreak, which might not be as traumatic but still leaves you feeling disassembled and bruised.

As much as heartache hurts, having a heart that can break is a good thing. Because being able to break means your heart is unarmored, unshielded, and malleable enough to engage with life authentically.

It means you are in touch with qualities like empathy, compassion, and vulnerability and trying to live by those qualities in a confusing world that doesn't always seek to do the same.

It means you have wishes, dreams, and ideals you want to bring into being to live your best life and make the world a better place, and it hurts when those aren't realized.

It mostly means you are more invested in opening to life with love than closing yourself out of fear and control.

What a strange paradox heartbreak is: what breaks us is often that which we loved— whether that was a person, situation, or ideal. And it's also a strange paradox that out of the rubble of anything that breaks or is stripped away, something more beautiful, wild, and pristine resurrects itself in time.

Cheryl Strayed once wrote, "Be brave enough to break your own heart." And I would add to that expansive thought— be brave enough to let your heart break.

345

STARLIGHT AND STRANGE BEAUTY

Life is an ongoing process, and with any process, good and bad things will come. We keep learning that the true alchemy in life is how we choose to respond to life's processes.

Whether we choose to find the gifts that exist.

Whether we develop a relationship of entitlement or appreciation for our life.

Whether we keep refocusing on what we can cultivate and create or fall victim to the old programs of despair, disconnection, and hopelessness.

The onus of choice always comes back to us. Though we may have seasons of grief or stress to work through where we don't feel we can access our higher minds and stay open to life's gifts— we can still retain the knowledge that, at some point, the light will once again break through. When it does, we will reach for it.

We can always work with ourselves wherever we are. We can always find a way to chisel away at the hard materials life has given us. See if we can create a malleable matter that lends itself to finding a more expanded way of engaging with our lives with presence, creativity, and grace.

We can remember our true treasure lies within us and within our ability to cultivate inner wealth. Grow our hearts. Do inner work. Make love our purpose. Stay open to receiving our soul's higher plan. Dream our dreams, believe good things will happen, and choose to seek the light in the dark when life calls us into submergence.

Those things remain ours to cultivate, explore, and own. They are the anchors we can bring ourselves back to when we lose our bearings in life's ups and downs. They are the tools we have that allow us to utilize the experience and wisdom we gain on the journey and build castles of compassion, grace, and whimsy.

So, deep breath, dear ones. Keep returning to the treasure within and hold fast to the truth in your heart's sacred beat—

Remember that even if you should find yourself in the vast darkness, there is always a smattering of starlight and a strange beauty awaiting your discovery.

346

From Cocoon to Sky

This, too, is a task of the wild-hearted: to learn how to fully claim ourselves and belong to our whole selves. It's easy to learn to identify with and belong to what is beautiful, light, and joyful inside of ourselves, yet the journey of the wild heart also knows there is devotion and belonging to be found in our darker spaces.

We discover an unusual and dignified strength when we rock ourselves through anxiety-ridden nights or trace the circumference of our fears around our minds. We deepen our commitment to self when we've sat in ceremony with our mistakes, grievances, or judgment errors and learned to see them for what they are— simply another part of the journey that holds value and growth.

When we don't know how to face our pain yet find a way to stay present, we receive gifts of great value that cannot be acquired any other way except by accessing them through darkness. When the illusion of control falls away, we must find our way by intuition, trust, and whatever scraps we can kindle into a small spark of belief.

These are the moments we learn not to abandon ourselves and keep breathing in the dark. We learn to trust the stars in our souls to guide us. We learn to face what seems endless and terrible inside, compassionately witness, and keep faith in our inner light.

Over time, we see that something of the highest value was born in this underworld space. In the despair of the darkness, we realize that we came alive to our real beauty. Stripped of all pretenses, our soul was pure and beautiful and guided us true during the darkest hours of our need.

Please know, brave heart, as you emerge back into the light, you will have changed, and not everybody will get that. Others will likely not see or understand your work in the darkness. They will only see the completion and gifts of strength that came in the end, without realizing the struggle from the cocoon to the sky that led to growing your wings and your flight.

Just remember that some things are not for others to understand; they are for you to embody and live. You have nothing to prove. You are brave, strong, terribly clever, and have made it through and arrived at a more soulful place inside yourself.

You are living the truth of what it means to lay claim to the power of your heart and fully belong to yourself. You now shine with the sunlight and the moonlight. Both radiating off you in rivers of authenticity and quiet power.

347

Soul Retrieval

"The purpose of our journey is to restore ourselves to wholeness."
—Debbie Ford

We recover ourselves in bits and pieces— a push of momentum, a moment of hope, a flash of transcendence that raises us upwards over our heartbreaks, spillage, and grief.

For a minute, we are suspended on feathered wings, and we see the bigger picture and our whole. We can fly down and retrieve the pieces of ourselves we laid or dropped along the way, taking back anything we accidentally gave away.

We reclaim parts of ourselves we didn't even know we'd lost. Reintegrate aspects long forgotten. Recover and collect fragments of psyche and soul, which help us to remember our true selves and compose a deeper completion.

If this world doesn't work for you, you've got to rework your world. Sewing new wings of clarity, discovery, and fortitude so you can go on a treasure hunt for your truth.

In this process, you will learn that so much of what seems to glitter will not be your true gold. But you will surprise yourself with how many diamonds you find in the rough of your soul. You will surprise yourself with what you collect upon the way and where your truest treasure grows.

You will surprise yourself with your capacity for wingspan and flight. You become fuller and wider— with each descent and as-cent— as you continue to move in your direction of light.

348

WILD AND WISE

Whatever you do, do it from a place of love. That is the golden rule of how to transform the situations and ingredients in your life into alchemical gold.

By finding the love. It sounds so simple, and yet love is undefinable; it wears a million faces, and sometimes it doesn't feel very easy to find, especially when we feel caught in life's storms, and we can't find the light through the rain.

It can be a hard truth to surrender to: life is bigger than us, and we're often asked to yield to it. Yet there's grace in this truth as well— there is grace in yielding, realizing we're not in control or in charge, and surrendering to the greater process.

There's also grace in life's challenges. We can allow the challenges to be a storm, which sweeps through us and helps potentially press reset.

The storm's wisdom awakens and rearranges us. It's a difficult process, yet it can also be beautiful when we intuitively follow sorrow's flows and discover they lead back to love.

And love is wild and wise.

Love has an intelligence all its own. Love knows how to instinctually, inventively, and ingenuously heal the wounds within, fill our cracks with liquid gold, and help us become our true selves.

We don't have to try so hard to figure out how to mend; we just need to surrender to love's wisdom and know all things repair, renew, and return to the light in their own time.

349

THE BEAUTIFUL MESS

If it's messy and awkward and experience-laden with a lot of course corrections and re-navigations, then you're probably living life in a way that engages you in your growth and development, and what a beautiful thing.

Maybe it doesn't look neat, linear, or well-packaged, and that's perfectly alright. People are so hard on themselves for being human that they fail to recognize how hard it is to be human and how hard it can be to embody our space of self.

After all, it is a splendid yet difficult journey to learn to navigate our unique mix of mind, body, heart, and spirit and how that translates and transforms with our experiences.

It's a lot.

So, go gently. Find grace for your process. Empower yourself to keep taking responsibility for all parts of yourself as you navigate and map out your territory of self. Forgive often. Learn to laugh at the inelegant moments and see them for the growing pains they are as you stretch and reach and learn to be bigger.

Do you. And learn that while some things we do may require apology (mistakes are part of life, and repair work is necessary and healing), one thing you never have to apologize for is figuring yourself out and giving yourself permission to take the inner journey into a deeper you.

350
Rewilding Our Souls

We need to keep finding ways to return to ourselves. Life moves so quickly these days, and if we don't have practices that help us stay connected to our hearts and soul's voice, we begin to feel fragmented, anxious, and ungrounded.

Our energy fades. We might feel we are going through the motions, stuck in a rut, or boxed into constraints and routines. We begin to lose connection with our hearts and purpose. We lose our sense of vibrancy and begin to feel disconnected. We feel like a dried-up orange with no juice.

We need the juice— the delicious, vitalizing experiences that keep us connected to our heart space and soulful self— so we can tap into the vast wild within, receive from our hearts, reignite our vision and intention, and get a glow-up from our soul.

We need spaces where we can be a freer version of ourselves, dream and imagine, and open to new possibilities. We need spaces where we loosen the strings that keep us bound to schedules and responsibilities, so we have room to breathe and receive.

This is where we can transcend mental chatter and replant into the voice of our hearts. We can be poured into by life, love, the numinous, and our higher self.

There are many pathways to access this vital, wild part of ourselves. This is why some people take a pilgrimage. Travel to intriguing places. Trek up mountains or journey on endless forest trails. Seek out a new experience to facilitate the rewilding process and search for the unrestrained self.

But rewilding can be humble in scope as well. It can take place in our day-to-day lives. In the confines of our ordinary lives, we can still travel through different portals to find it. For example:

Imagination's streams of endless creativity. Walking barefoot on the earth, star gazing on velvet black nights. Remembering our wild self through following the moon's cycles and honoring the seasons. Meditation and quiet. Tarot and tea. Anything that gives us a sense of sacred ritual. Art, poetry, a soul-stirring read. Gifting ourselves a day of joy.

When life starts to wear us down, we need to return to the wilderness within. Know ourselves whole again— unrestrained, uncontained, and untamed. Allow our wild selves to break free and roam.

Wander through the caverns of our souls and find the places where wild things grow.

351
Wild and Free: A Tiny Essay on Rewilding

Henry David Thoreau penned this beautifully, "All good things are wild and free." It's true, I thought: Sometimes we must repattern, rewild, and reseed our soul.

Learn to see disruptions as life's way of breaking us out of our daily stream of consciousness and giving us space to see things from a new lens so we can be liberated from the dead roots of self that no longer serve our highest growth.

We must return to the soil of self and beat with the wild of the earth. Free ourselves from old paradigms, constraints, and beliefs. Allow ourselves to return to seed and dare to face the shock of new shoots so we can grow outrageous blooms.

"All good things are wild and free."

It's true, I thought: Nature, love, authenticity, moonlight, creativity, imagination, and dreams. Wild and free, tinged with butterfly wings and shades of the numinous, where we can slip in between worlds and experience the mysteries.

Nature returns, rewires, and rewilds: If you need a friend, talk to a tree. If you need joy, talk to a flower. If you need to ground, talk to the earth. If you need to flow and let go, talk to the sea.

And if you need to release all that would weigh you down and shackle you to lesser things that don't reflect the infinite truth of your soul? Walk outside with bare soles. Or take a bath and let the water heal your soul.

Let all be renewed and released as you remember in your heart the words of Thoreau: *"All good things are wild and free."*

352

CHOOSE LOVE

"The way we can allow ourselves to do what we need to, no matter what others may say or do, is to choose love and defy fear."
—Martha Beck

Choose love. It is the only choice you will make that will forever improve your life because love is the origin of every good thing. Each time we choose to love, we open ourselves up to that nucleus of goodness; everything else beautiful originates from there.

Learn to embody love's universal energy inside of yourself. Wrap it around you like a psychic shield, which gently radiates presence and protection wherever you go. Pretend you are the ocean, holding space for all who inhabit her streams.

Choose love. Forgive yourself when you've had a bad day and stress, judgment, or fatigue got the better of you, making you less than your most desired self. Send out the energy of soft pink light to anyone who may have been affected— start with yourself.

Look for opportunities to help somebody in a practical way. Thank the person who serves your coffee with warmth and sincerity. Let somebody go in front of you while you are in traffic. Smile. Release imaginary lanterns of peace into the sky; picture their light shining on humanity. Be kind to animals. Eat a cookie and delight in it. Do whatever you can with joy.

Fostering love isn't about perfection; it's about developing an eye for opportunities to do so. Realize each of us is doing our best on any given day. Remember, we don't know somebody's soul path, why they are here now, what lessons they must learn, or how they need to grow their hearts.

Choose love. Don't be perfect. Be beautifully and wonderfully you, and be okay with making a mess. Don't shortcut your humanity and spiritually dissociate by pretending it's all light if it's not. Learn to face yourself and know all parts of you are valuable.

Realize in the eyes of the universe, there is nothing we can do or not do that will make us deserving of love. Be relieved that you don't have to try so hard, then notice how much more grace you naturally extend to others because of the amount of grace flowing through you. Do whatever calls you to love, and know it is enough.

Choose love. Make a list of what that means to you. Write it down. Share your list with others. Let's transform the energy of this world in as many ways as possible— then see how love multiplies, magnifies, and rises when we become its catalyst of change.

353

Coffee Talk

"Too often we underestimate the power of a touch, a smile, a kind word, a listening ear, an honest compliment, or the smallest act of caring, all of which have the potential to turn a life around."
—Leo Buscaglia

You don't have to make a huge splash to make the world a better place.

Think about a stranger who gives you an easy smile and you find yourself smiling in return, or the latte you're handed with a sincere "have a great day," which makes your day feel a little bit better, or what it feels like to give and receive a random act of care.

Action matters. Energy matters. Kindness matters. You matter. We matter. And we often make it overly complicated and minimize our efforts. We think our contributions are insignificant and don't have value if they're not grand or big.

Yet the deer will thank the tree for sheltering it from the rain. The tree will thank the rain for giving it sustenance to grow. The rain will fill the ponds where the deer goes to drink. And nature reminds us that interdependence is the truth of existence, where all efforts have a place.

Remember next time you judge a deed as insignificant and small— each drop we cast into the pond of our world ripples out into all. Even something so seemingly small as a sincere exchange when buying coffee can change the course of another's day.

354

ENERGETIC FOOTPRINTS

Sometimes, this world shows you its worst, and you will have to decide how you want to continue showing up.

Do you still choose to show up in your integrity and heart? Do you choose to shut down and retreat for a time? Do you choose to show up in bitterness and anger that eventually leads to your worst?

There are no right or wrong answers to these questions, and there are a myriad of paths each of us could take. Sometimes, we take multiple paths simultaneously and vacillate between trying to stay open and optimistic one day and retreating into a deep well of pain and resentment the next.

You don't owe the world your best, your kindness of being, or your creative courage. You just owe yourself the right to try and choose the path that resonates most with you.

This is why many of us might still try to take the high road, even if lower ones are available. This is why many of us might spend time in the darkness yet fight to return to a space of joy and bravery and try to see life as a friend.

Sometimes, it can take many days, moon cycles, or seasons to find our way back to a space where we feel aligned and centered in our wholeness of being and can show up in our light. There is no timeline for our process. There is just our right to choose.

Our right to continue to set our compass to our true north and keep moving in the direction our soul calls us to go.

Our right to have a say about who we want to be in this world and to choose to dictate how we show up based on what is inside us.

Our right to set boundaries, make mistakes, and steer clear of the things that hurt and harm us.

Our right to explore the possibility of our being and to grow to understand how our choices make us feel and impact our somatic, emotional, psychological, relational, and spiritual health.

There is no right answer to the question of your soul and how you choose to express your essence. You choose how close to your heart you want to live and exercise your right to create the energetic footprint you wish to leave on your trail of becoming.

355

SPHERE

If you sit with all that is not fair in life long enough, you will discover two choices. Bitterness and disillusion or compassion and love.

While having moments of the former is inevitable, I keep striving for the latter. When life makes no sense to me, and I struggle with its circumstances, I strive to find radical, fierce compassion for the whole.

Strive to use my heart and not my ego. Step beyond all that doesn't seem fair, step outside of situations, and look for both the brokenness and the resilience, the decay and the life, the devastation and the consolation.

See the situation as a giant sphere filled with awful and beauty, grief and healing, unfairness and hope, and hate and love. See how opposing truths can occupy the same space and make peace amongst themselves.

I try to walk around that sphere looking at the different viewpoints without judgment, without the need to fix, and see how they are all connected and how they work together. See how love and grace bind the whole thing together, even when it doesn't feel like it.

If I take a step even further away, the sphere gets bigger. It is filled with the people I know, the people I don't know, the people who inhabit this space together. They are all working out their own sense of brokenness and resilience as they try to find the love that binds everything together— each in their own way.

There is exquisite wonder in that sphere if you learn to see it. Even with all the cracks and pain, it offers the potential to step back, look at the whole of who we are, and find beauty in the full sphere of being human.

If you learn to stare at that sphere long enough, you will focus less on how unfair things are and more on finding the same love that holds us all together— despite our differences and because of ourselves.

That is the crux of the energy of love: we don't have to do anything to merit it. It is already in us. Equally available to everything and all. We just need to learn to sit in its circle and receive.

356
RAISING THE POWER OF LOVE

One of the best things I have ever learned is that life expands when we choose to love. The kinder and more open-hearted I am, the more life blooms in accordance, and suddenly, days that seemed ordinary turn into days of connection, gratitude, and tiny miracles.

I have learned many powerful lessons about directing my energies to those who can respect, reciprocate, and receive that gift instead of those who would take it and empty me without giving back. And I don't regret the lessons because they have taught me so much about love in all its forms.

I learned to differentiate between imitation and the real thing. Here is what I've learned about the real thing: when we choose to love anyway— because we can— from a pure space of open-hearted courage inside of ourselves, love multiplies exponentially.

It's true. If you send love's energy into the world, open your heart, and live with boldness and courage, you will find that the energy returns to you and continues to pay itself forward.

Love will never guarantee that you won't get hurt, but it will guarantee that more love will keep rippling out and coming your way.

The more you love your beautiful self, the more you practice random acts of kindness, appreciate the beauty of the world we live in, cherish the people close to your heart, and move towards loving from an unconditional place—

The more the energy of your heart grows, the more love you hold inside, and the more you can't help but embody that energy.

Regardless of what others choose to do with their hearts, I keep learning to keep mine open. I keep learning that if I want the good things in life— if I want the magic, the warmth, the joy— then I must also take the lessons of grief, challenge, and heartbreak.

Ultimately, life is as big as our hearts allow it to be. We become the love we give.

357
HOW TO MAKE A DIFFERENCE

Sometimes, in a world that seems to be growing larger by the technological, media-saturated second, it is very easy to wonder what possible difference we can make in our tiny ponds when the larger ocean seems so vast, troubled, and deep.

To that, I would simply ask:

Did you do something kind today? Did you care for another being? Did you appreciate nature? Did you try to make someone smile? Did you do the best you knew to do?

Did you cast out love and compassion into the world in any shape or form? Did you do the work of a healer, a caretaker, a dreamer, an artist, a conscious human, an awakened being who realizes life is bigger than just the self?

Did you add hope, wishes, beauty, imagination, compassion, kindness, faith, nurture, care, guidance, and love to this world in any shape or form?

If you answered *yes*, then you are making a difference.

It's not that the world has become too big, jaded, or wounded to make a change. It's that our sense of impact has become too small. We diminish the power we hold inside ourselves to change the spaces we occupy through our energy, presence, aligned actions, and love.

We forget that the tiniest ripple can gain momentum and create a wave. We trick ourselves into thinking this world is too hardened and hopeless to help. We deny the innate authority given to us by the gift of life to rise and live and make a difference in any capacity we can.

It is not the world that is too big to change. It is us who think we are too small to make a difference. Change is about presence. Change is about the heart. Change is about love.

Change is about paying attention to our hearts, taking steps that are in heart-coherence, offering our love in the ways that we feel called, and making the difference that we can.

358

EARTH ANGELS

"If instead of a gem, or even a flower, we should cast the gift of a loving thought into the heart of a friend, that would be giving as the angels give."
—George MacDonald

Be an earth angel for someone else. Take time to lift them up. Send a card, send light, make a call, or spend time. Supporting others doesn't always require much effort, struggle, or mire. It just takes an intention followed by aligned action and sincere desire.

Be an earth angel for the planet. Talk to the animals and learn the gifts of the plants. Listen for their voices and belong to the land. Love the earth and treat her kindly. Thank the moon for her light and the sun for his rise. Find all sorts of big and tiny ways to care for the seas, the trees, and the skies.

Be an earth angel for the world. Stay open, pray often, and love hard. Look beyond divisions and sides. Stand up for what's right. Contribute and uplift— be practical, find somewhere to help out, and take a shift. Let your offering to humanity be an open heart that looks for ways to practice peace and generosity.

Be an earth angel for yourself. Tend to your heart, tend to your soul, tend your being, and tend your mind. Heal what still aches, grow deep roots of self-faith, and keep finding ways to reach new heights. Do good things for yourself without apology, knowing you deserve to shine bright.

Remember— we are each an ongoing work of evolving creativity deserving of our care and time. We can transcend old ways, become angels for each other, and change our world one small step at a time. We can care as we can— we are love's hands— and allow our wings to unfold through each act of joy, peace, and light.

359
On the Matter of Light

It's easy to minimize the power of our intentions and actions. It's easy to think that our deeds and works only hold value if recognized by many. It's easy to disregard the impact of our empathy, heartfelt intentions, quiet demonstrations of care, and how we keep showing up for love.

It's easy to get caught up in producing, achieving, and results. Sometimes, we think our contributions don't hold value if they're not being validated or acknowledged. We forget that what is most important isn't what happens when we shine our light but that we shine it in the first place.

We forget that all creation has innate value and belonging, no matter how small the creation may be. We disregard our efforts and feel that our art, poetry, small acts of service, doing the right thing, sincerities, smiles, kindnesses to nature and animals, and efforts of change are pointless. We forget that changing the energy inside of ourselves can impact the spaces we touch.

We forget that when we create and act from a place of light, there is innate value because the act of owning and working our light IS the point. Our light matters.

We've each been given truths and dreams and unique ways to contribute and shine. We've been given a heart to love and the conviction to keep working on making our heart a peaceful place.

At times, this might not be readily validated and seem very small in the scope of how big life can be. And yet they are our truths, dreams, and heart contributions, and we are the only ones who can find the courage to dream them and see them into being.

It can be challenging to have faith in your visions for your life, believe in your gifts and dreams, and feel what you do matters and makes a difference— we are inundated with so much noise that it is easy to feel small and insignificant. Yet, one little pinprick of light makes all the difference in a darkened room and inspires others to turn their lights on as well.

Our light matters. Your light matters. Please keep finding the courage to shine. This world needs your light. And you need your light. And I need your light. And humanity needs your light. Now more than ever.

360

Purpose is Multifold

A life of purpose can be multifold. We might feel we have a greater purpose and some kind of legacy, work, or offering of light we'd like to share with the world. This is an honorable purpose; it certainly can feel significant and weighty and move one toward action.

However, purpose can also be unassuming and plain. It can be as easy as being a grateful human or becoming a student of nature's ways. Purpose can be about learning to make the most of each day, staying present with ourselves, and fearlessly excavating our souls.

Purpose can mean making positive contributions through kindness, humility, goodness, and love. It can mean putting our hearts into each day and finding meaning. Purpose can be found in learning about pleasure and sorrow, the highs and the lows, and all the shades of muted moments and small slivers of ordinary that lay in between.

Our purpose can be whatever we make it to be and encompasses many things. It evolves with us and can span the spectrum of the character we develop, the offerings, work, and service we create, the light and love we give, the energy we cultivate, and who we choose to become.

As outstanding as it can feel to set our sights high and dream about grand visions and big purpose, a life of simplicity and appreciation can also be a life of noble purpose and intention. Most likely, we'll have a multi-tiered relationship with our purpose, and like a rainbow layer cake, each different layer and sense of purpose will be packed with a different color and flavor.

Remember, though, that your purpose can keep evolving, be redefined, and continually understood. It can be expansive and loud or tiny and gentle, and every layer and tier in between; it can be whatever you choose to purpose it to be.

But if you should ever find yourself getting too wrapped up in the idea of purpose and losing sight of feeling present in the day-to-day, it is never amiss to just bring it back to your heart and remember— going about the good work of love with sincerity, authenticity, and grace is a life of gorgeous-mad-purpose and would be well spent.

361
MY COMPASS, MY QUESTIONS

This is your life. What will you do with it? How will you shape it? What choices will you make? If you don't like the direction you're going and you realize you've gotten off course, how can you redirect yourself?

How can you make the most of what you have? How can you change something if you don't like it? If you can't change the 'thing,' how can you change your perspective so you can find greater peace and acceptance?

What makes a great life? How can you make your life great right now? How can you find purpose in the smallest things?

What will you do with your days? How will you shape your thoughts? How can you find gratitude and return to a space of humility when you find yourself wandering into victimhood or entitlement or feeling you're owed by life?

How can you turn an ordinary day into something extraordinary and keep redefining your relationship with what is extraordinary and magical? How can you keep ceding to life's process and embrace what is?

I think about these things a lot. I don't always have the answers, but they are the questions I ask myself to return to my heart and come back to my inner compass. Over the years, I have asked myself many things, but I keep returning to these because they are the best questions I have discovered to find my way back to my path when I get lost.

They've helped me find a higher perspective, realign my priorities when life's stress cycles hit, develop a life philosophy based on the heart's way, and remember that no matter where I'm at, I can always work on finding gratitude for the simple gifts of the day.

I share my questions here with you, hoping they might help you, too. I hope they support you in creating a compass of courage, compassion, and faith in your process. I hope they help you remember how to return to yourself and create sacred meaning in the extraordinary breaths of our everyday lives. I hope they help you find gratitude for life's rich gifts.

And I hope— that as we each live the answers to our questions— we keep finding ways to anchor into our hearts. Over time, we will realize that the answers to our questions will always lead us back to love and support us in uncaging our hearts into a greater expression.

Do that, and the world is bound to change because there is no limitation to be found when we allow love to direct our course.

362
LOVE IS A HOLY CIRCLE

Love as you can. It is enough. Even small acts have ripple effects, and we never know who we'll touch with our intentional deeds of compassion.

Find a higher and wiser perspective: use this as your touchstone whenever your personal perspectives are challenged. Let the two chisel away at one another as you become wiser in the process, and your higher perspective stretches and grows through trial and truth.

Be an activist for grace. Be an activist for kindness. Be an activist for love. Stand up for what you believe, yet work on refusing to feed the agenda of smugness, strife, and hate. Set good boundaries around those who do feed that agenda.

Take things back into yourself when you begin to lose yourself. Find your silence, drop into your truth, and listen. Be slow to react and quick to consider. A thoughtful pause can make all the difference between creative construction or divisive destruction.

Do the repair work when you realize you got it wrong. Remember, this repair work begins within. Build so many bridges inside of yourself that you are filled with rainbows of peace, then take that empathic connection out into the rest of the world and build more rainbows.

Know that "I don't know. I'm still figuring it out" is a perfectly acceptable response. Give yourself space to wrestle with uncertainty: your future self will thank you for allowing them room to grow.

If you don't like something, change it, and if you can't change it, then keep on changing you so you don't become like it.

Know that most people react out of a place of separation, hurt, and pain. The path of peace doesn't mean you can't set healthy borders around yourself when you encounter these people. It just means your wiser self sees what's going on in their soul. So, you keep working to forgive and release so you do not attach to their wounds and become that pain yourself.

Remember, love is a holy circle: There are no sides. Love needs no sides. Love knows no sides. Love has no sides.

363

SPOKES ON A WHEEL

They are all spokes on a wheel— pathways we can follow to explore different facets of heart wisdom and the human experience.

Authenticity and following our hearts. Dreams, hopes, and possibilities. Growth, transformation, and becoming. Self-love, self-trust, and self-belief. Being, receiving, and patience in the process. Relationships, connection, and love.

Compassion, sensitivity, courage, and grace. Healing, wholeness, and finding the light in the darkness. Grief, heartbreak, and loss. Embracing change and letting go. Happiness, creativity, and meaning. Purpose, impact, and wild-hearted living.

Each is a spoke on a greater wheel— an entry point for the wild-hearted that helps us excavate our inner terrain and chart our evolving map of self. We learn valuable lessons about the heart of being human every time we explore a new facet of experience, find a way to keep our hearts open, and embrace growth.

If we were to overlay and collage our maps of self into a greater picture, we would see that there are many spokes and many wheels. Intersecting, crisscrossing, and weaving into one another. All of them create a greater wheel that encompasses all experiences— an infinite web of shimmering lights.

Love is at the epicenter— always reaching for us, revealing itself to us, unveiling itself to us, and showing its face in new forms. Both knowable and undefinable, love continues to free itself to become a higher expression and supports us in doing the same. We don't have to do anything to receive it— love just exists, available to us all.

However, if we want to lead a life of love, if we want to become ambassadors of love, if we want to walk the way of the heart and claim this energy for ourselves, we learn to actively seek the face of love. We learn to discover the places where love resides and look for it in all things. We learn to embrace its gifts and allow them to continue to transform our hearts.

We know that even when we cannot see it, love is reaching out to us. Over time, we learn to live in such a way that we are continually reaching back. And we discover that just as much as love touches our hearts, we begin to touch the heart of love.

In this space of infinite possibilities— true magic awaits.

364

THE CALL OF THE WILD-HEARTED

"It began in mystery, and it will end in mystery, but what a savage and beautiful country lies in between."
—Diane Ackerman

And this, perhaps, is the challenge of living wild-hearted:

We are asked to form a healthy attachment to and identification with our current life stage and space so we can experience, learn, be present, and grow. All while knowing that, at some point, we will be called to let go. We will be called into our greater wilderness soul.

We will be called to release our attachment and identification so we can travel with ease and carry the wisdom gained, which now sits light as a feather in our hearts.

This is the contradiction, the tension, and the cusp of the wild-hearted.

In the one hand, we hold all that has been, all that we have loved, and all the growth and experience in our current incarnation. In the other hand, we hold our willingness to let it all go—our willingness to pack up our bags and move onwards when life calls us into a new cavern of soul.

This does not mean we cannot create stability, family, community, or a place we call home. We can love with fierce passion the beautiful things that encompass our lives. We can till our soul of self, mine our moments for all they are worth, and belong to the moments of these precious days.

This simply means that we exist within our lives with the understanding of what it is to be on a journey of the soul. We hold the sacred knowledge that we will be called onwards and inwards at any time to travel deeper into the vast wilderness of love and the infinite nature of our soul.

We cannot know how this ongoing calling of the wild-hearted will manifest in external changes in our lives. We must trust. Trust the cusp and tension between what is and what shall be. Trust that our hearts will guide us true, that whatever is meant to last will, indeed, last, and that whatever we're meant to shed will pass.

Answering the call of the wild-hearted is that simple and that hard: We are asked to stand at an ongoing crossroads of self and forever choose the wild way of the heart.

365

A New Cycle of Light

"My dear girl, of course, it hurts to say goodbye to something that held you in its stead. But every ending is also the soil for a beginning, and so too do you have your own turn of seasons.
With permission to embrace the bittersweet diaphanous pain of change, finding gratitude for all that has been, and allowing what's next to begin to arrange.
For there is always something around the bend waiting to be discovered, and if you keep your heart open to life, you will see that there is more life waiting to be uncovered.
Deep breath. Chin up. Heart open wide. Allow what's passed to slip from your grasp and prepare to receive a new cycle of light."
—Sunshine in Winter

I wrote those words after something ended that had comforted and contained me during a transitional time in my life. I felt a vast sense of emptiness that it had come to an end. I didn't quite know who I was or what was next without it taking up space in my life.

Sometimes, we want to hold on to what was. We might not even realize how much we're holding on until we feel an amorphous sense of loss and fear about how things seem to be changing before our eyes. It hurts our hearts to realize we can't do anything to stop the process.

Letting go is not easy; it truly takes courage to live with an open heart, face and feel our feelings, and trust that when we release, we also receive.

There is no great secret to how we find this kind of courage. There is no magic elixir, easy answers, philosophy, or belief system that negates our human necessity and soul responsibility of feeling grief, learning to tolerate the oceans of ambiguity, and choosing to move forward and trust.

There is love, though. There is always love, which helps soften the pain and supports us in finding hope and peace as we work on letting go.

Sometimes, I like to visualize, in some other realm and on some other plane, that there is a higher and wiser version of myself who is smiling and laughing kindly as human me works on untangling and unknotting the sticky threads of attachment that make me want to hang onto how things have been.

She already knows that I'll eventually figure it out, that it's all going to be okay, and that I'll keep finding my way to the next bend and uncovering new adventures.

Most importantly, she knows we are never separated from love and that every time we lose something, it will come back around in a new form, and life will weave a new cycle of light into our pattern.

So, she laughs with joy at the beauty of it all, with reassurance in her heart that love has got this, and that I have got this.

And so do you, my friend. So do you. We do have this. We will find our way.

We can learn to embrace the diaphanous nature of change, find gratitude for all that has been, and allow ourselves to be arranged as we allow what's passed to slip from our grasp, and in so doing, we will keep finding in hundreds of shapes, surprises, and forms—

There is always love.

EPILOGUE
It's Going to Be Beautiful

Guess what? Today is a spectacular day to be fully present in your life.

Your life is happening right now. It's not happening back in the bittersweet memories of yesterday. It's not happening at a nebulous "I can finally be happy when—" point in the future.

This day is for you. This moment. This love. This present time.

You may grieve for what has passed, but know the ending is also the beginning, and today is your day for a new beginning. You are being called onwards in life's ongoing ouroboros of love, and you are still journeying and exploring.

So, keep surrounding yourself with noble and beautiful things. Take a step today in a new direction— do something that makes you smile, tell somebody how much they matter to you, or sit in the rain and feel it fall on your face.

Keep it simple. Make it magical. Look for tiny pockets of joy. Make your own sunshine or dive into your inner ocean to understand your emotional depths. Buy yourself flowers. Pet a fur friend.

Dance in nature. Laugh in the snow. Discover courage in change. Find the sacred in the mundane.

Whatever you do, remember that any day, every day, this day— Today— is your day, bright one. And we— life, the universe, humanity, your loved ones, your higher self— are all so glad you are here.

Welcome to your seat at the Great Tea Party of Life. Take a moment, have a cupcake to celebrate, and then get going!

For, don't you know, dear soul— magical things are waiting to happen for you. Today is your day. It's going to be beautiful.

Acknowledgments

A warm thank you to the team at Palmetto Press for your collective support, creativity, and expertise with the publication process. I am so grateful to have found a publishing platform for *Small Pearls*, and I appreciate the combined skillset and guidance you have provided.

Thank you to the following amazing women: Diane Logan, Jennifer Jepson, Ivory LaNoue, and Rebecca McKee for your support of *Small Pearls*. I'm grateful to know each of you, and I appreciate the positive energy, inspiration, and dedication each of you brings to the amazing things you do.

A special thank you to Carolyn Riker for your keen editorial eye and creative support on this project. Your friendship is a rich and beautiful blessing in my life, and I am beyond grateful.

Last, thank you to my readers and all those who have encouraged, inspired and offered words of support for my work. I am deeply appreciative of your presence, kindness, and light.

Addendum

The following essays were previously published in the following books and online sources. Some of them have been revised and adapted since their original publication.

Freebird Fridays: a love story, Golden Dragonfly Press, 2016.

Anyway
Fields Unseen
Jump
No Longer Willing
The Whole Story

Heliotrope Nights: starlight for the mind and soul, Golden Dragonfly Press, 2017.

Excess Baggage
How To Know Your Soul
In Nature, We Remember Ourselves [In Nature I Remember Myself]
Lighthouses of Hope
My Serenity Prayer
Red Doors
Sacred Spaces
Superheroes
To See and Receive the Answers [To See the Answers]
Who We'll Be [Who I'll Be]

Lamentations of The Sea: 111 passages on grief, love, loss and letting go, Golden Dragonfly Press, 2017.

All That is Shabby and Bright
Balloons
Becoming
BIG
Blank Spaces
Bloom
Break
Bounce
Brambles AND Roses
Creatures of the Deep
Dancing Leaves
Eclipse
Exit Plan Out of the Ghostlands [Forgiveness]
Get Over It
Forever
Heart
Home
Honor Them
How to Grieve
How to Swim
If You Strike Me Down
Illumination
I'm Just Not Myself
It is All Sacred [Sacred]
Learning to Lean [Lean]
Shine
Sphere
Sunshine in Winter

Tangled
The Love Inside
The Thick
The Wasteland
Tricksters
We Will Have Joy
Wildflowers
With Hope

Revelations of The Sky: 133 passages on the alchemy of grief,
Golden Dragonfly Press, 2020.

A Blessing of Peace [August Blessing]
Broken and Whole
Bruises and Pearls [Bruises]
Canon in Trust
Creative Adaptation
Deep Sea Diving
Ecosystem
Grit and Glitter
Leap
Life Cycles of Grief and Love [Cycles]
Love is a Holy Circle
Manifesto of Belief
Moving Forward
Nomads in Time
Rose Gardens in the Stars
Strings
That's Hope
The Beautiful Mess
The Butterfly Effect

The Nature of You
The Trifecta of Heart, Psyche, and Soul [Soul Musings]
What Loss Has to Teach Us
Wild and Free [Reseeding Our Soul]
Wild and Wise
Your Heart is Magic
We Are Golden [52 Weeks, Part II]

Things of That Nature: words for the mystic heart, Golden Dragonfly Press, 2019.

Cartwheels and Spirals
Compassionate Detachment [Lovingkindness Meditation]
Earth Angels
Galactic-Hearted Supernova [Supernova]
Gaze
Grace Rebels
Grief's Doorway
Hope's Hum
Into the Woods
Keys
Let the Shadows Fall Behind You
Manifesto of Hope
May Grace Flow [Duet of Possibility]
Metamorphosis
My Dear One, I Believe in You
Paint the Sky with Stars
Shadowlands
Snowflakes
Starlight and Strange Beauty
Soul Retrieval

To Learn Self-Trust
We Belong to Love [Rose Gardens]

Transformations of the Sun: 122 passages on finding new life after loss, Golden Dragonfly Press, 2018.

Breaking Out
Broken Birds
Dream Your World, Create a Beautiful Reality [Wildflowers]
Everywhere
Experts
Great Expectations
Grief, The Great Equalizer
Just Take Class [Flow]
Labyrinth
Magicians
Making Broken Things Whole
Mud or Stars
New Wings
Non-Sequitur
Noodles
Reidentification
Sacred Circles
Seed of Possibility
Self-Forgiveness
Sideways
The Essence of Grief
The Gifts of Loneliness
The Place Joy Lives
The Signature of Hope
The Vibrancy is Here [Vibrancy]

The Wild Unknown
Those That Shine the Brightest [Soul Callings]
Tides
Watchtowers of Love
You Are the Art

Other Publications:

Choose Love [We Are the Revolution, Choosing One Act of Love at a Time], Urban Howl, 2017
A Single Breath, self-published in Cranberry Dusk, 2016.
Joy is Vital to Our Souls, Spiritual Tree via Medium, 2020.
Rewilding Our Souls [Rewilding Our Hearts], Spiritual Tree via Medium, 2020.
This World Needs Your Light, Finding Your Heart Magic eCourse, *2019.*
Write About the World We Wish to See, Akashic Magic Newsletter, June 2021

Sunshine In Winter Blog @sunshineinwinter.blog

Aim for Peace [Year of The Peaceful Heart], January 2013.
Breathing Our Way Through Anything [Breath and the Art of Un-Zen], January 2015.
On Leave-takings, Becoming, and New Springs, April 2013.
Snow Falling on Happy, September 2013.

Words from the Blog @bethannekw.com/blog

A Life of Appreciation is a Life Well Lived, April 2020.
Darkness is Magic, Too, April 2021.

Happiness is the Act of Being Whole, May 2020.
Gratitude is a Gateway [Grace, Growth, and Gratitude], October 2023.
On Underdogs and Finding Inspiration in Quiet Ways [Superheroes], March 2019.
Parachutes, May 2020.
Purpose It to Love, May 2021.
Start, Just Start [It Begins in You], June 2020.
The Bold Stroke of Reinvention [The Red Pain of Reinvention], August 2021.
To Find Our Way Home [Finding Home], September 2021.

Connect With Me

Website: bethannekw.com

Podcast: Your Heart Magic @ https://www.yourheartmagic.com/

Monthly Akashic Magic Letter @ https://www.bethannekw.com/akashic

IG: @dr.bethannekw and @yourheartmagic

FB: Dr. BethAnne KW